PROBLEMS AND ISSUES IN MICROECONOMICS:

a STUDY GUIDE for

THE APPLIED THEORY OF PRICE, *Second Edition*

JOEL D. SCHERAGA

Department of Economics
Rutgers University

Macmillan Publishing Company
New York

Collier Macmillan Publishers
London

Printed in the United States of America

Macmillan Publishing Company
866 Third Avenue, New York, New York 10022

Collier Macmillan Canada, Inc.

ISBN 0-02-378500-4

Printing: 1 2 3 4 5 6 7 8 Year: 5 6 7 8 9 0 1 2 3

A Message to the Student

Intermediate microeconomics is considered by many students to be the hardest course in an economics curriculum. This fear arises because of the large amount of theory that must be learned. Students are often overwhelmed by the many graphs, equations, and new concepts to which they are introduced. The failure of many textbooks and courses to expand upon the usefulness of the theory for solving interesting problems in economics has only worsened the problem. Too many students are left wondering about the value of the theory for "solving real-world economic problems." Unfortunately, many students also abandon their hopes of becoming economists because of an inability to overcome their fears and confusion.

There is an old saying in the teaching profession that the only way to truly learn any material is to teach it and explain it to a group of students. There is another old saying that the only way to properly learn economic theory is to use it, practice it, and solve real economic problems. There are two ways to learn theory. One way is to memorize it. The other way is to use it. The philosophy upon which this study guide and the textbook by Donald McCloskey is based is that you must apply the theory to real economic problems in order to fully understand it.

In this study guide, you are encouraged to think for yourself and to think like an economist. Economic *intuition* is developed through problem solving. It is not enough for you to just learn the mechanics of solving equations and drawing graphs. Problems are presented that are topical and drawn from recent economic events. Many of the problems will seem hard. You will have to use economic theory to logically decide how to solve the problems. Only then will you also use the graphs and equations to mechanically solve the problems.

Economics is another language, just like mathematics or the Basic computer language. It is a way of clearly and concisely expressing ideas. But it is not a substitute for being able to think and clearly express the same ideas in plain English. When you are working on a problem in this study guide, pretend that you are walking down the street and a person who does not know any economics has come up to you and asked the same question. You would never tell a person in this situation that "the demand for gasoline is inelastic and therefore prices are what they are." The person would probably give you a very strange look and quickly walk away. Your answer would have to be in clear English. That is how you should try to think about and answer the problems in this book.

The chapters in this study guide are numbered so that they correspond to the same chapters in the McCloskey textbook. But the study guide is also designed to stand alone and can be used as a self-contained manual with any textbook on intermediate microeconomics. Each chapter consists of several sections. An overview summarizes the basic points presented in the corresponding chapter of the textbook. A list of key concepts follows the overview. Answers are presented to the "What To Read For" questions that appear before each section in the textbook. Each question precedes its answer for the ease of the student. Multiple choice questions give you the opportunity to test your knowledge of the technical details of the theory. Exercises require you to apply your knowledge of the theory to real problems in economics. Finally, the problem that appears at the end of each chapter is more lengthy and difficult, and it challenges your ability to extend the theory to more advanced concepts. Many of the problems and exercises deal with recent events that were reported in *The Wall Street Journal.*

Economics can be fun, fulfilling, and challenging. There is nothing frightening or mysterious about it. With studying and a lot of practice, you can become a competent and confident economist. Good luck!

Acknowledgments

The writing of this Study Guide proved to be a very rewarding and educational task for me. It gave me the opportunity to make a worthwhile contribution to the teaching of microeconomic theory. My enjoyment of teaching and belief that our undergraduate students deserve the very best education that our profession has to offer made my commitment to this project easy and the outcome fulfilling. This work is dedicated to undergraduate students, and I hope that it will help them to more clearly understand and appreciate intermediate microeconomic theory, and eliminate the frequent fear of learning this material.

I am very grateful to Chip Price, Executive Editor of the College Division at Macmillan, for giving me the opportunity to write this Study Guide. I am especially indebted to Don McCloskey for his faith in my abilities and his trust in allowing me to edit his text and write this accompanying Study Guide. Don has provided me with much guidance and encouragement with my work and my career. I have learned a lot from this scholar and good friend.

The writing of this book was a time-consuming task that required the patience, support, and assistance of many people, especially my closest friends. My father, who is always there when I need him, was very supportive. Joseph Seneca, my colleague and Chair of the Economics Department at Rutgers University, was enthusiastic from the start of this project and allowed me to teach intermediate micro theory classes to facilitate the development of this work. Sondra Palmieri provided expert secretarial assistance and was always patient and good-natured, despite many unreasonable requests and deadlines. Her enthusiasm for this project has been special. My thanks go to Andy Rozum and Dave Pristash, both of Computrol Corporation, for rescuing my Osborne computer from the edge of extinction at a very crucial stage of this project. Steve and Roni Kansagor have been the best of friends during the year it took to complete this project. Their friendship and encouragement helped me to keep a proper perspective.

Finally, I would like to thank all of my students at Rutgers University who have enthusiastically participated in my micro theory classes and provided useful suggestions. It is their success that has ultimately made this effort worthwhile.

Contents

PART I. DEMAND

CHAPTER 1

The Budget Line

I. OVERVIEW

Economics is the science that studies the allocation of scarce resources among unlimited human wants. A thing is scarce if it is desirable but limited in quantity. Alternatively, a thing is scarce if to obtain it resources must be used up that could be used to produce other things. For example, oil is scarce because it is not renewable. There exists a limited amount of it in the ground and once it is used it is gone. Gasoline that is used to power automobiles is a scarce resource because it is made from oil that could have been used to produce other products, such as home heating fuel.

The notion of scarcity can be captured in a diagram known as a budget line. Since a consumer or a society is not infinitely wealthy, there is a limit to the number of goods and services that can be consumed. The budget line depicts this constraint on consumption. It separates the bundles of goods that are attainable from those that are unattainable.

Every bundle of goods that lies on the budget line just exhausts the consumer's limited income. If the consumer wants more of one of the goods, then she must give up some of the other available goods. The slope of the budget line is the cost of one good in terms of the other goods. In other words, the slope of the budget line represents the opportunity cost of consuming more of one good, measured in terms of the other goods that must be foregone.

The concept of opportunity cost is central to economics. A person is always consuming something at the expense of something else. For example, if you choose to spend all of your money income on concert tickets and food, you do this knowing that you must forego purchasing nice furniture for your apartment, new clothing, and a new car. There is even an opportunity cost involved in the way you spend your limited available time. If you choose to spend three hours standing on line waiting to buy limited concert tickets, then you do so at the expense of the income you could be earning by spending that time at work. Time is also a scarce resource.

Since opportunity cost is the cost of one item in terms of the others, it makes sense to speak of the relative price of one item in terms of all other goods. Although the absolute money price of a glass of wine may be $2.00, it tells you nothing about the number of glasses of beer that you gave up in order to buy that one glass of wine. A relative price of 4 beers per glass of wine though, does capture the true opportunity cost of the wine.

The essence of scarcity is captured in the budget line. Opportunity cost, which is a result of scarcity, is represented by the slope of the budget line. The slope of the budget line measures the cost of one item in terms of the others; that is, the slope of the budget line measures the relative prices of the goods. Changes in relative prices are therefore represented by changes in the slope of the budget line. This is known as the <u>price effect.</u> The <u>law of demand</u> says that one would expect that more of a good will be demanded when its relative price falls.

The position of the budget line (as opposed to the slope) measures the income of the consumer. Changes in income alone, holding relative prices constant, are represented by parallel shifts of the budget line. The effect that a change in income alone has on the amount of a good that a consumer buys is known as the <u>income effect.</u> It can be positive or negative. If the income effect is positive, so that an increase in income leads to an increase in the amount of a particular good that the consumer buys, then the good is called a <u>normal good.</u> If the income effect is negative, then the good is known as an <u>inferior good.</u> Whether the good is a normal good or an inferior good to any particular consumer depends upon that consumer's own preferences.

<u>SUMMARY OF KEY CONCEPTS</u>

scarcity	budget line
fungibility	relative price
income effect	normal good
inferior good	revealed preference
law of demand	

II. <u>ANSWERS TO "WHAT TO READ FOR"</u>

1.1 SCARCITY AND THE BUDGET LINE

1. <u>What do economists mean by scarcity?</u> Anything is scarce if it is desirable but limited in quantity.

2. <u>Are most things scarce?</u> Scarcity is very common. Although certain things like the oxygen we breath (desirable but not

limited) and radioactive waste (limited but not desirable) are not scarce, the unpleasant fact is that many things are scarce.

3. <u>What are fungible goods and how is this concept related to scarcity?</u> Scarce goods are fungible if one of the goods may be replaced by, or substituted for, another of the goods. For example, stalks of wheat are fungible. Dollar bills are also fungible.

4. <u>What unit sets the value of a pile of goods?</u> Because of fungibility, the value of the last increment to a pile of goods sets the value of the whole.

5. <u>What is a budget line, and how is it related to scarcity?</u> In a world of scarce resources, one cannot consume unlimited quantities of goods and services. The budget line is a downward sloping curve that captures this notion of scarcity. It bounds the attainable goods and services. It is also known as a <u>transformation curve</u>, <u>production possibility curve</u>, <u>trade-off curve</u>, or a <u>production frontier</u>.

6. <u>What is opportunity cost?</u> The opportunity cost of consuming a good is the maximum amount of other scarce things that are sacrificed by choosing the good.

7. <u>What is its relation to the price of one thing in terms of another?</u> Opportunity cost is the cost of one item in terms of another.

8. <u>How do you calculate relative price, given two money prices?</u> Relative price is the rate at which one item can be substituted for another item. It is equal to the ratio of the two money prices.

9. <u>In a two-good diagram, how is a rise in the price of one of the goods (and a fall in the price of the other) represented using a budget line?</u> The slope of the budget line measures the relative price of one item in terms of the other. In a two-good diagram, a rise in the price of one of the goods is represented by a change in the slope of the budget line.

1.2 INCOME IN THE BUDGET LINE

1. <u>How is income represented in a budget line?</u> The position of the budget line measures the income of the consumer.

2. <u>Is income in the form of particular goods (housing, food) as useful to the consumer as the same value in money?</u> Most economists agree that income in the form of particular goods is not as useful to a consumer as the same value in money. It is

always desirable to have access to the whole of a higher budget line (a gift in cash) rather than to only part of it (a gift in the form of goods).

3. <u>Do people with higher incomes face lower prices?</u> People with higher incomes do not face lower prices. The budget line for a richer person will be farther out than the budget line for a poorer person, but both face the same relative prices. Although the positions of their budget lines are different, the slopes are the same.

4. <u>In a two-good diagram, how does one represent a rise in income using a budget line?</u> In a two-good diagram, a rise in income is represented by a parallel shift outward in the budget line.

5. <u>What is the income effect?</u> The effect of an increase of income alone on the amount of a good or service consumed is known as the income effect. Relative prices are held constant.

6. <u>What is a normal good?</u> If an increase in income leads to an increase in the amount of a particular good consumed, the good is a normal good. The income effect is positive.

7. <u>An inferior good?</u> If an increase in income leads to a decrease in the amount of a particular good consumed, the good is an inferior good. The income effect is negative.

8. <u>How do you express budget lines in algebra?</u> One equation for the budget line is: $P_G Q_G + P_A Q_A = Y$, where Q_G is the quantity of some good G, Q_A is the quantity of all other goods, P_G is the price of G, P_A is the price of all other goods, and Y is the consumer's income.

1.3 PRICES IN THE BUDGET LINE: THE LAW OF DEMAND

1. <u>What happens to the amount of a good demanded when its price changes?</u> The quantity of a good demanded varies inversely with changes in its price.

2. <u>What is the Law of Demand?</u> The law of demand says that more is demanded of a thing when its relative price falls.

3. <u>Do consumers do what they do out of habit?</u> Consumer behavior is determined by price and not by habit.

4. <u>Is gold more expensive than a haircut?</u> It is meaningless to

say that gold is more expensive than a haircut. The law of demand does not apply to comparisons between different goods.

5. <u>How do money prices and relative prices figure in the Law of Demand?</u> The law of demand speaks of relative prices and not of money prices.

6. <u>Does the ratio of prices or the difference between prices matter to how much is consumed?</u> The ratio of prices, not their difference, is what determines how much is consumed.

7. <u>Does an equiproportional increase in all prices and money income have any effect on amounts consumed?</u> An equiproportional increase in all prices and money income does not have any effect on amounts consumed.

8. <u>Why should you believe the Law of Demand?</u> The Law of Demand is only a working hypothesis, but one which is hard to disbelieve. It is equivalent to the Weak Axiom of Revealed Preference which asserts that consumers are consistent in their behavior.

9. <u>What is the Weak Axiom of Revealed Preference?</u> The Weak Axiom of Revealed Preference asserts that if a consumer is presented with an opportunity to purchase some bundle A, yet chooses to buy another bundle B, then she will never choose to purchase A if B is also affordable.

10. <u>What is a demand curve?</u> A demand curve is another alternative representation of the law of demand. It shows the relationship between the relative price of a good and the quantity of the good consumed.

11. <u>How is it related to budget lines?</u> The slope of the budget line corresponds to a particular relative price. As the slope of the budget line changes, the relative price of the good changes as well as the quantity demanded. For each budget line there corresponds a price along the demand curve.

III. <u>MULTIPLE-CHOICE</u>

1. The shape of a budget line in an economy depends upon
   (a) the prices of the resources needed to produce the goods
   (b) the degree of fungibility of the goods
   (c) the money prices of the goods
   (d) the technology for producing the goods

2. Opportunity cost is the result of
   (a) unlimited human wants and needs
   (b) scarcity

(c) high money prices for some goods and low money prices for others
(d) too many poor people

3. The opportunity cost of a good is simply
(a) its money price
(b) its importance to society
(c) its price along the budget line
(d) related to how many units of the good exist

4. The slope of the budget line measures
(a) the relative price of one good in terms of another
(b) the amount of disposable income a consumer has
(c) the number of attainable goods in society
(d) the amount of each good the consumer will buy

5. The position of the budget line
(a) depends upon the cost of an additional unit of one item in terms of other items
(b) measures the income of the consumer
(c) depends upon the amount of each good the consumer will buy
(d) changes if the goods produced by society are normal goods or inferior goods

6. The effect of an increase in income alone on the amount of a good consumed
(a) is always positive
(b) is always negative
(c) is positive if the good is a normal good
(d) is positive if the good is an inferior good

7. The law of demand
(a) allows real income to vary
(b) applies to comparisons between different goods
(c) says that more is demanded of a good when its money price falls
(d) says that more is demanded of a good when its relative price falls

8. Sid Stone buys only two goods, beer and pizza. If the prices Sid faces double, including the wage he earns working after classes, then
(a) the amounts of beer and pizza he consumes must rise
(b) the amounts of beer and bizza he consumes will stay the same
(c) the amount of beer consumed will rise and pizza consumed will decline
(d) the amount of beer consumed will decline and pizza consumed will rise

9. An equiproportional increase in money income and money prices
(a) causes real income to change

(b) has no effect on consumer behavior
(c) causes a leftward shift in the budget line
(d) causes a rightward shift in the budget line

10. William Morris consumes cigars and food. If the relative price of food increases and his real income remains constant then
(a) the number of cigars he purchases will rise
(b) the amount of food he consumes will rise
(c) the amount of food and cigars he consumes will rise
(d) the amount of food and cigars he consumes will decline

IV. EXERCISES

1. In the late 1970's, the state of New Jersey became one of the first states to institute legalized gambling in the form of a state lottery. After considerable debate, the state legislature passed the necessary legislation to legalize the state lottery system. Agreement was reached only after the condition was set that a large percentage of the expected profits from the lottery would be earmarked specifically for higher education.

Although the state lottery system eventually became very profitable, the allocation of state funds for higher education did not grow at the same rate. This led to complaints from the general public in the late 1970's and early 1980's that the state university system had been cheated and that funds that were earmarked for higher education in New Jersey were being diverted to uses elsewhere in the state.

Is the general public correct in its belief that revenues from the state lottery are being diverted to other uses? Is it meaningful to speak of funds being "earmarked" for a specific use? What can you conclude about the true substance of the condition set by legislators for the passage of the state lottery legislation?

2. The 20 Cent Photo Company began a promotional campaign in 1983 to lure customers to their film developing business. Every time a customer sent them a roll of film for processing, they received a bonus coupon. When the customer collected 9 bonus coupons, she was entitled to free developing and printing of the tenth roll of film. This promotional offer was valid through December 1984.

In January 1984 Mary Read collected her ninth bonus coupon. After using up a tenth roll of film, Mary concluded that the pictures she had taken were not very interesting. She decided that it was silly to waste her free developing on that roll of film and would wait instead to use it on the next roll she exposed. Instead of using the free developing to which she was entitled, she paid for the development and printing of the roll with cash and saved her bonus coupons.

Comment on Mary's decision. Did it really make any difference which roll of film was developed using the bonus coupons? Why?

3. In November 1983, disposable personal income in the United States, which is after-tax income, was $2.423 trillion. In December 1983, disposable personal income rose to $2.433 trillion. This represented a 0.8% increase. The December increase was partly a result of increases in employment and higher average hourly earnings. This rise in disposable income led to a 1.3% increase in personal spending on retail goods and on services.

Use a two-dimensional budget line to depict the change in consumption opportunities from November to December.

4. Consider the two different situations drawn in Figure 1.1. Jim Hogan and Jeremy Stone consume Food and Other Goods. Over time, the price of Food has risen and the price of Other Goods has fallen. The dashed budget lines represent Hogan's and Stone's respective budget constraints before the price changes, and the solid lines represent their respective budgets after the price changes. In each diagram, A is the bundle of goods that was chosen before the price changes and point B is the bundle of goods that was chosen after the price changes.

Do Hogan's and Stone's behavior each satisfy the Weak Axiom of Revealed Preference? Why? What do their respective consumption patterns imply about the law of demand?

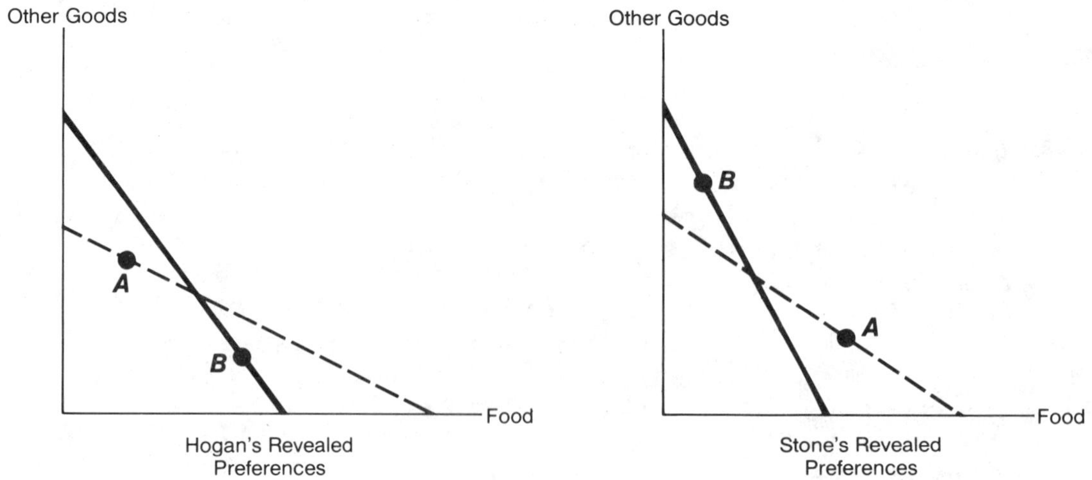

FIGURE 1.1

5. John Linkletter is a freshman at Drexel University. He is able to attend Drexel because he receives a $3000 annual stipend from the university. Drexel requires that every student purchase a personal computer upon entering the university. Consequently, John has decided to allocate his stipend between his purchase of a computer and textbooks for his courses. Suppose that the average price of a personal computer is $500 and the average price of a college textbook is $25.

(a) What is the equation for John Linkletter's budget constraint?

(b) What is the relative price of a personal computer in terms of college textbooks? How is this related to the slope of the budget line?

(c) What is the opportunity cost to John of purchasing one more textbook?

(d) If John decides to spend his entire stipend on books, what is the maximum number of books that he can possibly purchase? How is this number related to the value of the intercept of the budget line?

6. The state legislature in New Jersey is contemplating implementing a five cent per gallon tax on gasoline in order to raise additional revenues for the state. The sales tax on all other goods will remain unchanged. If the new tax law is passed, what will happen to the price of gasoline relative to all other goods? Show this using a budget line for gasoline and all other goods.

7. In 1977, legislation was passed by the federal government that made food stamps free to all recipients. Eleanor Reynolds is a food stamp recipient. Because of her low income level, she qualifies for $200 worth of food stamps every month. Although Eleanor is willing to accept the food stamps, she would rather not spend so much on food even when she is subsidized by the federal government. She therefore uses as many of the food stamps as she wants and then sells the remaining stamps to her friends at a discounted price. Is Eleanor as well off as if the government had simply given her a cash transfer equal to the money value of the food stamps she uses plus the amount of money she receives by selling the extra stamps?

V. PROBLEM

Election 1984: Democrats versus Republicans on Defense Spending

The Democratic presidential primary races in 1984 reflected a fundamental change in the attitudes of candidates about defense spending. In recent elections, Democratic contenders had usually advocated cutting the defense budget. But in 1984, six of the eight Democratic candidates favored increased defense spending by the federal government. Ben Wattenberg, a scholar at the American Enterprise Institute noted, "...the party has collectively changed its view ... Suddenly in the Democratic party it has become a bonus to attack a guy for being soft on defense."

Prior to the 1984 campaign, President Reagan proposed a 13% real, inflation-adjusted, boost in defense spending. John Glenn took the toughest stance on defense spending within the Democratic party and advocated a 6% increase in real spending. Senator Alan Cranston took a more moderate view and argued for a 4% annual increase, while Walter Mondale called for a real increase of 3% to 4%. The two major exceptions were George McGovern and the Rev. Jesse Jackson, who called for spending cuts. Mr. McGovern advocated a 25% cut in spending.

A major reason for the switch in attitudes by most Democratic candidates was due to the experience the Democrats had during the 1980 presidential campaign against Ronald Reagan. As Mr. Wattenberg noted, "We got burned by Ronald Reagan in 1980 making the case the Democrats were generally the limp-wristed party."

(a) Draw a production possibility curve for the United States showing the trade-off between production of defense and social welfare programs.

(b) What is the opportunity cost to society of spending more of its scarce resources on defense? How is this represented by the production possibility curve?

(c) Is it possible for the federal government to maintain the same number of social welfare programs and at the same time increase its expenditures on defense? (Assume that taxes remain unchanged.) How is this represented in the production possibility diagram?

(d) Suppose the Congress adheres to the popular view and increases defense outlays. What will happen to the opportunity cost of defense expenditures by society as more federal funds are spent on defense and less on social welfare programs?

(e) Technological advances are frequently made in the defense industry and are reflected in lower prices for existing military equipment. If a major technological breakthrough occurs in 1985, what will happen to the production possibility curve for the United States?

(f) Advancing technology also often leads to increased productivity within the economy. Private firms are able to produce more goods and services from the same amount of resources. If this occurs over time, what will happen to the production frontier for the United States?

CHAPTER 2

The Consumer's Choice

I. OVERVIEW

Consumers derive satisfaction or utility from the goods and services that they consume. A basic assumption that is made in economics is that consumers behave so as to maximize their utility, subject to the limitations imposed by their budget constraints.

In order to maximize utility, a consumer must be able to rank her preferences for different commodity bundles. It is assumed that a typical consumer is always able to compare the utility gained from any two bundles A and B. Either the consumer will prefer one bundle over the other or she will be indifferent between the two. The hill of utility (or utility function) is a way of representing the consumer's preferences. Utility is an ordinal measure. Since happiness cannot be measured, economists do not generally attempt to assign a cardinal measure of happiness to every bundle of goods that the consumer might choose to consume. The hill of utility simply shows the order in which a consumer prefers different bundles of commodities. The further up the hill the consumer is, the higher is her level of satisfaction. The peak of the hill, or "bliss" point, is the point of saturation.

Indifference curves are constant utility contours. They correspond to a particular distance up the hill. All of the bundles of commodities that lie on a particular indifference curve provide the consumer with the same level of utility. The consumer is indifferent between these bundles. Indifference curves, like the utility functions themselves, convey relevant ordinal information about the consumer's preferences.

The shape of the hill of utility and its correspoding indifference curves depend upon the types of goods between which the consumer must choose. In general, indifference curves are convex. They are bowed toward the origin. But there are two limiting cases: perfect complements and perfect substitutes. If the goods are perfect complements, like right shoes and left shoes, then the indifference curves will have corners. If the goods are substitutes, like butter and margarine, then the indifference curves will be straight lines.

Indifference curves are useful tools that can be combined with the budget line to determine the utility-maximizing, or equilibrium, bundle of goods. The consumer purchases goods and services so as to maximize her satisfaction. She wants to get as far up the hill of utility as she possibly can. She is constrained not to exceed her fixed, limited, and scarce money income. In other words, the consumer cannot consume a bundle of goods that lies beyond her budget line. The equilibrium bundle is on the highest indifference curve that she can get to without going beyond her budget constraint. The bundle of goods that gives her the maximum attainable satisfaction is at the point of tangency between the budget line and the highest attainable indifference curve. These points of tangency are also points on her demand curves for the different goods.

The concept of total utility leads to the related concept of marginal utility. Simply put, marginal utility is the additional utility that a consumer gains by consuming an additional unit of a good. The condition for utility maximization can be expressed in terms of marginal utilities. The rule of rational life is equivalent to such an expression: Pursue an activity until the marginal benefit is equal to the marginal cost of pursuing it further. If the consumer purchases less or more than the rule dictates, she will be foregoing attainable happiness.

SUMMARY OF KEY CONCEPTS

utility	consumer equilibrium
indifference curves	goods and bads
perfect complements	perfect substitutes
convexity	marginal utility

II. ANSWERS TO "WHAT TO READ FOR"

2.1 THE PURSUIT OF HAPPINESS

1. How does a consumer choose between different combinations of goods? The consumer chooses the bundle of goods that is at the highest point on her hill of utility that she can reach, without going beyond her budget line.

2. What is the hill of utility? The hill of utility is a way of representing a consumer's preferences. Every point on the hill corresponds to a different bundle of goods. The higher up the hill, the higher is the consumer's level of happiness.

3. Indifference curves? An indifference curve is a contour on

the hill of utility. It shows all of the bundles of goods that provide the consumer with the same level of happiness.

4. How do you represent people with preferences for one good over another? People with preferences for one good over another are represented by a particular hill of utility. Different preferences or tastes are represented by hills of utility that have different shapes.

5. How do the indifference curves look between a good and a "bad"? The indifference curves between a good and a "bad" slope upwards.

6. How are indifference curves useful for making choices? The indifference curve framework is applicable to any choice.

2.2 THE SHAPE OF INDIFFERENCE CURVES

1. What does an indifference curve usually look like? Indifference curves for goods (as opposed to bads) are usually convex to the origin.

2. What are the extremes within which the shape of a typical indifference curve must fall? The extremes within which the shape of a typical indifference curve must fall are right-angles and straight lines.

3. What does an indifference curve between two perfect complements look like? An indifference curve between two complements is a right angle.

4. Between two perfect substitutes? An indifference curve between two perfect substitutes is a straight line.

5. When two goods are complements, does the pricing of either good alone matter to the consumer? When two goods are complements, the pricing of either good alone does not matter to the consumer.

6. Can the prices of substitutes vary relative to each other? The prices of substitutes move together. They cannot vary relative to each other.

7. What is the marginal rate of indifferent substitution, or the marginal valuation? The marginal rate of indifferent substitution is the rate at which a consumer is willing to give up one good in order to obtain one more unit of another good. It is also known as the marginal valuation of one good in terms of the other.

8. <u>How does it vary along an indifference curve?</u> The marginal valuation of good A decreases as you move along any given indifference curve in the direction of increasing good A and decreasing good B.

2.3 THE USES OF INDIFFERENCE CONTOURS

1. <u>Do economists actually have precise measurements of the shapes of indifference curves?</u> Economists do not have precise measurements of the shapes of indifference curves.

2. <u>If not, why bother with the idea?</u> Even though economists do not have precise measurements of the shapes of indifference curves, the idea that indifference curves are convex is enough to shed light on many social questions.

3. <u>Is it possible to answer interesting social questions using indifference curves, even though we don't precisely know their shapes?</u> Yes, it is possible to answer interesting social questions using indifference curves.

4. <u>Is it better to give small towns cheap mail or direct cash subsidies?</u> A subsidy to income is always better than a subsidy to a price. It is therefore better to give small towns direct cash benefits rather than cheap mail.

5. <u>Can an offer of free, public education sometimes lower the amount of education consumed?</u> Depending upon consumer preferences and the shapes of the corresponding indifference curves, it is possible that an offer of free, public education will lower the amount of education consumed.

6. <u>How do indifference curves answer such questions?</u> The indifference curve diagram is a tool to assist your thinking. For any particular question, a correct indifference curve diagram must be set up. Once this is done, a budget line between the two goods can be drawn on the indifference curve diagram and a point mutually exclusive to the budget line can be found. The problem is then solved.

2.4 MEASURABLE UTILITY

1. <u>What is marginal utility?</u> Marginal utility is the additional utility gained by consuming one more unit of a commodity.

2. <u>How is it related to total utility?</u> The marginal utility

curve is the slope of the total utility curve.

3. <u>What is the Rule of Rational Life?</u> The Rule of Rational Life says that an activity should be pursued until the marginal benefit is equal to the marginal cost of pursuing it further.

4. <u>What is marginal cost?</u> Marginal cost is the additional cost incurred by pursuing an activity one step further.

5. <u>How does marginal utility guide the consumer to a correct utility-maximizing choice?</u> In order to make a correct, utility-maximizing choice, the consumer should continue to purchase a commodity until the marginal utility gained from an additional unit of the good is equal to the marginal cost of consuming it.

6. <u>How does one show that the theory of marginal utilities is the same as the theory of indifference curves?</u> The Rule of Rational Life, expressed in terms of marginal utilities, is equivalent to the tangency condition for an optimum in the theory of indifference curves. The consumer's marginal valuation of a particular good is equal to the slope of a given indifference curve at a particular point. The marginal cost to the consumer of consuming an additional unit of a good is equal to the slope of the budget line. The Rule of Rational Life is therefore equal to the tangency condition.

III. <u>MULTIPLE CHOICE</u>

1. Mary Jane would move to the point of saturation in her consumption
   (a) only in a two-commodity world
   (b) were it not for the scarcity of her resources
   (c) only when it corresponds to a point on her budget line
   (d) only when it corresponds to a point below her budget line

2. The bundle of commodities that Ralph Edwards chooses to consume is called an equilibrium. This equilibrium bundle
   (a) is the best position Ralph can imagine
   (b) corresponds to the point of saturation
   (c) is the best bundle Ralph can attain given his income and the commodity prices he faces
   (d) lies below Ralph's budget constraint

3. The Ohio Power and Electric Company produces electricity for residents in the state of Ohio. A large portion of this electricity is generated by burning coal. A serious side effect of this burning is sulfur dioxide that pollutes the atmosphere that the residents of Ohio (and other states) must breathe. If

one were to draw community indifference curves between electricity and sulfur dioxide pollution for the residents of Ohio,

(a) they would be downward sloping
(b) they would be upward sloping
(c) they would intersect
(d) one would find that they can't exist

4. Sam Frederickson is caught up in the latest computer rage and is anxious to buy his own home computer. When he shops around for a computer, he discovers that the computer hardware (that is, the machinery) is useless unless he also buys the computer software (that is, the programs) that are specifically designed to run the computer hardware. Computer hardware and software are therefore

(a) perfect complements, represented by straight line indifference curves
(b) perfect substitutes, represented by straight line indifference curves
(c) perfect complements, represented by indifference curves with corners
(d) perfect substitutes, represented by indifference curves with corners

5. If two goods, such as left and right shoes, are perfect complements then

(a) increasing the quantity of either good will increase utility
(b) increasing the quantity of one without increasing the minimum quantity of both will decrease utility
(c) increasing the quantity of one without increasing the maximum quantity of both will increase utility
(d) increasing the quantity of one without increasing the minimum quantity of both will not increase utility

6. If goods are perfect substitutes and the consumer faces constant prices, then

(a) the consumer should specialize in only the cheaper of the goods
(b) the consumer should consume some of both goods in order to minimize the risk of shortages
(c) the consumer should never buy more of one good without buying more of the other
(d) increasing the quantity of one without increasing the minimum quantity of both will not increase utility

7. A frequent debate among economists is whether it is preferable to subsidize the cost of medical care for the elderly or to simply provide the needy elderly with a monetary subsidy to their income. The answer is that

(a) it really makes no difference since the elderly can afford to purchase needed medical care under either plan
(b) a subsidy to income is always better than a subsidy to

price
(c) a subsidy to price is always better than a subsidy to income
(d) the answer depends upon the particular preferences of the elderly

8. Tina Hall has been a student her whole life. Even after she graduated from college and found a job, she always forced herself to set aside a few hours every night to read and study books. Tina's friends think that she is a bookworm and should stop spending so much time reading now that she is out of college. The rule of rational life says that Tina
(a) should stop studying while the marginal benefit is still greater than the marginal cost of pursuing it further
(b) should continue studying until the marginal benefit is equal to the marginal cost of pursuing it further
(c) should continue studying until the marginal benefit of pursuing it further becomes zero
(d) should continue studying until the marginal cost of pursuing it further becomes zero

9. The rule of rational life
(a) is identical in content to the theory of indifference curves
(b) is contained within the formulation of the budget line
(c) can only be applied to economic problems
(d) can only be applied to the consumption of goods but never bads

10. If marginal utilities depends only on the ratio of the two goods consumed, then
(a) the consumer will alter the ratio of goods consumed when her income increases
(b) the consumer will not alter the ratio of goods consumed when her income increases
(c) the consumer will not alter the ratio of goods consumed when the prices she faces increase
(d) the consumer will always consume the identical bundle of commodities

IV. EXERCISES

1. Hilda Washingame has preferences for food and clothing that can be represented by the utility function U=X+Y, where U is utility, X is ounces of food consumed, and Y is the number of pieces of clothing. Demonstrate that this functional representation of her preferences is not unique by deriving another utility function that represents these same preferences.

2. Indifference curves are constant utility contours along the hill of utility. The indifference map conveys the same ordinal information about the consumer's preferences as does the utility function itself. Consider again Hilda Washingame's utility function in exercise 1.

(a) What is the general equation for Hilda's indifference curves?

(b) Demonstrate that the indifference curves representing Hilda's preferences are also not unique by deriving another indifference map that represents her preferences.

3. The bundle of goods that will maximize Hilda's utility is at the point of tangency between her budget line and the highest indifference curve she can attain. Yet, the functional representation of her preferences is not unique. What does this imply about the relationship between the utility maximizing bundle and the choice of utility function that is used to represent Hilda's preferences?

4. Suppose that the average prices of food and clothing double. At the same time, in order to compensate Hilda for inflation, her employer doubles her income. What will happen to the utility maximizing bundle of food and clothing?

5. Indifference curves have properties that reflect certain assumptions that have been made about consumer behavior. The following questions are intended to investigate some of these properties.

(a) What implicit assumption about consumer behavior guarantee that there must be an indifference curve through each point in commodity space?

(b) Prove that indifference curves cannot intersect.

(c) The assumption of non-satiation is often made in economics. The consumer always prefers more to less. What does this assumption imply about the shape of the hill of utility?

6. Suppose Ted Thurber is considering buying 10 shares of IBM stock and 20 shares of AT&T stock. Suppose the price per share of IBM stock is $100 and the price per share of AT&T stock is $50. The particular combination of stock that Ted is considering buying is such that his marginal valuation of IBM stock in terms of AT&T stock is 4. Is the combination of 10 IBM shares and 20 AT&T shares an optimal choice for Ted? Explain.

V. PROBLEM

Food Stamps

The problem of domestic hunger is a major policy issue in the United States. The efficiency and fairness of the food stamp program is the frequent subject of public debate.

During the Nixon administration, food stamps were made a true national entitlement. All participating households received a sufficient number of food stamps to purchase an adequate amount of food each month. The food stamp allotment depended upon the size of the household. The amount the household had to pay for the stamps depended upon the household's income. Very poor families received their food stamp allotment for free. Families that were better off financially had to pay for as much as 85% of the face value of the food stamps.

In 1977, during the Carter administration, the food stamp program underwent a basic structural change. The requirement that recipients pay for the food stamps was eliminated. Food stamps were free to all recipients. Households that were the same size but had different incomes received different numbers of food stamps. A principal motivation for this change was to increase household freedom.

It was observed that the structural change in the food stamp program had little effect on the poorer families. Under the old system, they were required to pay a very small amount of money for their food stamp allotment. Under the new system, they received a slightly smaller allotment for free. Some less poor households, however, spent as much or more than their food stamp allotment on food, but less than the food stamp allotment they would have received under the old Nixon administration program.

(a) Using indifference curve analysis, show how the food stamp program functioned during the Nixon administration. Indicate how the allocation of food stamps to an eligible household affected its optimal choice of food and all other goods.

(b) Many eligible families failed to participate in the food stamp program during the Nixon years. What possible reasons could explain this observed phenomenon?

(c) Why did the behavior of less poor families change with the institution of the new food stamp program in 1977? (Use indifference curves in your answer.)

CHAPTER 3

The Measurement of Utility and the Economics of Risk

I. OVERVIEW

Utility is an ordinal concept. It is not possible to derive cardinal measures of happiness. Yet it is possible to use utility functions and indifference curves to describe observable consumer behavior that arises from individual preferences. None of the economist's uses of the indifference contours on the hill of utility depend upon the measurability of utility.

The shapes of the hill of utility and of the indifference curves are important. The theory of revealed preference asserts that the shapes of indifference curves can be ascertained from the observed behavior of consumers in the marketplace. It is not necessary for a consumer to explicitly rank different bundles of commodities in order for the economist to determine the shape of her indifference curves. By subjecting a consumer to different budget lines, she is induced to reveal the order in which she ranks different bundles of goods. Indifference curves and different bundles of commodities can be given a rank by observing the behavior of the consumer as revealed in the marketplace.

In 1944, John von Neumann and Oskar Morgenstern demonstrated that although utility is an ordinal concept, it is possible to assign numbers to indifference curves. The method that is used for assigning numbers to indifference curves makes use of gambling. By subjecting a consumer to various gambles that have uncertain outcomes with different probabilities, she is induced to reveal the utility levels she attaches to the bundles of goods. These numbers are not absolute measures of happiness. They depend on the scale that is chosen for measuring happiness. Since no single scale is uniquely correct, the units in which marginal utility or total utility is measured has no absolute significance. But the rate of change of marginal utility is uniquely measurable.

Utility measures also cannot be compared between individuals. It is meaningless to say that one individual gets more units of happiness from an additional unit of a commodity than does another individual. One also cannot make interpersonal comparisons of rates of change of marginal utility.

The debate about whether or not utility is measurable has

led to the development of a tool that is useful for understanding consumer behavior. This tool is the utility-of-income curve. The shape of this curve has meaning in the world of uncertainty in which we live. It plots income against the utility of income (measured in terms of all other goods). The shape of this curve can describe a consumer's behavior toward risky activities. A person who prefers fair gambles to a secure income is said to exhibit a preference for risk, and the marginal utility of income is rising. A person who will pay not to gamble (that is, accept unfair insurance) is said to exhibit an aversion to risk, and the marginal utility of income is declining. This framework is applicable to many different risky activities such as gambling, insurance, crime and punishment, and investment in risky projects.

SUMMARY OF KEY CONCEPTS

nonmeasurable utility	measurable utility
risk preference	probabilities of prospects
expansion path	utility of income curve
insurance	

II. ANSWERS TO WHAT TO READ FOR

3.1 PARADISE LOST: NONMEASURABLE UTILITY

1. Can one really measure utility, or marginal utility? No. Since "happiness" is not quantifiable, utility and marginal utility cannot really be measured.

2. What, then, does an indifference curve say? An indifference curve illustrates the bundles of commodities among which a consumer is unable to choose. It does not show the amount of happiness that the consumer derives from the different bundles. An indifference map shows a consumer's rankings of different bundles of goods.

3. Do indifference curves need to be ordinal or cardinal to describe sensible consumer behavior? Indifference curves only need be ordinal in order to describe rational consumer behavior. What is important is the consumer's rankings of the bundles, not the absolute amount of happiness she derives from the bundles.

4. Is it possible to draw indifference curves by simply observing the behavior of consumers? How? Yes, it is possible

to draw a consumer's indifference map by observing her behavior as revealed in the marketplace. By subjecting her to different price scenarios (that is, budget lines), the consumer is induced to reveal the order in which she ranks different bundles of commodities.

3.2 PARADISE REGAINED: MEASURABLE UTILITY

1. What is average utility? When a consumer takes a gamble with uncertain outcome, it is impossible to say with certainty what will be the level of utility that the consumer will get from the outcome. Economists therefore speak of the average utility from the gamble. This is equal to the probability of winning the gamble times the utility from winning, plus the probability of losing times the utility gained from the losing outcome.

2. How is average utility related to gambling? In order to speak of average utility, one must be considering uncertain outcomes. A gamble has an uncertain outcome.

3. In terms of average utility, when will a smart gambler take a gamble? A smart gambler will take a gamble only when she thinks that the utility she will end up with on average is greater than the utility she started with.

4. Why is "the" utility not unique? Is temperature unique? The utility is not unique because utility is not measurable on an absolute scale. Cardinal values can be given to utility once an arbitrary scale for utility is chosen. Similarly, temperature measures are not unique. Consider that there are at least three different scales for temperature: the Celsius, Fahrenheit and Kelvin scales. Once an arbitrary scale for temperature measures has been chosen, changes in temperature are measurable.

3.3 IMPERFECTIONS IN PARADISE?

1. Would units other than joys be suitable for measuring utility? Absolutely. One could measure utility in terms of happys, funs, or smiles.

2. Is a scale of utility of joys for Field unique? No. A scale of joys used for measuring utility is arbitrary. Any other scale would be appropriate. Total utility and marginal utility are not measurable uniquely. But the rate of change of marginal utility is measurable uniquely.

3.4 LIVING IN PARADISE: THE USES OF MEASURABLE UTILITY

1. <u>What is the utility of income?</u> The utility of income curve plots income against the utility of income (measured in terms of all other goods).

2. <u>What role does it play in thinking about gambling?</u> The utility of income curve is useful for thinking about uncertain outcomes. The curve reduces all commodities into a single commodity called income. Income has a level of utility associated with it. The curve therefore enables one to analyze a consumer's condition in various circumstances.

3. <u>What is risk aversion?</u> Risk aversion is a description of a consumer's attitudes towards risky activities and uncertain outcomes. A person who prefers fair gambles to a secure income is said to have a preference for risk. A person who will pay not to gamble is risk averse.

4. <u>How is it related to the shape of the utility of income curve?</u> The shape of the utility of income curve describes a person's behavior toward risky activities. A person whose preferences exhibit increasing marginal utility is a preferer of risk. A risk averter exhibits declining marginal utility of income. A person who is risk neutral exhibits constant marginal utility of income.

5. <u>What is fair insurance?</u> The insurance that a consumer buys is fair if the cost of the insurance is equal to the income she expects to lose on average from taking a gamble.

6. <u>Why does a criminal take a chance on being caught?</u> Crime is a gamble. A criminal takes a chance on being caught because she believes that the gamble will raise her income on average. Notice that a criminal can be risk averse and still take a chance on crime.

7. <u>Why shouldn't you put all your eggs in one basket?</u> Safety is costly. A consumer who is trying to maximize her income might not choose a perfectly safe income (such as a federally insured savings account) if her average income can be increased by accepting some variability of income (for example, by putting some money in the stock market).

III. <u>MULTIPLE CHOICE</u>

1. Mary Decker and Carl Lewis find a gold coin lying on the ground while they are out running. The gold coin has a value of $300. Since they both want the coin, they decide to flip the

coin to see who gets it. If the coin comes up heads, then Mary wins the coin. If the coin comes up tales, then Carl wins the coin. The money that Mary and Carl each end up with on average is

(a) $300
(b) $600
(c) $0
(d) $150

2. Suppose in problem #1, Carl Lewis was the first to find the gold coin, but still agrees to accept the gamble with Mary. In this case, Carl Lewis is

(a) risk neutral
(b) risk averse
(c) behaving like a smart gambler
(d) not behaving like a smart gambler

3. Crime in the United States can be reduced by

(a) giving all potential criminals more money through a welfare system
(b) spending more taxpayer money on crime prevention
(c) making living conditions in jails poorer
(d) all of the above

4. Although utility is not quantifiable uniquely,

(a) marginal utility is uniquely measurable
(b) changes in marginal utility are measurable uniquely
(c) changes in total utility are measurable uniquely
(d) interpersonal comparisons of utility can be made

5. The marginal utility of income curve

(a) is unique
(b) plots income against the utility of income
(c) is the slope at an irregular slice up the utility hill
(d) does not vary with the degree of risk aversion

IV. EXERCISES

1. The Ganav Insurance Company is a major seller of car insurance in the United States. Most of their accident insurance policies are sold to risk prefering car owners. The annual premium for car insurance from Ganav is $700. This insurance covers the insured motorist for up to $100,000 of damages incurred in an accident. Ganav knows from market studies that for its clientele, there is a 1 in 100 chance of a major accident.

(a) On average, how much money does each driver expect to lose from taking a gamble of not carrying any insurance?

(b) Is the insurance policy offered by the Ganav Insurance Company fair in the technical sense?

(c) If the typical motorist was risk neutral, would the insurance policy still be fair?

2. A major problem in several states is the existence of uninsured motorists. These are car owners who illegaly drive cars without owning any insurance. The extent of this problem varies between states.

(a) What are some of the possible explanations for the existence of this problem?

(b) Why is the uninsured motorist problem more prevalent in some states than in others?

3. During the 1960s, Carl Morton was a very conservative investor. Despite the encouragement of his financial advisor, he refused to ever purchase stocks or bonds. He chose instead to put all of his money into a federally insured savings account paying 5% interest per annum. In the 1980s, Morton decided to shift all of his money into a money market fund that payed 15% interest per annum, even though his money was no longer insured. <u>True or False:</u> Morton's shift in investment strategy indicated a change in risk preference.

V. PROBLEM

The Space Insurance Industry

Satellites and other space payloads have been insured against damage or failure for over 20 years. The importance of this insurance industry has grown rapidly in recent years as numerous communications satellites have been placed into orbit. It has been projected that owners of space payloads will pay at least $2.5 billion in insurance premiums by 1995.

At the beginning of 1984, owners of satellites that were launched from the U.S. Space Shuttle paid insurance premiums of less than 6% on the total amount of coverage. But several failures of shuttle-launched satellites during the early months of 1984 forced insurers to raise their premiums to a new level of 9% to 12% of total coverage. Insurance claims for satellite failures during that period alone totaled $300 million. James Barrett, the president of International Technology Underwriters was quoted as saying, "...if you're asking me to risk the capital of my company, then I've got to be comfortable that you're going to succeed. If we're not comfortable, we're not going to insure it, or we'll charge you like hell for it." Mr. Barrett was further quoted as saying, "In the future there will be fewer underwriting groups, and those that are successful will be very large."

(a) Does the increase in premiums reflect a change in risk preference on the part of the insurance companies?

(b) Explain fully why premiums rose after the satellite failures in early 1983.

(c) If premiums did not rise, what reaction might one expect on the part of the insured owners of the satellites?

(d) After the failures in early 1983, many insurers demanded a greater say over new space technology that they thought was too risky. Why?

CHAPTER 4

Indifference Curves and Demand

I. OVERVIEW

The law of demand says that the quantity of a good that is demanded is inversely related to its price. This relationship is depicted by a downward-sloping demand curve. The indifference curve framework provides an alternative way of looking at demand curves that is useful for understanding the law of demand. It enables one to easily decompose the total effect of a price change into two component effects: the income effect and the substitution effect.

Consider a fall in the price of a commodity. The fall in price causes the consumer's real income to rise. After the price decline the consumer can afford to purchase more of each good. This is the income effect. In terms of indifference curves, the income effect is represented by a jump from one indifference curve to a higher indifference curve. The consumer's real purchasing power is higher so her level of utility is higher. The decline in price also causes the relative price of the commodity to fall. The good becomes cheaper in terms of all other goods. The consumer therefore substitutes the cheaper good in place of some of the other goods. This is the pure substitution effect. In terms of indifference curves, the substitution effect is represented by a movement along a particular indifference curve.

The direction of the substitution effect is unambiguous. A fall in the price of a commodity causes the consumer to substitute more of the cheaper good in place of some of the other goods. The direction of the income effect however, is ambiguous. Consider a fall in the price of a commodity that leads to an increase in real income. For a normal good, the rise in real income results in an increase in the amount of the good purchased. In this case, the income effect reinforces the substitution effect. For an inferior good, the rise in real income leads the consumer to purchase less of the commodity. This effect offsets to some degree the substitution effect. But the substitution effect still dominates the income effect. A Giffen good is a special case of an inferior good for which the income effect overwhelms the substitution effect. The fall in the price of the good results in a decrease in the quantity demanded. This perverse case is represented by an upward sloping demand curve.

SUMMARY OF KEY CONCEPTS

offer curve	income-compensated demand curve
Giffen good	uncompensated demand curve
income effect	substitution effect

II. ANSWERS TO WHAT TO READ FOR

1. What exactly happens when a consumer faces a drop in the price of something, say transportation? Assume that transportation is a normal good. When the price of transportation falls, the quantity of transportation demanded rises. This total effect consists of two components: an income effect and a substitution effect. The income effect results from the increase in the consumer's real purchasing power (that is, real income) given the fall in the price of transportation. The consumer can afford to buy more transportation, more of all other goods, or more of both. The substitution effect results from the change in the relative price of transportation. Since the relative price of transportation has fallen, the consumer substitutes more transportation in place of all other goods.

2. Is he made virtually richer? Yes. The consumer is made virtually richer by the fall in the price of transportation.

3. How much income would the consumer be willing to give up to get the privilege of buying the transportation at the lower price? The consumer would be willing to give up an amount of money equal to the income effect of the fall in price.

4. How do membership fees relate to this amount? A membership fee is a charge for the right to buy any amount of the product at the new, lower price. The largest membership fee that could be charged and still interest the consumer in the offer is equal to the income effect.

5. What is the substitution effect? The substitution effect shows how sensitive the consumer is at a given real income to changes in the price of the commodity. It corresponds to the degree of curvature of an indifference curve.

6. What is the income effect? The income effect shows how sensitive the consumer is at a given price to changes in real income. It corresponds to the amount of the good the consumer buys as she moves up to a higher indifference curve.

7. In an indifference curve diagram, how can a fall in the price of one commodity be broken into the price (or substitution)

effect and the income effect? In an indifference curve diagram, the price effect corresponds to a movement along a particular indifference curve due to the change in relative prices. The income effect corresponds to the jump from one indifference curve to a higher indifference curve as the consumer's real income rises.

8. In a demand curve? The ordinary demand curve consists of both the income and the substitution effects. The income compensated demand curve takes away the income effect. It is the demand curve holding real income constant and therefore shows the substitution effect.

9. What is a compensated demand curve? A compensated demand curve compensates for the income effect.

10. What is an uncompensated demand curve? An uncompensated demand curve contains both the income and the substitution effects.

11. How is an ordinary demand curve related to income-compensated curves? Each point on an ordinary demand curve corresponds to a different indifference curve and therefore lies on a different compensated demand curve. (Recall that the income-compensated demand curve shows only the pure substitution effect because it holds the consumer on one particular indifference curve.)

12. What are Giffen goods? A Giffen good is a commodity for which the negative income effect overwhelms the positive substitution effect. The demand curve corresponding to such a good has an upward slope.

13. Do they exist? Although the existence of Giffen goods is conceivable, they are factually unimportant.

14. What is a "need" for a good? Economists use the word "need" to mean that a consumer will never voluntarily consume less of the good. "Need" depends upon the shape of the consumer's indifference curves and the corresponding demand curve.

III. MULTIPLE CHOICE

1. The income-compensated demand curve shows only the pure substitution effect because
   (a) the income effect is zero
   (b) the substitution effect usually dominates the income effect
   (c) it holds the consumer on a single indifference curve

(d) the consumer jumps from one indifference curve to a higher indifference curve

2. An uncompensated fall in price includes
   (a) an income effect
   (b) a substitution effect
   (c) income and substitution effects
   (d) uncompensated income effects

3. Each point on the ordinary demand curve
   (a) lies on a different compensated demand curve
   (b) corresponds to the same indifference curve
   (c) shows only the pure substitution effect
   (d) shows only the income effect

4. An offer curve is
   (a) a locus of points at which the marginal utility of income is constant
   (b) a locus of points at which the marginal utility of all other goods is zero
   (c) a locus of points at which the marginal utility of all other goods is constant
   (d) a locus of tangency points between the consumer's indifference curves and all possible budget lines drawn for a particular endowment of all other goods

5. If food is a normal good for Jim Barnes then
   (a) his ordinary demand curve for food has a lower slope than any of his income-compensated curves
   (b) his ordinary demand curve for food has a higher slope than any of his income-compensated curves
   (c) his ordinary demand curve for food has the same slope as any of his income-compensated curves
   (d) his ordinary demand curve is identical to the income-compensated curve

IV. EXERCISES

1. In November 1983, Senator Robert Dole sponsored a measure in the United States Senate which would have provided tax credits to parents of children attending private and parochial schools. This tax credit was intended to provide as much as $300 in tax credits per child. This plan was supported by Senator Daniel P. Moynihan who argued that defeat of the measure would weaken the education system of the U.S. The plan however, was ultimately defeated in the Senate by a vote of 59-38.

(a) Suppose the tax credit bill had been passed. Using the indifference curve framework (with education on one axis and all other goods on the other axis), locate the equilibrium quantity demanded of education by a typical American family before and after enactment of the tax bill.

(b) On the same graph, show the income effect and the substitution effect due to the enactment of the tax bill.

(c) Is education a normal good, an inferior good, or a Giffen good? Explain.

2. The country of Narnia experienced an average annual rate of inflation of 5% from 1965 through 1970. During that period of time, the price of gasoline charged at the pumps remained unchanged.

(a) What happened to the relative price of gasoline and all other goods in Narnia from 1965 through 1970?

(b) Sketch an indifference curve map for a typical Narnian consumer, placing gasoline on the horizontal axis and all other goods on the vertical axis. Suppose that the relative price of all other goods in terms of gasoline was 100 in 1965. Construct the offer curve, assuming that the typical consumer perceived gasoline as a normal good from 1965-1970.

(c) Given this offer curve, sketch the uncompensated demand curve for gasoline.

V. PROBLEM

The Irish Potatoe Famine

Numerous economists have (erroneously) claimed that the Irish potatoe famine in 1845 is an empirical example of the violation of the law of demand. This argument is attributed to Sir Robert Giffen, a Victorian economist.

During the potatoe famine in 1845, the price of potatoes fell. Although the law of demand predicts that the quantity of potatoes demanded should have risen, Giffen claimed that the opposite actually occurred. He argued that the potatoe was a strongly inferior good to the poor Irish peasants. Prior to 1845, Irish families consumed a lot of potatoes because they were too poor to be able to afford meat. Further, few other substitutes for the potatoe were available to the peasants. During the famine, potatoe prices fell. This raised the peasants' purchasing power and caused a large income effect that tended to decrease the consumption of potatoes (since potatoes were viewed as an inferior good). Giffen argued that the income effect overwhelmed the substitution effect, so that the quantity of potatoes demanded fell as the price fell.

(a) Using an indifference curve framework, show how the violation of the law of demand during the potatoe famine is a theoretical possibility.

(b) On the same graph, locate the income effect and the substitution effect.

(c) Assume that the price of potatoes fell continuously during the period of the famine. Construct an offer curve for the typical Irish family.

(d) Using this offer curve, construct the ordinary (uncompensated) demand curve for Irish potatoes. Is the law of demand violated? Explain.

PART II. EXCHANGE

CHAPTER 5

Trade

I. OVERVIEW

The framework for analyzing individual consumer behavior can be used to study the problem of exchange between consumers. The fact that trade occurs between people suggests that an individual consumer can be a supplier of some goods and a demander of others. Whether the consumer is a supplier or a demander of a particular good depends upon her initial endowment of the good and the prevailing market price. If the difference between her initial endowment and the quantity of the good she demands at the prevailing market price is positive, then the consumer will be a supplier. If the difference is negative, then she will be a demander. Exchange between a demander and a supplier actually takes place when the supplier's marginal valuation of the good is less than the demander's.

The Edgeworth box is a graphical tool used by economists to depict all of the possibilities for exchange between two consumers. This box contains both consumers' indifference maps. Points of tangency between the consumers' indifference curves represent efficient allocations of the goods. It is beneficial for the consumers to continue trading until they reach an efficient allocation because both consumers can be made better off by the exchange without anyone being made worse off. Once the consumers have traded to any of the efficient allocations, no further exchanges can be made that will make one consumer better off without making the other worse off. The contract curve is the locus of all such efficient points.

Consumers are price takers. The actions of any particular consumer have a negligible effect on prevailing market prices. The consumer takes the market price of a good as given and "selfishly" maximizes her own utility. Since all consumers are price takers, market supply and demand curves can be found by adding up the individual supply and demand curves. The market is in equilibrium when market supply is equal to market demand.

A central theorem in economics that was first stated by Adam Smith in 1776, asserts that an efficient market equilibrium prevails when trade occurs between consumers who are acting selfishly. Selfishness leads onto the contract curve. That is, the free interaction of supply and demand leads to one of the efficient points on the contract curve. But efficient allocations of goods are not necessarily equitable allocations.

Although the free market mechanism leads to efficient outcomes, social bliss is not guaranteed.

SUMMARY OF KEY CONCEPTS

net demander	net supplier
Say's law	Walras' law
Edgeworth box	mutually beneficial exchange
contract curve	Pareto optimum
efficient outcomes	price taker
market offer curves	Adam Smith's Theorem

II. ANSWERS TO "WHAT TO READ FOR"

5.1 SUPPLY AND DEMAND

1. How can a demander of goods at the same time be a supplier? Exchange involves the budget constraint. Since every consumer is constrained by her budget, the value of the goods she supplies to someone else in an exchange must be equal to the value of the goods she receives from the person. Whether a consumer is a demander or supplier of any particular good depends on her initial endowment of the good and the quantity of the good she demands at the prevailing market price.

2. What is the veil of money? Money is simply a medium of exchange that makes the physical bartering of goods unnecessary. Even though consumers usually exchange money for goods, the money is just a convenient intermediate step in the exchange process. In reality, goods are exchanged for goods. The money is simply a "veil" over the true transaction.

3. Do consumers value the goods that money can buy, or the little green pieces of paper the money is printed on? The consumers value the goods that money can buy. The money is just a medium of exchange.

4. How can one relate the usual indifference curve diagram to a consumer's demand curve for one commodity and her supply curve of all other goods? At a particular relative price, a consumer will be self-sufficient. That is, the quantity of a good that she demands will be exactly equal to her initial endowment. This corresponds to a particular point of tangency between an indifference curve and the budget line corresponding to the self-sufficient price. This also corresponds to a particular point on

her supply-demand curve. At prices above the self-sufficient price she will be a net supplier of the good. At prices below the self-sufficient price she will be a net demander.

5. Is a balance-of-payments deficit a Bad Thing? No. In fact, a balance-of-payments deficit can be a good thing. Deficits occur because countries also trade in money. One country is often willing to give up goods in exchange for the currency of another country. The willingness of countries to give up goods in exchange for paper money enables the country issuing the paper money to consume beyond its budget constraint.

6. Is American self-sufficiency good? Self-sufficiency is not always good. Self-sufficiency prevents America from taking advantage of the benefits from exchange. By becoming a net demander and net supplier of goods, it is possible for America and other countries to make themselves better off without making either worse off.

7. At what price does one become a demander? At what price a supplier? One becomes a demander at prices below the self-sufficient price. One becomes a supplier at prices above the self-sufficient price.

5.2 EXCHANGE BETWEEN TWO PEOPLE OR NATIONS

1. Why is exchange mutually beneficial? Exchange is mutually beneficial because it enables two parties to trade goods that each values less at the margin than the other party. Such a trade makes both parties better off without making anyone worse off.

2. How can this be represented with indifferences curves? This can be represented in an Edgeworth box that contains the indifference maps for both parties. Exchange is mutually beneficial whenever the existing allocation of goods between the two parties is off of the contract curve. It is mutually beneficial for both parties to trade until they reach an efficient allocation on the contract curve.

3. Is a starving farmer who takes a loan from a moneylender in order to survive being "exploited?" No. The starving farmer is clearly made better off by the loan. Having the choice of taking the loan is better than no choice at all.

4. What is an Edgeworth box? An Edgeworth box contains the indifference maps for both parties to an exchange. It is used by economists to represent all mutually advantageous exchanges between two consumers.

5. <u>What is the contract curve?</u> In the Edgeworth box, the locus of all tangency points between the indifference curves of the two consumers is called the contract curve. This curve represents all efficient allocations of the goods.

6. <u>What is a Pareto optimal point? An efficient point?</u> A Pareto optimal point is an allocation of goods at which no further exchanges can be made that will make one consumer better off without making the other consumer worse off. A Pareto optimal point is also an efficient point.

7. <u>Is there any best point?</u> There is no best point. There are many efficient exchanges that will leave two parties unwilling to exchange further.

8. <u>Does the Edgeworth box tell where bargaining between two people will end up? Why?</u> No. The point on the contract curve at which two people will end up depends upon the initial endowments of the goods and each individual's bargaining abilities.

5.3 TRADE AMONG MANY PEOPLE: BEHAVIOR

1. <u>Why don't you bargain and haggle over most deals?</u> You don't bargain over most deals because you are a price taker. You recognize that the size of your purchases and sales of goods are insignificant relative to the size of the entire market. You exercise an insignificant amount of power over the prevailing market price.

2. <u>How much influence over the going market price of bread do you have when you purchase bread?</u> An insignificant amount.

3. <u>What is a price taker?</u> A price taker is an economic agent who has an imperceptible affect over the terms on which she buys a particular commodity.

4. <u>What is the one-man-one-toilet principle?</u> The principle says that just as one man is limited in his influence over the water supply in a city, so too is he limited in his influence over the prevailing market price of any commodity.

5. <u>What was the definition of the offer curve given in an earlier chapter?</u> The offer curve was defined as a set of tangency points between the consumer's indifference contours and all possible budget lines drawn for a given endowment of all other goods.

6. <u>How is it used here to show the equilibrium achieved in a</u>

market of many buyers and sellers? Market offer curves can be drawn for many buyers and sellers just as they are drawn for individual consumers. The market equilibrium is at the point of intersection of the buyers' offer curve and the sellers' offer curve. That is, market equilibrium is at the point for which the offer made by all sellers as a group is consistent with the offer made by all consumers as a group, at the prevailing price.

7. Is a price that is less than the equilibrium price sustainable? No. A low price induces sellers as a group to offer a lower quantity than buyers as a group are induced to demand.

8. Who is to blame for the equilibrium? No one is to blame. The process is blind. No individual economic agent intends for the equilibrium to occur, but it happens anyway.

5.4 TRADE AMONG MANY PEOPLE: HAPPINESS

1. Is the equilibrium also the best the society can do? The equilibrium is an efficient outcome. But capitalism does not guarantee social bliss. It does not guarantee a "best" outcome. Efficient outcomes should not be confused with equitable outcomes.

2. In what sense of "best"? The equilibrium is a best outcome in an efficiency sense.

3. What is Adam Smith's Theorem? Adam Smith's Theorem asserts that the exchange brought about by the pursuit of self-interest in a market of price takers is efficient.

4. What is the relationship between the equilibrium point of intersection of the offer curves, and the point of intersection of the demand and supply curves corresponding to the offer curves? The equilibrium price at which demand is equal to supply is the same as the price corresponding to the equilibrium price line that passes through the point of intersection of the offer curves. The equilibrium allocation of goods at the point of intersection of the offer curves is identical to the equilibrium allocation of goods in the supply-demand framework.

5. Do people have to be unselfish to achieve efficiency? No. Selfishness leads onto the contract curve. Selfishness leads to efficiency.

6. Is efficiency good? Points on the contract curve are not necessarily good. Efficient distributions of goods are not necessarily best in a moral sense.

7. Should we always let the market work freely? No. The final efficient distribution of goods depends upon the initial endowments of the goods. Changes in the initial endowments change the offer curves, and this changes the final equilibrium. Since points on the contract curve are not necessarily morally best, we should not always let the market work freely.

8. What is the economist's way of fixing bad results of markets? The economist's way is to change the initial distribution of goods and then let the market work to achieve an efficient outcome.

9. How does this compare to the noneconomist's way? The noneconomist would argue for direct interference in the market.

III. MULTIPLE CHOICE

1. When applied to whole economies, Say's law says that
   (a) the value of goods you provide to someone else in an exchange must be equal to the value of the goods you receive in return
   (b) the summed monetary value of the goods and money you provide to someone in an exchange must be equal to the monetary value of the goods and services you receive in return
   (c) Walras's law must always be satisfied
   (d) Walras's law can never be satisfied

2. An exchange that results in a move from a point off the contract curve to a point on the contract curve
   (a) makes someone better off but others worse off
   (b) makes someone better off without making anyone worse off
   (c) makes no one better off
   (d) is possible only if endowments are changed

3. All points on the contract curve are
   (a) efficient
   (b) Pareto optimal
   (c) possible equilibrium points
   (d) all of the above

4. Pareto optimal points
   (a) are efficient
   (b) leave one consumer unable to make herself better off without making the other consumer worse off
   (c) are not necessarily equitable
   (d) all of the above

5. If the prevailing market price is lower than the equilibrium

price at which the two offer curves intersect
- (a) the price will rise
- (b) the price will fall
- (c) consumers will be induced to demand less than suppliers are willing to sell
- (d) the prevailing market price will still be sustainable

6. Exchange in a free market of price takers will lead to
   - (a) an efficient outcome
   - (b) a Pareto optimal outcome
   - (c) a situation in which neither suppliers nor demanders can be made better off without making the other worse off
   - (d) all of the above

7. Adam Smith's Theorem prevails because
   - (a) consumers are price takers and producers are price setters
   - (b) all economic agents are price setters
   - (c) all economic agents are price takers
   - (d) suppliers' offer curve is tangent to consumers' offer curve

8. A supplier's offer curve
   - (a) is constructed from her indifference curves
   - (b) is always equal to the consumer's offer curve
   - (c) is invariant with respect to income
   - (d) shifts as market prices change

9. The Edgeworth box
   - (a) shows only the efficient outcomes of exchange
   - (b) shows only the equitable outcomes of exchange
   - (c) shows all possible trades that can be made between two parties
   - (d) shows the point of social bliss

10. Changes in the initial endowments of goods
    - (a) change the supply and demand curves
    - (b) change the offer curves
    - (c) change the final distribution of goods
    - (d) all of the above

IV. EXERCISES

1. Fred Reagan and Simon Marx are two political scientists. Reagan is a staunch capitalist and Marx a socialist. Both agree that there is currrently a poverty problem in the United States that must be solved. Reagan argues that the best way to resolve the problem is to simply redistribute income from wealthier families to poorer families through the tax system. Marx feels that a more drastic solution is necessary. He feels that only a

complete transformation of the economy to a socialistic structure will solve the poverty problem.

(a) What are the advantages of the Reagan proposal? What are the disadvantages? (In your answer, be sure to address both efficiency and equity issues.)

(b) What are the advantages of the Marx proposal? What are the disadvantages?

(c) Does the Marx proposal really resolve the poverty problem? Explain.

2. In January 1984, Chinese Premier Zhao Ziyang visited the United States for ten days and met with business and political leaders. The visit indicated that a change in policy by the Chinese was occurring. It was seen as a signal that China wanted to obtain U.S. business and technology in order to modernize its economy, despite the American stand on the issue of Taiwan. In turn, the United States was anxious to negotiate with the Chinese in order to improve global stability and trade relations. At the time of Premier Ziyang's visit, U.S.-China trade was expected to rise between 25% and 35% from its depressed 1983 level.

In the context of an Edgeworth box diagram, explain why the U.S.-Chinese negotiations to improve trade relations was an efficient move.

V. PROBLEM

The GM-Toyota Pact

General Motors decided in 1983 to pursue the possibility of a joint venture with Toyota to make cars in California. The short-run goal of the joint venture was to build approximately 200,000 subcompact cars (the Sprinter) per year. This car was to be based on the design of Toyota's Corolla car. GM's hope was to benefit from Toyota's experience, production expertise, and ability to make a better small car. Cost figures indicated that Japanese automobile manufacturers had a $1,500 to $2,000 production-cost advantage per car.

At the same time that the joint venture was being negotiated, the major U.S. automobile companies were reporting record profits. These profits were attributed to improvements in management and production techniques and to quotas that had been placed on the importation of Japanese automobiles. Japanese automobile companies were also reporting record profits as they shifted their production for the U.S. market to more profitable mid-size cars.

(a) Discuss why it was in the interests of both GM and Toyota to pursue the joint venture.

(b) If both GM and Toyota were reporting record profits, why did it make sense for them to alter their production strategies?

(c) Use an Edgeworth box diagram to illustrate your answers to parts (a) and (b).

CHAPTER 6

Using Market Supply and Demand

I. OVERVIEW

The fundamental problem of economics deals with the allocation of scarce resources amongst unlimited human wants. Useful tools for studying this problem are supply curves and demand curves, which apply to markets of price takers. The usefulness of these curves lies in the assertion that the market must clear. The price mechanism will ration existing supplies of scarce resources amongst the unlimited human desires for these resources. Prices will adjust so that quantities supplied will always equal quantities demanded. Another way of saying this is the law of one price. If the market has cleared, so that it is in equilibrium, all participants in the market will be paying or receiving the same price. One price clears the market. If more than one price prevails, then arbitrage possibilities exist and the market has not yet cleared.

The law of one price enables economists to add up individual demand curves to obtain market demand, and individual supply curves to obtain market supply. Each demander is a price taker, and at any given price she will want to buy a certain quantity. At each price, the quantity demanded in the entire market is equal to the sum of all the individual quantities demanded at that given price. The entire market demand curve is therefore the horizontal sum at all prices of the individual demand curves. The same procedure leads to the market supply curve. Market supply is the horizontal sum of the supply curves of the individual firms in the market. Market equilibrium occurs at the point where market supply equals market demand; that is, where the upward sloping market supply curve intersects the downward sloping market demand curve.

Market supply and demand curves can be used for thinking about related markets. Markets can be related through their supply and demand functions. For example, a change in the relative price of two complementary goods can be analyzed by looking at how the market demand curves for the two commodities shift in response to the relative price change. Market demand curves can also be derived for two commodities that are jointly supplied. Consider the case of wool and mutton that are derived from sheep. When two goods (wool and mutton) are jointly supplied, the market demand curve for the whole thing (sheep) is the vertical sum of the demand curves for the two separate goods (wool and mutton). The individual demand curves for wool and mutton show the willingness of consumers to pay for a particular product. Since the individual wool and mutton products are jointly supplied from the whole sheep, the demand curve for the sheep must be the vertical sum of the willingness of consumers to pay for the individual characteristics of the sheep. Similarly, the supply curve for a joint product (like a house which is made of wood and nails) is the vertical sum of the willingness of firms to supply each individual input (wood and nails) at any given price.

SUMMARY OF KEY CONCEPTS

- supply and demand curves
- law of one price
- adding up supply and demand
- shifts in supply
- related markets
- market clearing
- market equilibrium
- shifts in demand
- joint supply

II. ANSWERS TO "WHAT TO READ FOR"

6.1 THE USES OF EQUILIBRIUM

1. <u>What determines the position of someone's demand curve for football tickets?</u> The position of someone's demand curve for football tickets is determined by how much income the person has. It also depends upon the person's preferences or tastes for the good.

2. <u>Is a demander always a demander, regardless of how the price or his initial number of tickets change?</u> A demander is not always a demander. Whether a person is a demander or a supplier depends upon her initial allotment of tickets and her preferences for tickets.

3. <u>Why is allocation of tickets necessary?</u> Allocation of tickets is necessary because tickets are scarce. Everything scarce needs to be allocated. Scarcity implies that not everyone who has a positive demand for tickets can get them.

4. <u>Are tickets scarce?</u> Yes, tickets are scarce.

5. <u>What are some alternative ways of allocating tickets?</u> There are alternative ways to allocate tickets. One way is to allocate them randomly. They can be allocated on a first-come- first-serve basis. Another way is to allocate the tickets by strength

or beauty. They can even be allocated to those who make the most persuasive case that they "need" them the most.

6. Is bribery always bad? Bribery is not always bad. If bribery is allowed to work, then suppliers and demanders will make deals. The people to whom the bribes are offered become willing recipients for services rendered. The deals that are made put the good in the hands of those individuals who value them the most.

7. Is there a victim in an exchange? There is no victim in an exchange. Market exchanges are good because every person who ends up having the good values the good more than anyone who does not have it.

8. Is scalping of tickets bad? Scalping of tickets is not bad because it permits the tickets to be reallocated so that they are put in the hands of those who value them the most. Permitting scalping allows the market to work.

9. Why do economists favor making tickets resellable? Economists favor making tickets resellable because this allows the market to work. The market is voluntary. And when the market is allowed to work it puts the tickets into the hands of those who value them the most.

10. When the market is allowed to work, who ultimately gets the tickets? When the market is allowed to work, those individuals who value the tickets the most ultimately get them.

6.2 ADDING UP SUPPLY AND DEMAND: EQUILIBRIUM

1. How do you go from a single person's demand curve to a whole market's demand curve? The market demand curve is the horizontal sum of the demand curves of all individual demanders. At any given market price, the quantity demanded by the market will be the sum of all the individual quantities demanded.

2. The market's supply curve? The market supply curve is the horizontal sum of the supply curves of all individual suppliers.

3. What is equilibrium, geometrically speaking? Geometrically speaking, the intersection of the market demand and market supply curves determines the equilibrium price and quantity for the entire market.

4. What is the significance of the phrase "the market must clear"? The simple assertion that "markets must clear" says that the market price adjusts to make quantities supplied and quantities demanded equal.

5. <u>What is true about quantities supplied and quantities demanded at the equilibrium price?</u> At the equilibrium price, quantities supplied are equal to quantities demanded. This is the price at which the supply curve crosses the demand curve.

6. <u>How do movements in the price and quantity depend on shifts in the supply schedule?</u> When the supply schedule shifts outward and the demand schedule remains fixed, price falls and quantity rises. When the supply schedule shifts inward and the demand schedule remains fixed, price rises and quantity falls.

7. <u>How do movements in the price and quantity depend on shifts in the demand schedule?</u> When the demand schedule shifts outward and the supply schedule remains fixed, price and quantity rise. When the demand schedule shifts inward and the supply schedule remains fixed, price and quantity fall.

8. <u>How can one infer from price and quantity movements what has happened to the market supply and demand curves?</u> Knowing how price and quantity depend on shifts in the demand and supply schedules enables one to infer from price and quantity movements what has happened to the market supply and demand curves. For example, if one observes that price and quantity are greater than once before, one can conclude that the cause must be an outward shift in the demand curve. (Recall that when the demand schedule shifts ourward and the supply schedule remains fixed, price and quantity rise.) It is possible that the supply curve also shifted out. But the shift in supply must have been less than the shift in the demand curve.

6.3 ADDING UP SUPPLY AND DEMAND: THE DIAGRAMS FOR ANALYSES

1. <u>What is the law of one price?</u> The law of one price says that in equilibrium, all participants in a market must be paying or getting the same price.

2. <u>Why is it necessary for using supply and demand curves?</u> The law of one price is necessary for the adding up of the supply and demand curves. The adding up is done horizontally <u>at one price</u>.

3. <u>What is the general technique for handling questions involving supply and demand?</u> The general technique for handling questions involving supply and demand is: (1) to identify all the suppliers and demanders in the market and to group them into relevant categories; (2) to write down the condition for equilibrium; (3) to draw the corresponding diagram; and (4) to answer the question.

4. <u>How does the equilibrium price determine how much is demanded or supplied by each segment of the demanders or the suppliers?</u>

One of the uses of summing supplies and demands is that when the separateness of different segments of the demanders or the suppliers is important, the curves can be separated. Separate supply curves and demand curves can be drawn for the different segments. These separate curves can then be used to determine from the single market equilibrium price the quantities supplied and demanded by the different segments.

5. _How do you prove that a small demander or supplier should think of herself as a price taker?_ The logic of supply and demand itself justifies the assumption of price-taking in the case of large numbers of participants in a market. One can _prove_ that a small demander or supplier should think of herself as a price taker by manipulating the equation that "the sum of all supplies must equal the sum of all demands." For example, the logic of adding and subtracting supply and demand curves implies that an individual consumer faces a supply curve that is virtually horizontal.

6.4 EXTENSIONS OF SUPPLY AND DEMAND

1. _How can "substitute" and "complement" be defined in terms of the effect of price on quantity demanded?_ Consider two substitutes. An outward shift in the supply curve of one good causes a fall in the price of the good. This causes a downward shift in the demand curve for the other good. Consider two complements. An outward shift in the supply curve of one good causes a fall in the price of the good. This causes an upward shift in the demand curve for the other curve.

2. _How is this type of definition related to the earlier definitions of "substitute" and "complement" given in terms of the shapes of indifference curves?_ This type of definition is equivalent to the earlier definitions of "substitute" and "complement" given in terms of the shapes of the indifference curves. A demand curve is a schedule of the price that people are willing to pay at a given quantity. The price along a demand curve for a particular good is the marginal valuation of the good at various quantities. An indifference curve contains the identical information about the consumer's preferences.

3. _What are related markets?_ Related markets are markets that are connected through their demand or supply functions.

4. _When things like wool or mutton are jointly supplied, why is the demand curve for the whole thing (sheep) the vertical sum of the separate demand curves?_ The demand curves for wool and mutton slope downward. If wool and mutton are jointly supplied in the form of sheep, then the demand curve for sheep also slopes downward. The demand curve for sheep is the vertical sum of the

wool and mutton demand curves.

5. <u>Why is a supply curve the vertical sum of the willingness to accept each input into the good?</u> The supply curves for each input into a good slope upward. If several inputs are used jointly to produce a single product, then the supply curve for the final product also slopes upward. The supply curve for the final product is the vertical sum of the willingness to accept each input into the good.

III. MULTIPLE CHOICE

1. In the country of Shangri-La it has been observed that the price of an automobile has been rising over the last ten years. At the same time, the quantity of automobiles sold has also been steadily rising. The cause must be
   (a) an outward shift in the demand curve
   (b) an outward shift in the supply curve
   (c) a rotation of the demand curve
   (d) a rotation of the supply curve

2. Simon Asch is an avid football fan. Simon is also a very wealthy individual.
   (a) Simon will always be a net demander of football tickets
   (b) Simon will always be a net supplier of football tickets
   (c) Simon is both a net supplier and net demander of football tickets
   (d) Simon can become a net supplier of football tickets only if his initial allocation of tickets is very large

3. Tickets to a recent John Denver concert were sold on a first-come-first-serve basis. Under this system of allocation, it is likely that
   (a) the tickets were allocated to those people that "needed" them the most
   (b) the tickets were put in the hands of those who valued them the most
   (c) the tickets were put in the hands of those with the most political influence
   (d) the tickets were put in the hands of those best able to compete with patience for standing in line

4. John Adamson and George Jefferson both enjoy consuming Breyer's ice cream. But John is willing to pay a higher price for any given amount of Breyer's ice cream. This means that
   (a) there is more than one price that clears the market for Breyer's ice cream
   (b) John is richer than George
   (c) John is poorer than George
   (d) John is more of an ice cream lover than George

5. In 1971 the Nixon Administration froze the price per barrel of domestic crude oil at existing levels. If the true market clearing price for domestic oil then rose over time
(a) the quantity of oil supplied at the frozen price would still be equal to the quantity demanded because the market must clear
(b) the quantity of oil supplied at the frozen price would be greater than the quantity demanded
(c) the quantity of oil supplied at the frozen price would be less than the quantity demanded
(d) there would be a glut of oil in the domestic market

6. Suppose transistor radios can move freely and costlessly between the American and Japanese markets. Then
(a) the same market equilibrium price will prevail in both markets
(b) excess demand in the American market will be matched by excess demand in the Japanese market
(c) excess supply in the American market will be matched by excess supply in the Japanese market
(d) a single price will clear the American market and a single but different price will clear the Japanese market

7. Butter and margarine are substitutes. If the supply of margarine rises then
(a) the supply of butter must also rise
(b) the supply of butter must fall
(c) the demand for butter will rise
(d) the demand for butter will fall

8. A recent freeze in Brazil severely damaged the coffee bean crops. The world supply of coffee beans fell. Coffee and sugar are complements. The fall in the world supply of coffee beans therefore caused
(a) the demand for coffee to rise
(b) the demand for coffee to fall
(c) the demand for sugar to rise
(d) the demand for sugar to fall

9. A typical meat packer is willing to pay $20 for the amount of mutton that comes from 10 sheep. A typical fabric company is willing to pay $15 for the amount of wool that comes from 10 sheep. One can therefore conclude that
(a) the price people are willing to pay for 10 sheep is $35
(b) the price people are willing to pay for 10 sheep is $5
(c) the equilibrium price in the market for sheep is $35
(d) the equilibrium price in the market for sheep is $5

10. Suppose that condominiums and furniture are jointly supplied.
(a) A rise in the cost of condominiums will raise the price of furniture
(b) A fall in the cost of condominiums will lower the price of furniture

(c) The cost of condominiums is independent of the price of furniture
(d) A rise in the cost of condominiums will lower the price of furniture

IV. EXERCISES

1. In 1984, Super Bowl XVIII pitted the Los Angeles Raiders against the Washington Redskins. The game was played at Tampa stadium in Tampa, Florida. About 40,000 football fans were interested in either watching the game on television or attending the game in person. Tampa stadium has a capacity of 72,000 seats. The NFL does not permit the market to distribute the available seats. The NFL rations the tickets. The Redskins and Raiders each got 18,000 seats for distribution to season-ticket holders at $60 per ticket. 18,000 tickets were given to the other teams who distributed them to owners, players, coaches and a few season-ticket holders. Tampa Bay, the host team, got 7,200 tickets. 10,800 tickets went to the NFL office.

The lucky recipients of the tickets are allowed to resell their tickets. In Washington, ticket dealers were reselling the tickets for as much as $400 each. Newspaper ads offered from $350 to $900 for a ticket. The final equilibrium price after all the reselling appeared to be around $500 per ticket.

(a) Draw the supply curve for Super Bowl tickets prior to the distribution of the tickets by the NFL.

(b) On the same diagram, sketch in the market demand curve for tickets. Indicate where the $60 NFL price is and comment on the prevailing situation in the market.

(c) Scalping of the tickets occurred after the initial distribution by the NFL. On the same graph, show what happened to the market price for Super Bowl tickets as they were resold. Where was the final equilibrium?

(d) Who benefitted from the NFL's ticket allocation system? Why?

(e) Was the reselling of tickets bad after the initial allocation of tickets? Who ultimately got the Super Bowl tickets?

2. Silicon semiconductor chips are electronic components that are used in most computers. The availability of these chips has become very important to the computer industry, especially since there has been a sudden boom in personal computers and other

electronics products that use the chips. At the same time, illicit traffic in silicon chips has been growing. A new "gray market" has been flourishing in which the most needed chips bring as much as 10 times their regular price. Some of the chips sold on this "gray market" were stolen. Others however, are chips that are simply being resold by the original purchasers.

(a) Why does the "gray market" exist?

(b) Is the existence of the gray market bad?

V. PROBLEM

The Market For Energy

In December 1971 the Ford Foundation authorized the organization of the Energy Policy Project. The general purpose of this project, which received appropriations totaling $4 million, was to study the need for a national energy policy.

The final report of the Energy Policy Project was published in 1974. It concluded that there is an energy crisis, that it did not come and go in 1973-74, that it will last a long time, and that conservation is as important as supply. The Report also concluded that there is a need for an integrated national energy policy. Political control of energy markets in the United States is required due to a widening gap between energy consumption and domestic production, growing dependence on foreign supplies of energy, inefficient uses of energy, and soaring energy prices.

The Report recommended a zero rate of growth in energy use between 1975 and 2000. This proposal was made because it was "desirable, technically feasible, and economical to reduce the rate of energy growth [to] 2 percent annually," and "provides benefits in every major area of concern, avoiding shortages, protecting the environment, avoiding problems with other nations, and keeping the real social costs as low as possible."

In 1975 the Institute for Contemporary Studies published a response to the final report of the Energy Policy Project. It concluded that the Report "is inexcusably ignorant of economics" and "is so fatally dosed with economic error, fallacy, and confusion at critical stages as to border on dishonesty." It pointed out that a serious analytic error was the Report's refusal to recognize that the amount of energy demanded can be reduced by a higher price to match supplies that are available at that price.

(a) Proponents of the Ford Foundation Report have argued

that people "need" energy to survive. People "require" oil to heat their homes, natural gas with which to cook, and gasoline to run their automobiles. What does the law of demand say about such "needs" and "requirements"?

(b) Petroleum has many different uses. The crude oil that is pumped out of the ground is refined into home heating oil, gasoline, motor oil, petroleum jelly, and many other commodities. In a free market economy, is it possible that existing supplies will not cover all of these needs? Under what conditions could shortages exist in a free market economy?

(c) Political control over the consumer's use of the available supplies of energy is often argued for in the belief that there is a fixed supply of energy. Comment on the validity of this argument.

(d) Suppose that in 1973 the price of petroleum was $4 per barrel. At this price, the amount of petroleum "needed" by consumers exactly equaled the quantity supplied. In 1975 the OPEC cartel restricted output from existing petroleum sources. Using a graph, depict the effect of the oil cartel's output restriction. In a free market economy, what effect does the output restriction have on the prevailing market price for petroleum? Are consumers' needs still satisfied?

(e) Suppose the federal government decides to control the price of petroleum in order to "protect" consumers from high energy prices. It fixes the price of petroleum at the 1973 price level of $4 per barrel. After the OPEC restriction on output, will consumers' needs still be satisfied?

CHAPTER 7

Measuring Supply and Demand

I. OVERVIEW

The law of demand asserts that price and quantity demanded are inversely related. Demand curves are downward sloping. When the price of a good rises, the quantity of it demanded falls. When price falls, quantity demanded rises. But the law of demand does not indicate how much quantity demanded changes when price changes. The law of demand tells us the direction in which quantity demanded changes. It does not indicate the extent of the change.

Consider the two scenarios depicted in Figure 7.1.

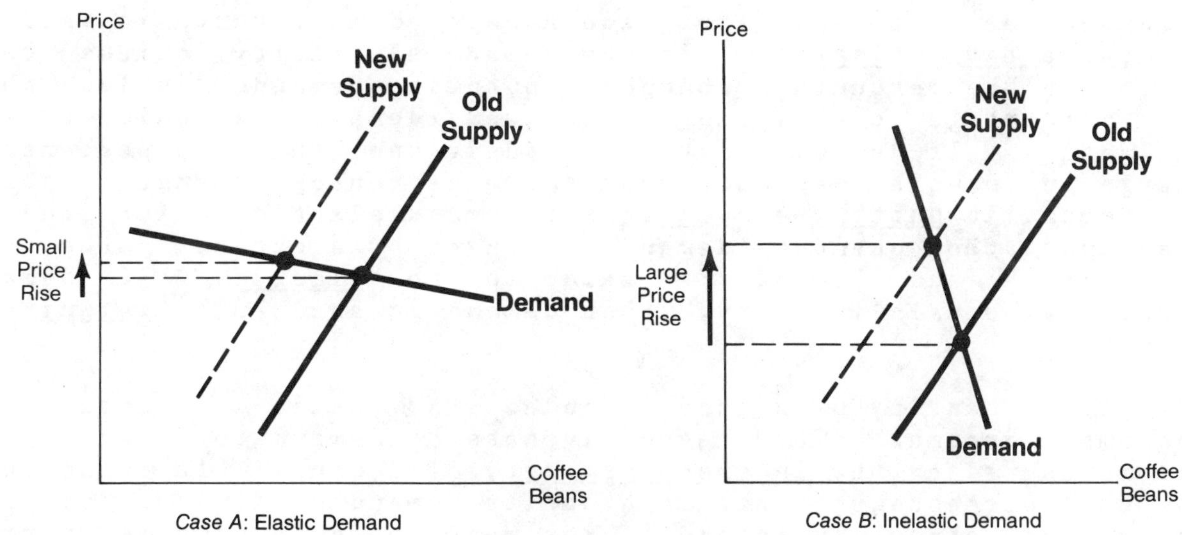

FIGURE 7.1

In both cases, a fall in the supply of coffee beans has occurred, creating an excess demand for beans at the prevailing market price. In case A, the demand curve is drawn so that quantity demanded varies greatly with price. In case B, quantity demanded varies only slightly with price. The difference in the shapes of the two demand curves indicates a difference in the degree of responsiveness of demand to changes in price. This difference has important implications for the price change that is necessary to restore equilibrium in the market for coffee beans. In case A, given the fall in the supply of coffee beans, a small rise in price will eliminate the excess demand and restore equilibrium. In case B, since quantity demanded is insensitive to price changes, a large price rise is needed to restore equilibrium. A shift in supply can have very different effects depending on the shape of the demand curve.

The price elaticity of demand describes the shape of a demand curve. It is a measure of the responsiveness of demand to price changes. The price elasticity of demand is defined as the percentage change in quantity demanded divided by the percentage change in price. It provides a numerical measure of the degree to which demand responds to changes in price. Since there is an inverse relationship between price and quantity demanded, the elasticity of demand is technically a negative number. But since this inverse relationship is understood, the negative sign is ignored. The elasticity of demand therefore ranges from zero to infinity.

The more responsive demand is to price changes, the greater is the elasticity of demand and the higher is the numerical measure. If demand elasticity equals zero, then quantity demanded does not vary with price and the demand curve is said to be perfectly inelastic. If the demand elasticity is less than one, then the percentage change in quantity demanded is less than the percentage change in price and demand is said to be inelastic. If demand elasticity equals one, then the percentage change in quantity demanded equals the percentage change in price and demand is unitary elastic. If demand elasticity is greater than one, then quantity demanded changes by a greater percentage than price and demand is said to be elastic. If demand elasticity equals infinity, then demand is said to be infinitely elastic.

The quantity of a good demanded also varies with changes in consumer income. The responsiveness of demand to changes in income is called the income elasticity of demand. It is defined as the percentage change in quantity demanded divided by the percentage change in income. For most goods, known as normal goods, an increase in income leads to increases in demand. Demand therefore has a positive income elasticity. Goods for which consumption decreases in response to a rise in income are called inferior goods. These have negative income elasticities.

SUMMARY OF KEY CONCEPTS

average propensity to consumer
income elasticity of demand
marginal propensity to consume
price elasticity of demand

constant price elasticity
rate of change transformation
Engel curve

II. ANSWERS TO WHAT TO READ FOR

7.1 ELASTICITIES OF SUPPLY AND DEMAND: THE ESSENTIAL IDEAS

1. How sensitive is consumption to changes in income? To changes in price? The sensitivity of consumption to changes in income and to changes in price varies between consumers. Michael Bordo's consumption of wine may be more sensitive to changes in income than Ann Carlos' wine consumption.

2. What is the elasticity with respect to income? The elasticity of demand with respect to income describes the responsiveness of demand to changes in income. It is defined as the percentage change in quantity demanded divided by the percentage change in income.

3. What is the elasticity with respect to price? The price elasticity of demand is a measure of the responsiveness of quantity demanded to price changes. It is defined as the percentage change in quantity demanded divided by the percentage change in price.

4. What is an Engel Curve? An Engel Curve is a curve that plots the amount of a good purchased against income.

5. What shapes do curves of infinite, zero, or unit elasticity have? A curve that is infinitely elastic is horizontal. A curve that has zero elasticity is vertical. A curve with unit elasticity has an exponential form.

6. How do you know if a point on a demand curve is an elastic or an inelastic point? There are three ways to determine the elasticity of demand at a particular point. First, one can examine the change in the area of the rectangle under the demand curve that represents revenues as price changes. Second, one can compare the slope of the tangent at the point to the slope of the diagonal (Q/P in Figure 7.4 in the text). Third, one can compare the size of the line segment $P(\Delta Q/\Delta P)$ to the line segment Q (in Figure 7.4 in the text).

7. Why is an elasticity of 1.0 significant? If the price elasticity of demand is 1.0, then the percentage change in quantitiy demanded is equal to the percentage change in price. Total expenditure on the good remains constant whenever price changes.

7.2 CONSTANT ELASTICITIES

1. <u>What does a formula for a demand curve look like that has unchanging elasticity throughout its length?</u> The demand curve has an exponential form.

2. <u>What is the relationship between elasticities and the exponents in multiplicative functions?</u> The exponent is the absolute value of the elasticity of demand with respect to price.

3. <u>What is the significance of the rate of change transformation in thinking about curves with constant elasticities?</u> The rate of change transformation is useful for connecting known and unknown elasticities.

4. <u>If you know the elasticities of a market's supply and demand curves, can you infer the elasticities facing individual suppliers or demanders?</u> Yes. The rate of change transformation leads to an equation in elasticities that can be used to find the elasticities facing individual suppliers or demanders.

5. <u>What is the procedure, exactly?</u> Write down the equilibrium condition (quantity supplied equals quantity demanded). Take the rate of change of this expression by taking the logarithm of both sides of the equation. Divide this expression by the rate of change of price. The resulting equation is in elasticities. This equation can then be applied to problems of finding the elasticities facing individual suppliers or demanders.

III. <u>MULTIPLE CHOICE</u>

1. A demand curve in the form of a straight line
   (a) has a constant price elasticity of demand
   (b) has varying elasticity at various different points
   (c) has a lower price elasticity at higher prices
   (d) has a higher price elasticity at lower prices

2. The own price elasticity of demand describes the
   (a) responsiveness of demand to changes in income
   (b) responsiveness of demand to changes in the price of another good
   (c) responsiveness of demand to changes in the commodity's own price
   (d) direction of slope of the demand curve

3. The cross price elasticity of demand describes the
   (a) responsiveness of demand to changes in income
   (b) responsiveness of demand to changes in the price of

another good
(c) responsiveness of demand to changes in the commodity's own price
(d) direction of slope of the demand curve

4. If the price of Corvettes rises, then total expenditures on Corvettes
(a) will always fall
(b) will always rise
(c) will always stay the same
(d) might rise or fall

5. If demand is elastic, then a fall in price
(a) increases total expenditures
(b) decreases total expenditures
(c) leaves total expenditures unchanged
(d) has an ambiguous effect on total expenditures

6. If demand is inelastic, then a rise in price
(a) increases total expenditures
(b) decreases total expenditures
(c) leaves total expenditures unchanged
(d) has an ambiguous effect on total expenditures

7. If the cross price elasticity of demand is negative, then
(a) the two goods are normal goods
(b) the two goods are inferior goods
(c) the two goods are complements
(d) the two goods are substitutes

8. If Lester Guidry's consumption of chocolate bars decreases in response to a rise in income then
(a) chocolate bars are normal goods to Lester
(b) chocolate bars are inferior goods to Lester
(c) the law of demand is violated
(d) demand has unitary price elasticity

9. If the income elasticity of demand is greater than one, then the good is
(a) an inferior good
(b) a Giffen good
(c) a necessity
(d) a luxury good

10. The income elasticity of demand is equal to
(a) the rate of change of the average propensity to consume
(b) the rate of change of the marginal propensity to consume
(c) the average propensity divided by the marginal propensity
(d) the marginal propensity divided by the average propensity

IV. EXERCISES

1. In words, explain fully the relationship between price elasticity of demand and total expenditures.

2. Suppose the price of apples increases 5% and the price elasticity for apples is 0.5. What will happen to the quantity of apples demanded? What will happen to total expenditures on apples?

3. Suppose per capita income in the country of Grand Fenwick increases by 1% and the income elasticity of flour is -0.36. What will happen to the quantity of flour demanded?

4. Consider the following hypothetical market demand schedule for wheat:

Observation	Price ($/bushel)	Quantity Demanded (billion bushels/year)
A	$5	2.5
B	4	3.5
C	3	5.0
D	2	7.0
E	1	10.0

Find the elasticity of the market demand curve between points A and B, B and E, and A and D. Indicate which sections are elastic, inelastic, and unitary elastic.

V. PROBLEM

Physician Services

Dr. Livingston is a physician with a practice in the small town of Sayreville. Since Dr. Livingston is a benevolent person, he is willing to keep his fees low in the belief that he will still earn large revenues by doing a large volume business. In contrast, Dr. Stanley (whose office is located across the street from Dr. Livingston's) is selfish and always charges premium rates for his services. Dr. Stanley has taken courses in economics and is familiar with consumer theory and the law of demand. He knows that consumers will demand a smaller quantity of his services given his high fees. But he believes that the reduced quantity demanded will be offset by his higher rates so that he will earn the same large revenues as Dr. Livingston. Under what circumstances is Dr. Stanley's strategy correct? Dr. Livingston's?

PART III. PRODUCTION AND WELFARE

CHAPTER 8

Production Possibilities

I. OVERVIEW

The discussion so far has dealt with the theory of demand. We now turn our attention to the theory of supply. Recall that in the theory of demand a consumer is constrained by her budget. The budget line shows the opportunity cost of consuming one good instead of another. Similarly, the central idea in the theory of supply is opportunity cost. Productive resources are scarce. The amount of output that a firm or society can produce is limited by the available resources. The opportunity cost of producing one product is equal to the other possible products foregone.

The existence of opportunity costs in production make it essential that resources be used in the most efficient way possible. Opportunity costs must be minimized in order to obtain the maximum output of goods and services. The specialization theorem asserts that the total output of goods in a society can be made larger if people are permitted to specialize in production and to trade their products. Recall from the discussion of the Edgeworth box that free trade always leads to a Pareto optimal allocation of goods and services. Free trade leads to an efficient outcome. The specialization theorem says that free trade also results in the largest possible Edgeworth box.

The freedom to trade allows people to do what they do best and then to trade the fruits of their labors for other products. People are able to specialize in their own comparative advantage. This division of labor raises the production possibilities in society. The areas in which labor specializes depends upon the relative prices of different types of output. Supply theory asserts that at a higher relative price for a particular commodity, more resources will be devoted to the production of that commodity. More output is forthcoming only at higher relative prices.

Production processes typically require several different factors of production. The quantity of output depends upon -- or is a function of -- the quantities of factor inputs used. A production function associates physical output with input. It is an equation showing the maximum amount of output that can be produced from any specified set of inputs. The production function is a "hill of output" just as the utility function is a "hill of happiness."

A particular level of output can usually be produced by a wide variety of different input combinations. One input may be substituted for another while still maintaining the same level of output. An <u>isoquant</u> is a constant output contour on the hill of output. It shows all of the technologically efficient combinations of factor inputs that can produce a given level of output. That is, an isoquant shows the least amount of inputs required to produce a given level of output. Recall that points on the production possibility frontier are also efficient points of production. Along the production possibility frontier resources are being fully and efficiently employed. Points on the production possibility frontier therefore correspond to points on the production function. In turn, given the usual condition of <u>diminishing returns to scale</u> or <u>constant returns to scale</u>, the upward-sloping segments of a supply curve correspond to the outward-bulging segments of the production possibility curve.

The production possibility curve is a budget line for society. Its slope shows the relative prices of goods produced in the economy. The slope tells the price at which a given quantity of output will be supplied. Similarly, the slope of the indifference curve for society that is tangent to a point on the production possibility curve tells the price at which a given quantity of output will be demanded. The tangency point is therefore a point of equilibrium. At this point, the price at which a given quantity of output will be supplied is equal to the price at which it will be demanded. The marginal cost of producing the output is equal to the marginal valuation of it. At this equilbrium, supply is equal to demand. Society's utility is being maximized subject to the constraint of the production possibility curve.

<u>SUMMARY OF KEY CONCEPTS</u>

- specialization theorem
- division of labor
- production function
- factors of production
- returns to scale
- isoquant
- comparative advantage
- production possibility curve
- Leontief production function
- substitutability in production
- upward-sloping supply

II. ANSWERS TO WHAT TO READ FOR

8.1 PRODUCTION AND SPECIALIZATION

1. What is the specialization theorem? The specialization theorem asserts that total output can be made larger by permitting people to specialize in what they do best and to trade their products.

2. How is opportunity cost related to specialization? Communities face opportunities in production just as individual consumers face opportunities in consumption. Producing one commodity has an opportunity cost in terms of other types of output foregone. By allowing people to specialize and trade, opportunity costs are minimized.

3. What is the division of labor? Comparative advantage? The division of labor permits people to specialize in what they each do best. Labor in society is divided according to each individual's comparative advantage.

4. How is Free Trade related to specialization? Without free trade, it would not be practical for people to specialize in their comparative advantages. Comparative advantage matters because the decision to specialize and do what one does best depends on the ability to trade for products that others can produce at a lower cost.

5. Why is Free Trade good? Free Trade is good because it allows commodities to be produced in the cheapest way possible by those with a comparative advantage in the production of those goods.

6. Why does a society's production possibility curve bulge outward? A society's production possibility curve bulges outward because of specialization.

7. Why does its supply of, say, food slope upward? The outward bulge in the production possibility curve implies that the supply curve slopes upward. The outward bulge of the production possibility curve indicates that as more food is produced, the cost of food in terms of all other goods rises. This implies an upward slope for the supply curve of food.

8.2 THE PRODUCTION FUNCTION ALSO LEADS TO THE PRODUCTION POSSIBILITY CURVE

1. What is the production function? The production function is

a mathematical correspondence between inputs and the maximum output that can be produced using those inputs.

2. <u>Why is it more measurable than a utility function?</u> Ordinal utility functions are not measurable because levels of satisfaction are difficult to quantify. But production functions are measurable because levels of output and factors of production are quantifiable.

3. <u>What is a Leontief production function?</u> This is a production function that represents a production process in which inputs are used in fixed proportions to produce a given level of output.

4. <u>What is an isoquant?</u> An isoquant is a curve showing the technologically efficient means of producing a given level of output; that is, the least amount of inputs required to produce a given level of output.

5. <u>Why are isoquants usually curved instead of sharp-cornered?</u> Isoquants usually have this shape because possibilities exist for the substitution of one factor input for another.

6. <u>How does the idea that there is more than one way to skin a cat relate to isoquants?</u> The idea is that different combinations of inputs can be used to efficiently produce the same level of output.

7. <u>How exactly do production functions connect with the production possibility curve?</u> An Edgeworth box for production can be constructed by combining the isoquant maps for different commodities (see Figure 8.6 in the text). The points of tangency between isoquants are efficient points of production. More of one good cannot be produced without sacrificing some of the other. These efficient points form the contract curve. The levels of production of the goods at these efficient points are on the production possibility frontier.

8. <u>Why does the production possibility curve bulge out?</u> The production possibility curve bulges out because of constant or diminishing returns to scale in the production of output.

8.3 HOW AN ECONOMY WORKS IN THE LARGE

1. <u>What is the economy-wide demand curve corresponding to the economy-wide supply?</u> The demand curve is society's marginal valuation of the goods produced in the economy. It is equal to the slope along the production possibility curve of the community's indifference curves.

2. <u>What is the relationship between the supply curve and the economy's production possibility curve? Between the demand curve and the production possibility curve?</u> The supply curve is the marginal cost of production. It is the slope of society's production possibility curve. The demand curve is the marginal valuation of the goods produced. It is the slope along the production possibility curve of society's indifference curves.

3. <u>What's so great about the equilibrium points of supply and demand?</u> The point of equilibrium between supply and demand is an efficient outcome. All of the resources in society are being fully and efficiently employed.

4. <u>How can you use economy-wide pictures to analyze problems?</u> The economy-wide supply and demand pictures can be used to study the <u>general equilibrium</u> of an economy. The model can be used to portray the economy-wide links between different types of goods. Supply and demand models apply to entire economies as well as to single markets.

III. MULTIPLE CHOICE

1. Prohibiting trade between countries
   (a) always results in a Pareto optimum
   (b) always reduces total income
   (c) enables the protected country to benefit from its absolute advantage
   (d) always increases total income

2. John and Cindy Livingston are a newly married couple. Since they do not yet have much money, they have purchased an old, run down, four-room Dutch Colonial house that is in dire need of repair. They intend to slowly fix the house up during the evenings after they both come from work, with the hope of someday selling it at a profit and then buying a new house. Experience has shown that Cindy can vacuum and scrub floors faster, repair plumbing leeks more efficiently, and fix electrical wiring better than John. Since John and Cindy are anxious to do the best job of fixing up the house as they possibly can

   (a) Cindy should do all of the repair work while John supervises from his lounge chair and watches Monday Night Football on television
   (b) Cindy should insist that John scrub the floors, since it requires the least amount of skill
   (c) Cindy and John should share the workload and each do what they do best
   (d) John should spend time learning how to do all of the chores better so that he can share the work load equally with Cindy

3. The point of the specialization theorem is that
   (a) nations run the risk of embargoes by specializing in the production of only particular goods
   (b) a division of labor by comparative advantage raises a nation's production possibilities
   (c) specialization in the production of particular goods leads to a decline in national income
   (d) a nation's national income can be raised by specializing in its absolute advantage and then trading freely with other countries

4. The main difference between utility functions and production functions is that
   (a) although utility is not measurable in an unambiguous way, output from a production process is easily measurable
   (b) although any bundle of goods always results in a unique level of utility, a given level of output can often be produced by several different combinations of inputs
   (c) output can sometimes be produced only in fixed proportions, but a utility function can never have fixed proportions
   (d) utility functions relate to consumers and production functions relate to producers

5. The production of carbon dioxide entails a chemical process that combines two atoms of oxygen with one atom of carbon. If the ratio of oxygen to carbon in the chemical reaction is greater than this 2 to 1 fixed proportion
   (a) carbon dioxide will not be produced
   (b) carbon dioxide will be produced more rapidly and in larger quantities
   (c) carbon will be wasted
   (d) oxygen will be wasted

6. Technical efficiency in production requires
   (a) that the most technologically advanced type of capital be used in the production process
   (b) the quantity of one input cannot be reduced, holding the other inputs constant, without reducing the amount of output
   (c) production in fixed proportions
   (d) that the fewest different types of inputs be used to produce a given level of output

7. Points on the contract curve correspond to points on the production possibility curve because
   (a) at points of tangency between isoquants in the Edgeworth box, all resources are being fully employed
   (b) at points of tangency between isoquants in the Edgeworth box, society's most desired bundles of goods is being produced
   (c) at points of tangency between isoquants in the Edgeworth box, more of one good cannot be produced without sacrificing some of the other
   (d) for given output levels, the slope of the contract curve is the same as the slope of the production possibility curve

8. The point of tangency between a community indifference curve and society's production possibility curve
   (a) is one of several possible points of equilibrium
   (b) corresponds to the highest level of community utility attainable within the production possibility curve
   (c) is an inefficient point of production
   (d) is attainable only if some of the resources in the economy are left unemployed

9. When markets work well, the economy is driven by the self-interests of producers and consumers to
   (a) inefficient points of production
   (b) exchanges between producers and consumers at which marginal valuation is greater than marginal cost
   (c) exchanges between producers and consumers at which marginal valuation is less than marginal cost
   (d) efficiency both in consumption and production

10. When a technological breakthrough in the production of a good occurs
   (a) the relative price of the good must rise to cover the cost of the breakthrough
   (b) fewer goods can be produced in the economy
   (c) more of the good can be produced, in total, for any given amount of all other goods produced
   (d) more of all other goods can be produced, in total, for any given amount of technologically improved good that is produced

IV. EXERCISES

1. What sort of returns to scale are displayed by each of the production functions listed below? (In the equations for these functions, Q denotes output, L denotes labor, K denotes capital, and M denotes land.)

(a) $Q = 25L$

(b) $Q = 7KLM$

(c) $Q = L^2$

2. Many of the fastest growing multinational companies during the past two decades are largely from newly industrialized countries (NICs). Multinationals from the Third World have increased in number from a few dozen in 1960 to a few thousand today. Many of these multinationals went abroad to assemble and manufacture more of their product line outside of their home countries. Interestingly, a few American and Japanese firms have

agreed to joint operations with these new multinationals. Joint projects have developed in areas such as paint, synthetic fibers and electronic goods.

(a) What possible explanations might there be for the rapid development of these new multinationals?

(b) Why would it be in the interests of existing American and Japanese firms to operate jointly with these new multinationals, rather than trying to compete with them?

PROBLEM

The U.S. Synthetic Fuels Corporation

In 1980, the U.S. Congress and President Jimmy Carter created the U.S. Synthetic Fuels Corporation. It was initially intended that this project would receive $15 billion of federal taxpayer money. The establishment of the project was motivated by the limits-to-growth theories of the 1970s and the fear that inexpensive energy resources would be completely exhausted. The purpose of the project was to explore the development of alternative synthetic forms of energy, even though they were more costly than existing energy sources.

(a) What were the opportunity costs to society of committing $15 billion to the Synthetic Fuels Corporation?

(b) Using an isoquant map and a production possibility curve for the United States, explain the result of the establishment of the Synthetic Fuels Corporation. Are resources being used efficiently? Is society doing as well as it possibly can?

CHAPTER 9

The Economics of Welfare and Politics

I. OVERVIEW

Economists are concerned with two types of questions: positive and normative. Positive economics deals with questions of "what is." Questions of this sort can be answered by an appeal to facts. Normative economics deals with questions of "what should be." Answers to these questions require moral judgements that are based on individual tastes. Welfare economics is the economist's way of dealing with normative as well as positive economic questions. Modern welfare economics studies the impact of different programs and events on the welfare of individuals.

A central controversy in welfare economics concerns laissez faire. This doctrine has come to refer to a policy of removing the government from economic affairs. The argument in favor of laissez faire is that it leads to an efficient distribution of goods. If people are permitted to freely trade, then they will end up on the contract curve. Laissez faire puts society on the utility possibility curve.

The choice of a particular doctrine or social utility function is a value judgement. Alternatives to laissez faire exist. One such alternative is utilitarianism. This doctrine asserts that there is a social good that is achievable by balancing one person's happiness against another's. Distributions of goods that are achieved through free exchange no longer have any special moral claim. Society can rank various distributions of goods between the different members of society. Social indifference curves that represent this ranking can be drawn and superimposed on the utility possibility curve. Society's objective is to choose the distribution of goods that attains the highest social indifference curve within or on the utility possibility curve.

The shapes of social indifference curves can vary. These shapes are similar to those for a single consumer. Social indifference curves with corners, which correspond to the case of perfect complementarity, represent egalitarianism. Perfect egalitarianism views the level of social utility as being determined by the income of the poorest member of society. Society as a whole is no better off than is the poorest person in that society. At the opposite extreme is the classical utilitarian case. These indifference curves are straight lines and say that society is better off when income is higher, regardless of who gets it.

Utilitarianism assumes that economies are made up of a typical person. The problem of measuring society's happiness is therefore reduced to measuring the happiness of the typical person. Consider this problem. A single consumer is better off in any particular year if his consumption of every single good has risen. But in general a consumer's consumption of some goods will have increased and some decreased. The question of whether she is better off is complicated. To answer this question, one must determine what has happened to the consumer's ability to purchase goods.

For the society as a whole, the problem amounts to determining what has happened to <u>real national income</u>. National income is the sum of all expenditures by members of society on goods and services. It is equivalent to society's budget. But relative prices change from one year to the next and from one place to another. In order to compare levels of national income in two different years or between two different places, the prices that are used to evaluate each level of national income must be chosen to be the same. The <u>index number problem</u> involves the choice of the prices or weights that must be used in order to add up quantities into real national income. A <u>Laspeyres index</u> weights the quantitites of goods by earlier prices. A <u>Paasche index</u> weights the quantitites of goods by late prices. But the choice of which prices to use is arbitrary.

National income is one possible measure of a society's happiness. The question still remains as to what programs society wants to pursue in order to increase its happiness. Since a unanimity of opinions does not exist in any country, a method for making social decisions must be found. Majority voting is one such method. But majority voting does not always lead to a decision or to a decision that properly reflects the opinion of the voters. Economists are also skeptical of the moral claims of majority rule. In the absence of unanimity, someone will be outvoted and dissatisfied with the outcome of the vote. There is no reason for society to give the majority's satisfaction with the outcome greater moral weight than the minority's dissatisfaction. Unanimity is therefore required to determine if a project is desirable.

Unanimity is rare. Strict adherence to a rule of unanimity can paralyze any society. A simple alternative is to permit bribery and the buying of votes. If the gainers from a project share some of their gain with the losers and still have some net gain left over, then the project is mutually advantageous. Losers are compensated at the expense of the winners. Bargaining in this way makes politics into a market.

The making of politics into a market has some flaws. A rule

of unanimity encourages extortion since each person in the society is in a bargaining position with the rest of society. Members of society also have an incentive to lie about their marginal valuations of public goods when projects of this sort are being voted upon. The most fundamental flaw is that marginal valuations are dependent on the initial distribution of income in society. A rule of unanimity does not avoid the problem of making moral judgements about the distribution of income. The national income measure of a society's happiness is also not an uncontroversial measure since it ignores the distribution of income. But the measure is not worthless. Rather, it should be viewed as a partial measure of society's total utility.

SUMMARY OF KEY CONCEPTS

positive economics	normative economics
laissez faire	utility possibility curve
utilitarianism	egalitarianism
real national income	index number problem
Laspeyres index	Paasche index
majority voting	

II. ANSWERS TO "WHAT TO READ FOR"

9.1 THE ECONOMICS OF ETHICS

1. What is positive economics? Positive economics deals with questions about "what is." Positive economic questions can be answered by an appeal to facts.

2. What is normative economics? Normative economics deals with questions of "what should be." Normative economic questions cannot be answered simply by appealing to facts.

3. Should economists make moral judgements about the economy? Economists should make moral judgements about the economy. It is true that normative questions are less easy to answer than positive economic questions, but arguments should still be ultimately decided. Further, the tools that are used for arguing positive questions are really very similar to those used for moral arguments.

4. What is laissez-faire? Why might laissez-faire be a Good Thing? Laissez faire refers to the policy of removing government from economic affairs. It might be a Good Thing

because it can lead to an efficient distribution of goods. Traders will be on the contract curve. The goal of making each person as happy as possible without hurting other people will be achieved.

5. How do you show this with a utility possibility curve? Laissez faire will put society on the utility possibility curve.

6. What is utilitarianism? Utilitarianism is the doctrine that there is a social good that is achievable by balancing one person's happiness against another's.

7. What is the bliss point and how is it related to the laissez-faire point? The bliss point is the highest attainable level of social utility within or on the utility possibility curve. The laissez-faire point will not in general correspond to the bliss point.

8. How can you show tastes for equality? Tastes for equality can be shown with indifference curves that have corners.

9. What is an egalitarian? An egalitarian views the level of social utility as determined by the income of the poorest member of society.

9.2 NATIONAL INCOME AND ITS AMBIGUITIES

1. Can we measure increases in happiness? It is possible to measure increases in happiness by measuring changes in the ability to consume goods and services.

2. What is real income? Real income is the ability to purchase goods and services.

3. How is its change measured? Real national income is the sum of all expenditures by Americans on goods and services. Changes in real income can be measured by looking at changes in total expenditures on good and services.

4. What about differences of income from one place to another? Differences of income from one place to another must be considered when measuring real income. One income must be weighted with another to form an aggregate measure of real income. The prices that are used to evaluate each income must be chosen to be the same.

5. What is the index number problem? The index number problem involves the choosing of weights in order to add up quantities into real national income.

6. Is there a solution to the problem? The choice of weights is arbitrary. The index number problem is insoluble. But the choice must be made. This involves choosing a particular point of view for looking at the problem.

7. What are Laspeyres and Paasche indexes? A Laspeyres index weights the quantities of all goods by early prices. A Paasche index weights all goods by late prices.

9.3 THE ECONOMICS OF POLITICS

1. Is there a General Will in society? There is no General Will in society. No country has unanimity of opinions. Everyone does not have the same utility function.

2. Is majority vote always a good thing? Majority voting is not always a good thing. It does not always lead to a decision. When majority voting does lead to a decision, it does not always properly reflect the opinion of the voters.

3. Why does the judgement that a project is good require unanimous agreement? In the absence of unanimity, someone will be outvoted and dissatisfied with the outcome of the vote. There is no reason to give the minority's dissatisfaction less moral weight than the majority's satisfaction. The judgement that a project is good therefore requires unanimous agreement.

4. Is bribery and buying of votes always bad? Bribery and buying of votes is not always bad. A rule of unanimity, or even a strict rule of majority, can paralyze a decision making body and make it virtually impossible to make any decisions. Bribery and buying of votes allows the winners to share some of the gain with the losers and yet still have some net gain left over.

5. How do such activities get around the problem of unanimity? Such activities get around the problem of unanimity by making politics into a market. The general will becomes whatever money can buy.

6. But what then is the problem of extortion? Unanimity encourages extortion. Since one person's vote is essential, a rule of unanimity puts every person into a position of bargaining with the rest of the community.

7. And would people tell the truth about valuations of public goods? People have an incentive not to tell the truth about their valuations of public goods. A taxpayer paying voluntarily has an incentive to put too high of a marginal valuation on the public good when society is trying to decide whether or not to provide the public good. She also has an incentive to understate

her marginal valuation when the tax collector comes to the door.

8. <u>Can one measure social gain created by a project without making an implicit judgement about the desirability of the income distribution?</u> One cannot measure social gain created by a project without making an implicit judgement about the desirability of the income distribution. The national income measure of social gain is not an all-purpose measure of national happiness. It ignores the distribution of income. It implicitly treats the existing distribution of income as special.

III. MULTIPLE CHOICE

1. A laissez-faire economic system will always lead to
   (a) an efficient and equal distribution of goods
   (b) an efficient distribution of goods through trade
   (c) an equitable distribution of goods through trade
   (d) a point outside the Edgeworth box

2. Supporters of utilitarianism
   (a) believe that free exchange has no special moral claim
   (b) free exchange will not achieve an efficient distribution of goods
   (c) free exchange will never acieve an equitable distribution of goods
   (d) the only way to achieve an equitable distribution of goods is through a system of perfect egalitarianism

3. The utility possibility curve
   (a) is society's budget constraint
   (b) is a social indifference curve
   (c) can never be reached under a laissez-faire system
   (d) can never be reached under perfect egalitarianism

4. The bliss point
   (a) lies above the utility possibility curve
   (b) lies on the highest attainable social indifference contour within or on the utility possibility curve
   (c) usually corresponds to the laissez-faire point
   (d) can never be achieved

5. The social indifference curve for an egalitarian
   (a) is analogous to the case of perfect substitutes in the theory of a single consumer
   (b) is analogous to the case of perfect complementarity in the theory of a single consumer
   (c) is analogous to indifference curves between a good and a bad
   (d) can never reach the bliss point

6. Social indifference curves will be symmetrical around a 45° line
   (a) if and only if society is indifferent between who gets a higher income
   (b) if and only if society as a whole is no better off than the member of society who is the worst off
   (c) if and only if society has achieved an efficient distribution of goods through trade
   (d) if and only if society is at a point within the utility possibility curve

7. Real national income
   (a) is a meaningful measure only if society is using all of its resources efficiently
   (b) is a measure of how equitably income is distributed within society
   (c) cannot be compared between two different years because relative prices usually change
   (d) is a measure of society's well-being

8. The index number problem
   (a) is insoluble because there is no unique choice of weights that can be used to add up quantities into real nation income
   (b) was finally solved with the construction of the Laspeyres index
   (c) was finally solved with the construction of the Paasche index
   (d) is insoluble because real national income can never be compared between two different years

9. The theory of dollar votes
   (a) is superior to a rule of unanimity
   (b) accepts the utilitarian ethic that one person can be used as a means to another's end
   (c) solves the problem of how society can achieve an equitable distribution of income
   (d) depends on a premise that the original distribution of dollar votes in society is morally acceptable

10. Vote trading under a rule of unanimity
   (a) solves the problem of discerning the general will
   (b) enriches the winners at the expense of the losers
   (c) does not ensure the largest happiness from a given distribution of income
   (d) enriches the losers and reduces total happiness in society

IV. EXERCISES

1. Consider two states of an economy, x and y. The unanimity principle asserts that state x is "better" than state y if someone in society prefers x to y and no one prefers y to x. When x is better than y, state x is said to be Pareto superior to state y. When the unanimity principle does not apply, states x and y are said to be Pareto noncomparable.

Consider the Edgeworth diagram in Figure 9.1.

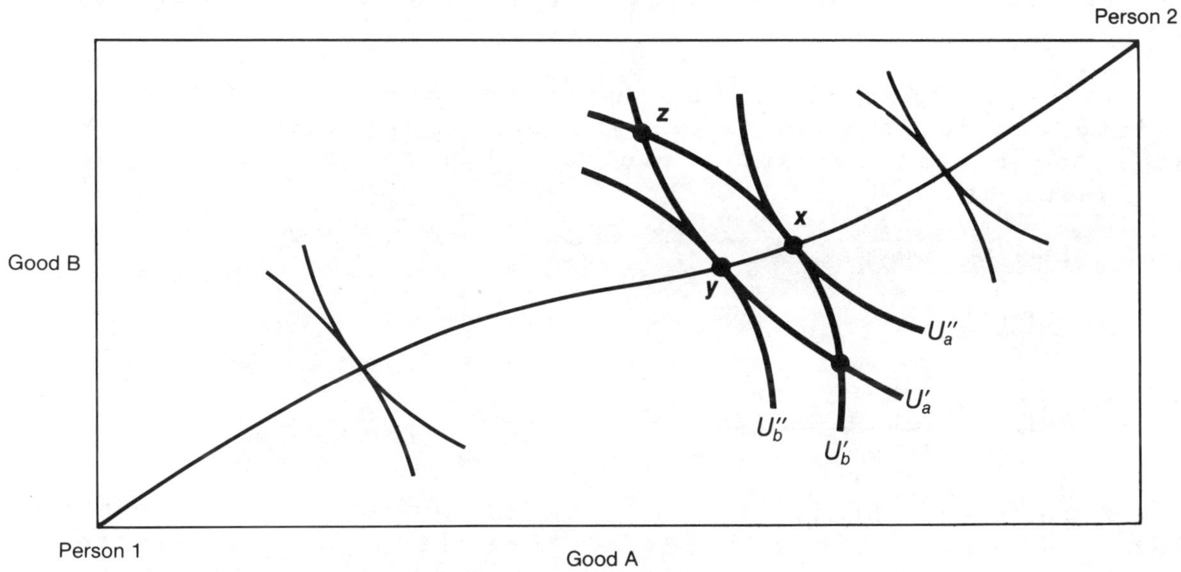

FIGURE 9.1

x, y and z are three different states of the economy.

(a) What is the relationship between state x and state y?

(b) What is the relationship between states x and y, and state z?

(c) Which of the three states are possible social optima? Why?

(d) Construct a diagram with a utility possibility curve and social indifference curves that depicts the relationships between states x, y and z.

2. The determination of socially optimal states requires the comparison of individuals' utilities. A <u>social welfare function</u> is a relationship between society's utility and the utilities of all individuals in society.

Consider the following two social welfare functions:

$$W(U_a, U_b) = U_a + U_b$$

$$W(U_a, U_b) = \min[U_a, U_b]$$

(a) What is the objective of each of these social welfare functions?

(b) For each of these functions, sketch a diagram using a utility possibility curve and a social indifference curve that shows the social optimum. Contrast the social optima for these two functions.

V. PROBLEM

The Paradox of Majority Voting

A famous economist by the name of Kenneth Arrow demonstrated that the democratic principle of selecting alternatives by majority vote might not result in socially optimal choices. Consider the case of the Wretched Wrench Tool Company. David Levy, Shaun Thompson and Mary Blair are the three executives who sit on the board of directors of the company. Their job is to elect a new chairman of the board from amongst three candidates: William Pennington, Joseph Reginald and Peter Columbo. The selection process is done through a majority vote.

David Levy prefers Pennington to Reginald, and Reginald to Columbo. Shaun Thompson prefers Reginald to Columbo, and Columbo to Pennington. Mary Blair prefers Columbo to Pennington, and Pennington to Reginald.

The agenda for the election is set by pairing the alternatives for the chairmanship. In the first round of the election, the members of the board will choose between William Pennington and Joseph Reginald. The members of the board will then choose between the winner of this vote and Peter Columbo.

(a) Under this agenda, who will be chosen as the new chairman of the board?

(b) Suppose a different agenda were set. Under the second agenda, the members of the board would first choose between Pennington and Columbo. The board members would then choose between the winner and Reginald. Who will be chosen as the new chairman?

(c) Under a third agenda, the board will first choose between Reginald and Columbo. The winner of this vote will then face Pennington. Under this agenda, who will be chosen as the chairman?

(d) What can you conclude about the outcome of the election from this example?

CHAPTER 10

Consumers' Surplus

I. OVERVIEW

Consumer welfare changes whenever prices change. We would like to obtain some unique dollar or income equivalent for the change in consumer utility. This type of dollar measure would be useful for cost-benefit studies, such as the evaluation of projects undertaken by a public agency, and the welfare losses to society of the existence of monopolies, oligopolies, and other market imperfections.

Consumers' surplus is the net gain to consumers from any trade. Value-in-exchange is the money value of the willingness of consumers to pay for a commodity at a particular price. Value-in-exchange is what the market price actually requires them to pay for the commodity. The difference between these two dollar amounts is consumers' surplus. Consumers' surplus is the area below the demand curve and above the market price. Similarly, producers' surplus is the producers' net gain from trade. It is the area above the supply curve and below the market price. The sum of consumers' surplus and producers' surplus is the total social gain from trade. Total social gain is maximized at a competitive equilibrium. Free trade maximizes social gain. At a competitive equilibrium, all mutually advantageous exchanges have been exploited.

The idea of consumers' and producers' surplus is useful for analyzing the role of middlemen in exchanges. Consumers view middlemen as bad because the middlemen often get the gains from trade. Middlemen store and resell products in order to "transport" them from regions of abundance and low prices to regions of scarcity and high prices. Middlemen try to arbitrage, which is the act of buying in low-price markets in order to sell in high-price markets. Consumers are correct in their dislike for middlemen because middlemen are bad for them. But who gets the gains from trade is irrelevant to the question of whether society as a whole gains. Middlemen increase net social surplus through arbitrage.

Changes in consumers' and producers' surplus are also useful for measuring the benefits to society from technological innovations. National income goes up after a technological innovation by the amount consumers' plus producers' surplus rises. The Laspeyres measure of national income is an upper bound on the benefit in consumers' surplus. The Paasche index is a lower bound on the benefit in consumers' surplus. But consumers' surplus and national income are questionable measures of social happiness.

SUMMARY OF KEY CONCEPTS

value-in-use	value-in-exchange
consumers' surplus	producers' surplus
rent control	arbitrage
middlemen	changes in national income
changes in surplus	

II. ANSWERS TO WHAT TO READ FOR

10.1 CONSUMERS' SURPLUS: THE ELEMENTS

1. What is value-in-exchange? Value-in-use? Consumers' surplus? Value-in-exchange is what the market price requires consumers to pay for a commodity. Value-in-use is the money value of the willingness of consumers to pay for the commodity. Consumers' surplus is the difference between value-in-use and value-in-exchange. It is the money value of the willingness of consumers to pay in excess of what the market price requires them to pay.

2. How is consumers' surplus related to the area under a demand curve? The area under the demand curve is the total willingness to pay (the value-in-use). The area under the demand curve below the market price is what the consumers actually must pay (the value-in-exchange). The area under the demand curve and above the market price is consumers' surplus. This area is the difference between value-in-use and value-in-exchange.

3. How is the area under a demand curve related to what society should pay for a bridge? The social value of a bridge is equal to the sum of the amounts that individuals are willing to pay for permits to cross the bridge. This is equal to the area under the demand curve for permits. If the bridge costs less than the money value of the satisfaction it brings (the area under the demand curve), then it should be built.

4. What price should be charged to cross a bridge? The best toll on a bridge is zero. A zero toll maximizes the social value of the bridge.

5. <u>What is producers' surplus?</u> Producers' surplus is the producers' net gain from trade. It is the area above the supply curve and below the market price.

6. <u>What are some alternative names for it?</u> Producers' surplus is also profit and economic rent.

7. <u>Why does competitive equilibrium make the sum of producers' and consumers' surplus as large as possible?</u> For quantitites less than the competitive equilibrium, the triangular areas representing consumers' surplus and producers' surplus are both truncated to trapezoidal areas. Both are made smaller. Their sum is therefore smaller. For quantitites greater than the competitive equilibrium, the gain to consumers of a large quantity and low price is more than offset by the consequent loss to sellers. The sum of consumers' surplus and producers' surplus is again smaller. The conclusion is that competitive equilibrium makes the sum of producers' surplus and consumers' surplus as large as possible.

8. <u>Does the equilibrium leave any mutually advantageous deals unexploited?</u> No. Free trade leads to the competitive equilibrium. Free trade exploits all mutually beneficial deals.

9. <u>Why does rent control leave advantageous deals unexploited?</u> Rent control often leads to a quantity smaller than the competitive equilibrium. At such quantities, mutually advantageous deals are left unexploited.

10.2 FURTHER USES OF CONSUMERS' SURPLUS: MIDDLEMEN AND OTHER EXCHANGES

1. <u>What is arbitrage?</u> Arbitrage is the act of buying in a low-price market in order to sell in a high-price market.

2. <u>Why is storage and resale of coffee like transporting coffee from a low-price town to a high-price town?</u> The storage and resale of coffee allows a middleman in coffee to withdraw coffee from lower-valued uses and to store it for higher-valued uses. The lower-valued use is consumption in a good year. The higher-valued use is consumption in a bad year. This is like transporting coffee from a low-price town to a high-price town.

3. <u>Is the transporting good?</u> Yes. The transporting allows the middleman to increase net social surplus. Society as a whole gains from the stabilization of output.

4. <u>When does the transporting stop?</u> If arbitrage and storage have zero costs, then the transporting stops when the prices in the two years are equal.

5. <u>Are middlemen, speculators, and so forth a good thing?</u> Middlemen, speculators, and so forth are on the whole good. They are good because trade is productive. They increase net social surplus. National income rises. There are gains from trade. Who exactly gets the gains is irrelevant to the question of whether society as a whole benefits.

6. <u>Are they good if they are mistaken about the future price?</u> Wrong arbitrage is bad. The storage and resale of a commodity (such as coffee) would be equivalent to the transport of the good from a region of scarcity and high prices to a region of abundance and low prices.

7. <u>Do consumers like middlemen? Are they justified in their dislike?</u> Consumers do not like middlemen because the net gain from trade often goes to the middlemen. They are justified in their dislike because middlemen are bad for <u>them</u>.

8. <u>Should society as a whole like middlemen?</u> Yes. Consumers are correct in their dislike of middlemen because middlemen are bad for consumers alone. But consumers are not the whole society. The storage and resale of a commodity by middlemen increases net social surplus.

9. <u>What is the use of horizontal as distinct from vertical consumers' surplus?</u> Horizontal consumers' surplus emphasizes the distribution of gains and losses. Vertical consumers' surplus emphasizes the sizes of gains and losses.

10. <u>Is it a good idea to restrict exports of corn when the American crop is bad?</u> Free trade increases Americans' wealth. It is not a good idea to restrict exports of corn when the American crop is bad. The gain to society in payments from foreigners is greater than the opportunity cost of foregone consumption.

10.3 A CHANGE IN CONSUMERS' AND PRODUCERS' SURPLUS IS THE SAME AS A CHANGE IN NATIONAL INCOME

1. <u>What is the benefit from cheaper railways, expressed in terms of consumers' surplus?</u> As a result of the coming of cheaper railways, the opportunity cost of transport per ton-mile or passenger mile fell. Society moved down the demand curve for transport. There was a net gain in consumers' surplus due to the fall in the cost of transport. Consumers of transport got the old quantity of transport at the new cheaper price, and they got additional transport at the lower price after railways.

2. <u>What is the relation between this benefit and the Laspeyres measure of the change of national income? The Paasche measure?</u>

National income goes up as a result of the coming of railways by exactly the same amount as the sum of producers' and consumers' surplus rises. The change in consumers' and producers' surplus lies between the Paasche and the Laspeyres measures of the change in national income.

3. Which is an easily observable upper bound on the "true" benefit from cheaper railways? The Laspeyres index is an easily observable upper bound.

4. Is the change in consumer surplus any more difficult to measure than the change in national income? The change in consumer surplus is difficult to measure unless one precisely knows the demand curve. For this reason, the bounding of consumers' surplus by the two measures of national income is the most common approach. But both national income and consumers' surplus face the index number problem.

III. MULTIPLE CHOICE

1. Consumers' surplus is
   (a) society's gain from trade
   (b) net social surplus
   (c) always greater than producers' surplus
   (c) the consumers' net gain from trade

2. Producers' surplus is
   (a) profit
   (b) supernormal profit
   (c) monopoly rents
   (d) always greater than consumers' surplus

3. At a competitive equilibrium, producers' surplus is
   (a) always equal to zero
   (b) always negative
   (c) maximized
   (d) less than it is under free trade

4. A quota on exports
   (a) increases producers' surplus
   (b) decreases producers' surplus
   (c) increases net social surplus
   (d) increases consumers' surplus

5. At output levels greater than the competitive equilibrium
   (a) consumers gain from a larger quantity and a lower price
   (b) consumers incur a loss from a larger quantity and a higher price
   (c) producers gain from a larger quantity and a lower price
   (d) producers gain from a larger quantity and a higher price

6. A competitive equilibrium is
   (a) best for consumers by themselves
   (b) best for producers by themselves
   (c) best for society
   (d) better for producers than consumers

7. The process of arbitrage continues until
   (a) the present and future prices are equal
   (b) the present price is greater than the future price
   (c) the future price is greater than the present price
   (d) the present quantity is greater than the future quantity

8. The Paasche measure of the gain in income due to a fall in price is
   (a) the fall in price times the new output
   (b) the old price times the new output
   (c) the fall in price times the old output
   (d) the old price times the old output

9. The change in consumers' and producers' surplus is
   (a) greater than the change in national income
   (b) the change in national income
   (c) less than the change in national income
   (d) unrelated to national income because of the index number problem

10. Horizontal consumers' surplus emphasizes
   (a) the size of the gains and losses
   (b) the size of the gains
   (c) the size of the losses
   (d) the distribution of gains and losses

IV. EXERCISES

1. Figure 10.1 depicts a demand curve for gasoline. Suppose that the price of gasoline falls from p^0 to p^1.

(a) What was the quantity of gasoline demanded prior to the fall in price?

(b) What is the direct savings on the original quantity of gasoline demanded, as a result of the fall in price?

(c) What is the quantity of gasoline demanded after the price decline? How much extra consumption can consumers do as a result of the fall in price?

(d) What is the value of the extra consumption?

(e) What is total consumers' surplus?

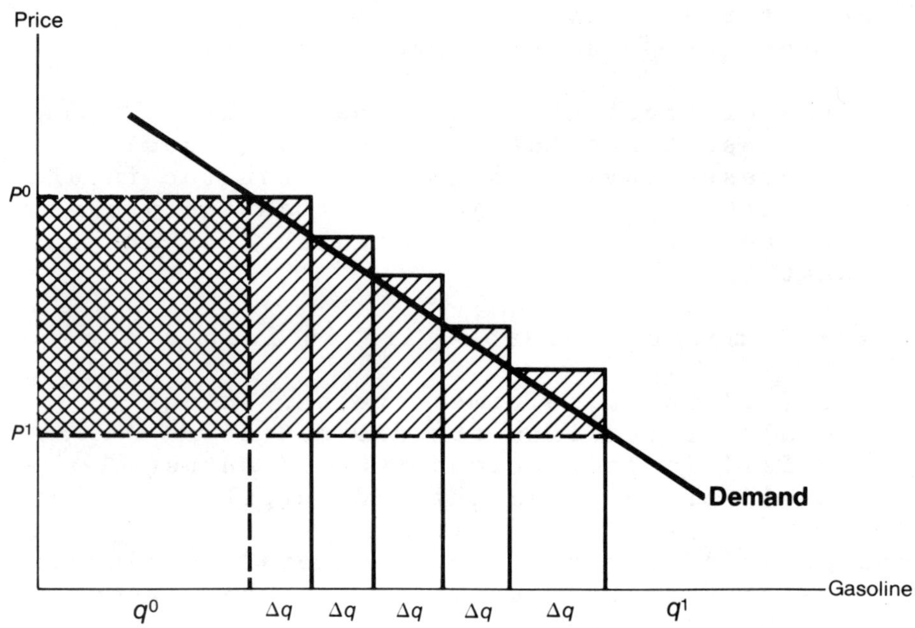

FIGURE 10.1

2. The <u>expenditure function</u> is a mathematical relationship that shows the minimum income (I) needed by a consumer to achieve a given level of utility (u) at prevailing prices (p). This function is useful for measuring consumer's surplus.

Suppose that Mary Jane is a coffee lover. At initial prices p^0, Mary's demand for coffee beans is $x(p^0)$. Suppose the price of coffee beans changes to p^1. At the new price level, Mary demands $x(p^1)$. Mary has constant money income I.

(a) How much would Mary have to be paid at the new price p^1 to make her as happy as at the price p^0? (This measure of consumers' surplus is known as <u>compensating variation</u>.)

(b) How much income would have to be taken away from Mary at the initial price p^0 to make her as well off as she would be at the price p^1. (This measure of consumers' surplus is called <u>equivalent variation</u>.)

(c) Briefly explain the difference between these two

measures of consumers' surplus.

V. PROBLEM

Rent Control

The rental housing in Santa Monica, California, is rent controlled. In 1984, a landlord in Santa Monica decided that he wanted to demolish a six-unit apartment building that he owned. He decided that it was preferable to destroy the fully tenanted building rather than continue to operate it under city rent controls. The city of Santa Monica contested his decision in court and refused to permit him to destroy the building.

The landlord argued that the building was his property and he had the constitutional right to do whatever he wanted with it, including shut it down. He contended that the "depressed value" of the housing that resulted from the rent controls forced him out of business.

It was also believed that the land would be more salable without the building on it. If the building were not destryoed, the property would have to be sold as rental property. But a clear parcel of land could be sold to someone who wanted to build and sell condominium apartments. The condominiums could be sold at a greater profit than the building sold as a rental property.

(a) Draw a supply-demand diagram to show the effects of rent controls on the Santa Monica rental housing market.

(b) What did the landlord mean by the "depressed value" of his property due to rent controls?

(c) The total cost incurred by a firm has many components including explicit costs (such as labor, land and capital) and implicit opportunity costs. What are the landlord's opportunity costs in this case? What effect does rent control have on a landlord's ability to cover his costs? Why would a landlord want to demolish his building?

(d) The Santa Monica rent-control board argued that the city's desire to preserve its rental housing superseded the landlord's right to demolish his building. In terms of producers' and social surplus, what is the city saying? Who gets the gains from trade under rent controls?

PART IV. PRODUCTION AND MARKETS

CHAPTER 11

The Firm

I. OVERVIEW

What economists call the "firm" lies between the individual consumer and the economy. It is important to understand that the people within a firm are agents of other people who own, work for, sell to, and buy from it. Households that purchase things from firms are really dealing with other households that sell their services to those same firms. Why then do firms exist? They exist because they can in general do what they do cheaper and better than some other way of doing it.

Economists are concerned with the things that motivate the owner of a firm. The simplest theory is that the owner of a firm tries to maximize money profits. Money making is not the only motivation for a firm in market economies. But the assumption of a money-making motive is useful for measuring in money terms the value of nonmonetary motives.

The owners of a firm do not always have control over the internal operations of the firm. The manager of a firm's operations does not necessarily value the profits of the owner to the same degree as the owner herself. If the owner could monitor the performance of the manager at no cost, then she could force the manager to run the firm in a profit maximizing way. But the nature of the agency problem is that this type of monitoring is costly. A firm does not always operate at the point of maximum money profits for the owner.

How do firms maximize their profits? A firm follows the rule of rational life. It maximizes profits by producing the level of output at which marginal cost is equal to marginal revenue. If the firm is producing a level of output less than this, marginal revenue exceeds marginal cost and profits can be increased by increasing output. When marginal revenue is greater than marginal cost, an additional unit of output will yield additional revenue that is greater than the additional cost of producing that unit of output. On the other hand, if the firm is producing a level of output that is greater than the profit-maximizing level, marginal cost will be greater than marginal revenue. The firm can increase profits by reducing the level of output. With every unit decrease in output, the firm reduces its costs by an amount that is greater than the sales revenue foregone.

The rule of rational life can also be used to guide the firm towards an efficient allocation of its resources. The principle of equimarginality says that a firm should allocate its resources so that marginal costs are equal in different activities. For example, if a firm operates three different plants, it can minimize its total costs by having the plants produce the output levels at which the marginal costs of the three plants are equal. If marginal costs are not equal, then the firm can lower its total costs by reallocating its resources between plants to increase the marginal costs in one plant and decrease the marginal costs in another. When marginal costs are equal, costs are minimized and profits are maximized.

SUMMARY OF KEY CONCEPTS

- wheel of wealth
- the agency problem
- marginal revenue
- rules of thumb
- inventory problem
- economies of scale
- the profit motive
- marginal cost
- average cost
- equimarginality
- two-plant problem

II. ANSWERS TO "WHAT TO READ FOR"

11.1 WHETHER AND WHY FIRMS EXIST

1. Whom do you buy from when you buy an Oldsmobile? When you buy an Oldsmobile, you are really dealing with other households. You purchase the automobile from a firm named Oldsmobile. But households really own Oldsmobile, work for it, and buy from it.

2. What is the wheel of wealth? The wheel of wealth shows how the firm stands between the individual households and the economy. On the bottom of the wheel are households. On the top of the wheel are firms. The firms are owned by the households. Money payments go around the wheel in one direction. Goods and services go around the wheel in the other direction. The households supply their services to the firms and receive income in return. The firms demand the services that they need to produce the goods that the households demand.

3. Does it mean that firms are without use? In what sense are firms "islands of conscious power in an ocean of unconscious cooperation? A market induces people to cooperate and specialize unconsciously. A firm induces people to cooperate and specialize consciously. Within the limits of the contracts to

which workers and managers of firms agree, the managers become the "bosses". They consciously force people to cooperate and specialize in certain areas. When firms exist within a market they are "islands of conscious power in the ocean of unconscious cooperation."

4. <u>What alternatives to firms exist?</u> One alternative to a firm is self-help. A second alternative is a market.

5. <u>When does society adopt the firm rather than self-help or the market?</u> Society adopts the firm rather than self-help or the market when certain marketing costs are saved. Firms exist because they do what they do best and most cheaply.

11.2 THE PROFIT MOTIVE

1. <u>What is the best guess that economics has about what motivates the owner of a firm?</u> The best guess that economics has is that money profit motivates the owner of a firm.

2. <u>Can you always believe people when they claim not to be motivated by money?</u> Peoples' declarations that they are not motivated by money may be honest and true, yet can all be consistent with the pursuit of money profit. Money buys many of the things that people seek, even if it is not the primary motive.

3. <u>Will a hired manager always care to do what is best for the owner?</u> A hired manager will not always care to do what is best for the owner. Yet, the manager is often forced by the market to be close to the owner in goals.

4. <u>How can the owner put a stop to the manager's lack of care?</u> The owner can put a stop to the manager's lack of care by monitoring and punishing the manager for failing to be a good agent.

5. <u>Can he completely stop it?</u> If detection and punishment is costly, then the owner is not motivated to ever completely stop it.

6. <u>How can the simple money-making theory be used as a standard against which to measure the value of nonpecuniary rewards?</u> Money making is not the only motive in market economies. But it can be used as a standard against which to measure the value of nonpecuniary rewards. When nonpecuniary goals are sought, managers and owners sacrifice maximum money profits. It is possible to compare the actual returns on an investment with the opportunity costs of the amount invested. The difference between the actual and potential returns is a measure in money terms of

the value of nonmonetary motives.

11.3 MARGINAL COST: WHY THE FIRM PRODUCES WHAT IT PRODUCES

1. What does the familiar rule of rational life have to do with the firm's decision on how much to produce? The firm's decision on how much to produce is consistent with the rule of rational life. A firm that is trying to maximize money profits will produce that level of output at which marginal cost is equal to marginal revenue.

2. What is the marginal cost of output? The marginal cost of output is equal to the additional cost incurred by the firm when it produces an additional unit of output.

3. What is marginal revenue? Marginal revenue is the additional revenue gained by the firm when it produces an additional unit of output.

4. What are fixed costs? Fixed costs are costs that do not vary with output. Examples of fixed costs are land rents, license fees, and the repayment of loans.

5. What areas in the diagram represent the losses from the wrong outputs? The firm should produce at the point where marginal revenue is equal to marginal cost. If it produces a level of output less than this, marginal revenue exceeds marginal cost and the area between the two curves is equal to potential profit foregone. If it produces a level of output greater than the profit-maximizing level, marginal cost exceeds marginal revenue and the area between the two curves is equal to profit that is sacrificed.

6. Do "profit margins" have anything to do with the decision on how much to produce? Profit margins have nothing to do with the decision on how much to produce. Marginal cost is not the same as average cost. Average cost (or profit margin) is no guide to how much to produce. The concept of average cost is only useful for expressing the desirability of going into business.

7. Do "short-run profits"? If a firm is trying to maximize long-run profits, then it also has an incentive to behave efficiently in the short-run. Maximizing total profit summed over all future years will maximize the price that people will be willing to pay for the firm today. It is therefore fallacious to argue that "the market maximizes short-run profits rather than long-run profits."

8. How close does the theory of marginal cost and revenue need to fit? In practice, profit maximization is not attained exactly.

When price is not exactly equal to marginal cost, profit is not exactly at a maximum. But the constant adjustment of output to the profit-maximizing level is costly. The closeness of the approximation of the theory of marginal cost and marginal revenue depends on the incentives within the firm to make it close. The theory is a good approximation of the motives of many firms because it is forced on firms by the market. The theory is testable against the facts. But it can also be used as a standard of comparison even when it is false.

11.4 EQUIMARGINALITY: HOW THE FIRM PRODUCES WHAT IT PRODUCES AT MINIMUM COST

1. <u>How does a firm decide how to allocate internally?</u> A firm allocates internally so that it equalizes the marginal value of each activity within the firm.

2. <u>How much does it take from each plant?</u> If a profit-maximizing firm operates several different plants, it wants to allocate production between the different plants in such a way that the marginal cost at each plant is equal to the marginal cost at every other plant. If marginal costs are not equal, then the firm can reduce its total costs by reallocating its resources between plants to increase the marginal costs at certain plants and decreasing the marginal costs in others.

3. <u>What is the Principle of Equimarginality?</u> The Principle of Equimarginality says that a firm should set marginal costs equal in different activities.

4. <u>Is the average cost of each plant relevant?</u> The average cost of each plant is irrelevant. Marginal, not average, cost is to be equalized.

5. <u>What is the don't-do-it-yourself principle?</u> The don't-do-it-yourself principle deals with the question of self-sufficiency. It is an application of the principle of equimarginality. It says that if self-sufficiency does not equalize marginal costs, then the firm should purchase certain resources from other firms. At some low price externally relative to a high price internally, the firm should buy all of a resource from another firm.

III. <u>MULTIPLE CHOICE</u>

1. A firm chooses a certain scale of activity because
   (a) firms produce as much as they can
   (b) it is usually constrained by engineering considerations

(c) at that scale the firm makes the most money
(d) at that scale marginal revenue is maximized

2. The agency problem in economic life is that
(a) marginal cost often exceeds marginal revenue
(b) marginal revenue often exceeds marginal cost
(c) detection and punishment are costly
(d) managers like to indulge their own tastes and have a large number of subordinates

3. The whole cost of producing a given level of output is equal to the
(a) area under the average cost curve out to the quantity produced
(b) area under the marginal cost curve out to the quantity produced
(c) area between the marginal revenue curve and the marginal cost curve, out to the quantity produced
(d) area between the marginal cost curve and the average cost curve, out to the quantity produced

4. A firm that produces too small an output sacrifices potential profit because
(a) marginal revenue is below marginal cost
(b) marginal revenue is equal to marginal cost
(c) marginal revenue is greater than marginal cost
(d) average revenue is below marginal revenue

5. Profit maximization is not attained exactly because
(a) price is rarely equal to marginal revenue exactly
(b) price is rarely equal to marginal cost exactly
(c) price is usually greater than marginal cost
(d) price is usually less than marginal cost

6. Marginal carrying cost is equal to
(a) total reordering cost
(b) total carrying and reordering cost
(c) the slope of total carrying cost
(d) the slope of average carrying cost

7. Consider two perfectly substitutable activities. Total costs are minimized if
(a) average fixed costs are equalized in both activities
(b) total costs are equalized in both activities
(c) average costs are equalized in both activities
(d) marginal costs are equalized in both activities

8. Self-sufficiency will in general
(a) equalize marginal costs
(b) not equalize marginal costs
(c) minimize total costs
(d) minimize average costs

9. The profits that middlemen make are usually
   (a) supernormal profits
   (b) monopoly profits
   (c) due to marginal revenue exceeding marginal cost
   (d) a result of the services that they perform

10. A firm maximizes profit by producing the output level at which
   (a) average revenue is equal to average cost
   (b) average profits are maximized
   (c) average revenue is equal to marginal cost
   (d) marginal revenue is equal to marginal cost

IV. EXERCISES

1. Figure 11.1 contains the total cost (TC) curve and total revenue (TR) firm for a typical firm.

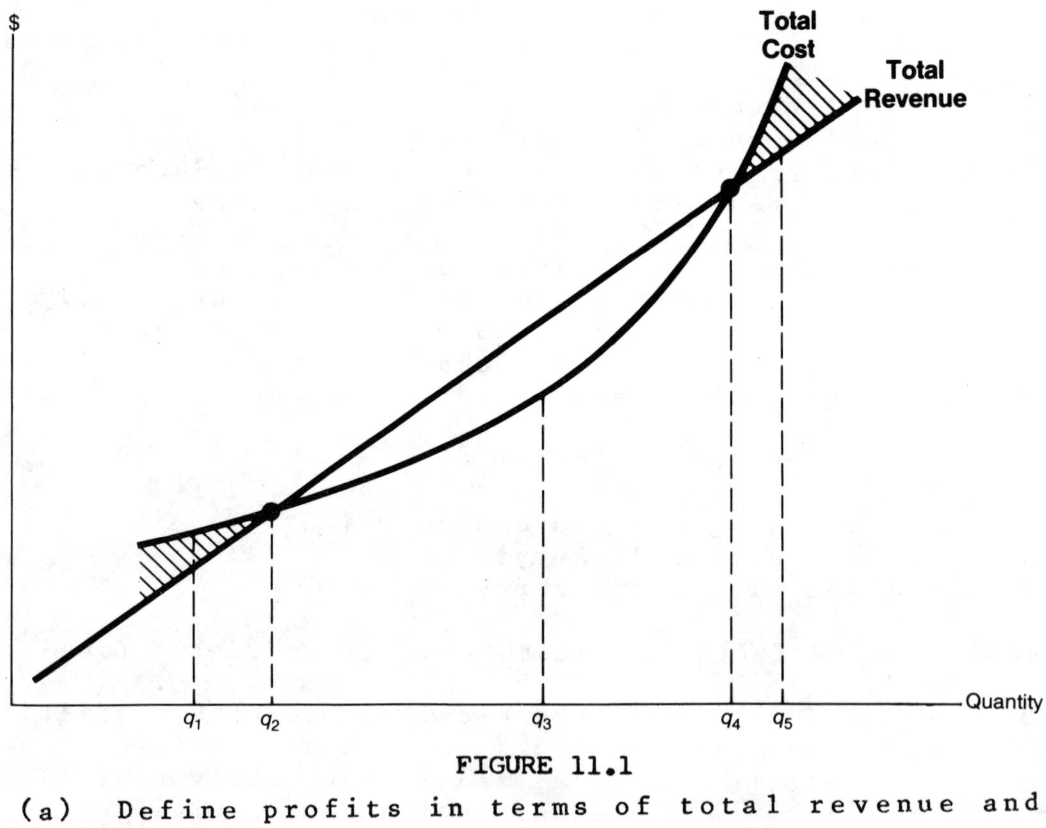

FIGURE 11.1

(a) Define profits in terms of total revenue and total cost.

(b) At what level of output are profits maximized?

(c) What is true about profits at output levels q_1 and q_5? What is true about profits at output levels q_2 and q_4? What is true about profits at q_3?

(d) What is true about the slopes of the two curves at the point of maximum profits? What "marginal" concepts are the slopes equal to?

(e) Graphically illustrate using a marginal revenue and a marginal cost curve the equilibrium point for a firm that is trying to maximize profits.

(f) If the firm produces to the left of the equilibrium point, what will happen to profits? Why?

(g) If the firm produces to the right of the equilibrium point, what will happen to profits? Why?

2. The Zazoom Toy Company produces toys by combining two variable inputs, labor (L) and plastic (P), with one fixed input, capital (K). Zazoom pays \$2 an hour for labor and \$1 for plastic. The fixed costs (including depreciation and interest) associated with its capital stock total \$150 per period. Write out a general equation for Zazoom's total costs.

3. The short-run total cost curve for the Number Crunching Computer Company can be written as follows:

$$TC = q^3 - 4q^2 + 20q + 40$$

where q is the quantity of computers produced. Using this equation, derive expressions for fixed costs (TFC), variable cost (TVC), average variable cost (AVC), and average fixed cost (AFC).

V. PROBLEM

The Duality of Profit Maximization and Cost Minimization

Consider a firm that employs only two factors of production, capital (K) and labor (L). The rental rate of capital is r and the wage rate for labor is w.

(a) Suppose the firm is constrained by its stockholders to spend only \$C on production. The firm wants to operate efficiently, subject to this cost constraint, by producing the maximum obtainable output. Using a diagram containing the firm's isocost curve and isoquant map, determine the equilibrium level of output for the firm. What is the equilibrium condition for a firm trying to maximize output subject to a cost constraint?

(b) Alternatively, suppose the firm is constrained by a regulatory agency to produce a particular level of output. The firm wants to minimize the cost of producing the output. Using a diagram containing the firm's isocost curve and isoquant map, locate the point of equilibrium for the firm. What is the equilibrium condition for a firm trying to minimize cost subject to a given output constraint?

(c) What can you conclude about the relationship between the two alternative equilibrium conditions?

(d) What is true about profits at both equilibrium points?

CHAPTER 12

Cost Curves of the Firm

I. OVERVIEW

The output of a firm depends upon the inputs that are used in its production processes. A production function is a mathematical expression that shows the maximum output that the firm can produce from any particular combination of inputs. A production function is a description of the type of production processes going on within a firm, and therefore has a particular shape and properties. One characteristic is that it exhibits eventually diminishing marginal returns to scale. A firm can attempt to produce more output by increasing the amounts of inputs that it is using. Initially, each additional increase in inputs will produce increasing amounts of output. The firm is experiencing increasing returns to scale. But as the firm adds more inputs, each additional dose of inputs eventually produces less additional output. The firm is experiencing diminishing returns to scale. Bigger is not always better.

Each input to production has a price. The firm incurs costs when it produces output. The cost function shows the least cost that the firm must incur in order to produce a given level of output. For a firm that is a price taker in the market for inputs, input prices will be fixed. Input prices are constraints faced by the firm. Increases in production that result from increasing the usage of inputs lead to increases in total cost. There is a connection between the types of production going on within the firm and the costs that it must incur to produce any given level of output. The shape of the production function determines the shape of the total cost function. If the prices of inputs are fixed, then the shape of the total cost curve is the same as the shape of the production function except for scale. There is a dual relationship between the firm's production function and its total cost function.

Marginal cost is defined as the change in total cost that results from a change in the quantity of output produced. The marginal cost curve initially declines, reaches a minimum, and then rises as output rises. This shape is a direct result of the returns to scale experienced by the firm. Consider the upward sloping portion of the marginal cost curve. This portion of the curve corresponds to the point of diminishing marginal returns. As the firm increases its usage of inputs, it gets smaller increments to output. This means that given increments to output will require larger and larger increments of inputs. This leads to higher and higher costs. Marginal cost is rising. Rising marginal cost can also result from rising delivery costs or from an inelastic supply of inputs. The fact that marginal cost eventually rises limits the optimal size of the firm.

Since the cost function shows the least cost way of producing any given level of output, a firm that is operating efficiently would always like to be producing on the cost function (the long-run total cost curve). In the short run however, it is not always possible for the firm to be at such points. Firms do not have full information. The lack of such information, which is costly, is one reason the firm is off of the long-run total cost curve. In the short-run, not all inputs are variable. The firm cannot instantaneously achieve the economically efficient factor input combination (that is, at the point where the marginal rate of substitution is equal to the input price ratio). This is another constraint that forces the firm to operate on a short-run total cost curve rather than the long-run total cost curve. There are many such short-run curves. Since the long-run cost curve is the lowest possible cost for any given level of output, it is the envelope of all the short-run curves. The long-run curve is a planning device for the firm when it is making decisions about the future.

The cost curves and production curves can be used to determine the level of output at which the firm will be maximizing its profits. The firm achieves maximum profits at the output level at which the gap between total revenue and total cost is the largest. In terms of the marginal curves, profit is maximized at the point where marginal revenue is equal to the marginal cost of production. This is just the rule of rational life.

SUMMARY OF KEY CONCEPTS

production function	increasing returns to scale
cost function	diminishingmarginalreturnsto scale
duality	marginal cost
long-run total cost	short-run total cost

II. ANSWERS TO "WHAT TO READ FOR"

12.1 PRODUCTION AND INPUT SUPPLY: WHY MARGINAL COST IS AS IT IS

1. What are the two fundamental messages of the idea of the

production function? The production function conveys two fundamental messages. The first idea is that output depends on input. The second message is that there are different combinations of inputs that can be used to produce the same level of output.

2. What are concavity and diminishing marginal returns to scale? Concavity is a description of the acceptable shape for a production function. Concave production functions exhibit diminishing marginal returns to scale. This says that as a firm attempts to produce more output by increasing the amount of inputs is uses, each additional amount of input produces less output.

3. What is the factual reason that economists assume diminishing marginal returns to scale? The factual reason that economists assume diminishing marginal returns to scale is that in cases in which returns to scale can be measured well, such as in farming, production functions do not exhibit continuously increasing returns to scale.

4. How do you derive a total cost curve from a production function and a price of the input? If the price of the input is constant, then the total cost curve and the production function will be identical in shape except for scale.

5. How do you derive marginal and average cost from the total cost? Marginal cost at a particular quantity is equal to the slope of the total cost curve at that quantity. Average cost at a particular quantity is equal to the slope of a straight line rya from the origin intersecting the total cost curve at the quantity.

6. What is the necessary relation between marginal and average cost curves? Marginal cost is equal to average cost only once. Marginal cost intersects the average cost curve at minimum average cost.

7. How does a firm behave if its marginal cost curve slopes down? If the marginal cost curve slopes down, then the firm will expand output without limit.

8. How can delivery costs and rising costs of inputs offset a perversely shaped marginal cost curve? Rising delivery costs and rising costs of inputs (diminishing returns to scale) can cause the marginal cost curve to slope upward.

9. What is duality? Duality describes the relationship between the cost function and the production function. The production functions shows the greatest amount of output that can be produced from a given amount of input. The cost function shows the least cost way of producing any given amount of output. Both functions describe the best thing for the firm to do. The two

are solutions to the same problem.

10. Why is it a consequence of the equality of cost and revenue? Duality is a consequence of the equality of cost and revenue because the firm is constrained by its budget constraint, PQ=wI, where P is the price of output, Q is quantity of output, w is the fixed input price, and I is the amount of the input used. Maximizing output for a given input is the same as minimizing input for a given output. The physical productivity of the inputs, Q/I, is maximized when the input cost per unit of output, w(I/Q), is minimized.

12.2 COST CURVES IN USE: THE LONG RUN AND THE SHORT RUN

1. What is the principle that adding constraints hurts? Firms are often above the long-run cost curve. In the short run, firms might be constrained to operate above the long-run cost curve because of costly short-run constraints. The short run is a situation with more constraints than in the long run.

2. How does the short-run cost curve of a firm illustrate the principle? The short-run total cost curve of the firm illustrates the principle that adding constraints hurts because it is always above the long-run cost curve.

3. What are the two reasons a firm will tolerate being on a higher cost, short-run curve? A firm will tolerate being on a higher cost, short-run cost curve if it believes that a change in output is going to be short lived. In this case, the firm will tolerate the higher short-run cost rather than purchase long-lived capital equipment to produce the higher output. Another reason the firm will tolerate the higher short-run costs even if the change is output is permanent, it may be cheaper to adjust to it slowly.

4. Would it tolerate it if there was a secondhand market in equipment? If there was a frictionless secondhand market in equipment, the firm would never tolerate higher short-run costs. There would be no distinction between the short run and the long run.

5. Why might a firm prefer an expensive but flexible plan to a cheap but inflexible one? A firm might prefer an expensive but flexible plan to a cheap but inflexible one if it often faces boom and bust periods in output.

6. What is the envelope of all short-run cost curves? The long-run total cost curve is the envelope of all short-run cost curves. The long-run curve shows the lowest cost way of producing any given level of output.

12.3 COST CURVES IN USE: FIXED AND VARIABLE COSTS

1. How do the total cost curve and the total revenue curve determine how much a firm wants to produce? The firm wants to produce the amount of output at which profits are maximized. This level of output corresponds to the points at which the gap between the total revenue curve and the total cost curve is the largest.

2. Are past, sunk costs relevant? Past, sunk costs are not relevant.

3. Why not? When a firm is trying to maximize profits, it is influenced only by future costs that can be altered by the amount of output. Sunk costs do not affect present and future costs.

4. Are fixed costs relevant? Fixed costs do not affect the output of the firm. Fixed and unavoidable costs have no effect on present and future decisions. Fixed and avoidable costs only affect the firm's decision about whether or not to produce anything. These costs are avoidable if one closes down entirely.

5. What are the two meanings of "fixed costs"? There are two types of fixed costs. The first type corresponds to fixed costs that are unavoidable. The second type corresponds to fixed costs that are avoidable.

III. MULTIPLE CHOICE

1. Economists assume that production functions are concave because
   - (a) increasing marginal returns are not possible
   - (b) marginal cost curves never slope downward
   - (c) empirical studies have shown that production functions do not exhibit continuously increasing returns to scale
   - (d) average cost is constantly increasing

2. If marginal cost were always falling then
   - (a) the firm would maximize profits where marginal cost equals marginal benefit
   - (b) the firm would increase output without limit because profits rise without limit
   - (c) the firm would never be able to obtain positive profits
   - (d) the firm would shut down and produce no output

3. If the production of a firm facing a horizontal demand curve exhibited constant returns to scale then it is possible that
   - (a) the firm would produce no output

(b) the firm would produce an infinite amount of output
(c) the firm would be indifferent to the amount it produced
(d) all of the above are possible

4. A flat or downward-sloping marginal cost curve at the plant in which production is taking place can be consistent with rising marginal cost at the place of use because
(a) constant returns to scale is inconsistent with a horizontal demand curve
(b) transport costs might be expensive and unequal
(c) the supply of inputs might be inelastic
(d) all of the above are possible

5. Maximizing output for a given input
(a) will put the firm on the long-run total cost curve
(b) is inconsistent with cost minimization
(c) is possible only if the firm is a natural monopoly
(d) is inconsistent with the behavior of nonexpansive market managers who attempt to minimize costs

6. The long-run total cost curve
(a) intersects the minimum points on all short-run cost curves
(b) is never below the short-run cost curves
(c) shows the least cost way of producing any given level of output
(d) can never be attained by a profit-maximizing firm

7. If a firm is producing at a point on its production function then
(a) it is also producing at a point on its long-run total cost function
(b) it cannot be producing at a point on its long-run total cost function
(c) it is also producing at the minimum point on its short-run cost function
(d) it is not producing efficiently

8. If a firm is producing at a point on the short-run cost curve then
(a) it is not trying to maximizing profits
(b) it is not a competitive firm
(c) it is not a natural monopoly
(d) it is unwilling to adjust immediately to a new scale of operation

9. Profit is equal to
(a) the difference between total revenue and the area under the marginal cost curve
(b) the difference between total revenue and the area under the average cost curve
(c) profit on fixed costs and variable costs
(d) the difference between fixed costs and variable costs

10. Average cost is relevant for
   (a) the determination of profit
   (b) the decision of whether to produce at all
   (c) the determination of the level of output at which to produce
   (d) the determination of total cost

IV. EXERCISES

1. Marginal cost, which is a description of the firm's cost structure, is defined as the addition to total cost due to the production of one additional unit of output. The marginal cost curve first declines, reaches a minimum, and then rises as output increases. Marginal product, which is a description of the firm's production technology, is the addition to total product due to the use of an additional unit of a specific input. Marginal product normally rises, reaches a minimum, and then declines as the usage of an input increases. Demonstrate that there is a dual relationship between these two curves; that is, that the shape of one curve is a result of the shape of the other.

2. Average variable cost is total cost divided by output. The average variable cost curve initially declines, reaches a minimum, and then rises as output increases. Average product is total product divided by the amount of an input that is being used. The average product curve first rises, reaches a maximum, and then falls as input usage increases. Show that there is a dual relationship between these two curves.

3. Upon graduation from college, Bob and Jeremy Stone decided to enter the computer business. As soon as they graduated, Bob and Jeremy took their combined savings of $15,000 and bought several pieces of electronic equipment that they needed to build computers with. They designed their own computer system using the knowledge that they gained in college. When they started to sell their computer system, Bob and Jeremy discovered that the computer market is competitive and that they had to charge the competitive market price for their system. They immediately discovered that the competitive price was below their average fixed costs. The market price was also below their average variable costs. Bob Stone argued that they should shut down their business immediately. Jeremy Stone argued that they should stay in business since they had already sunk their combined savings of $15,000 into the business. Who was making the correct decision?

V. PROBLEM

The Relationship Between Average and Marginal Measures

The small village of Stamford had a population of one hundred in 1980. Stamford was an unusual village in 1980 because every citizen had a $10,000 per year job. In 1981 Robert Shaun moved into Stamford and obtained a $15,050 per year job. In 1982 Wilma Josephson entered the Stamford community and found a new job paying her an annual salary of $10,050. In 1983 Paul Blair joined the community, but could only find an $8,000 per year job.

(a) What was the average income level for the Stamford community in 1980?

(b) What was the marginal contribution of Robert Shaun's income to total community income in 1981? What happened to the average income level in Stamford after Shaun's arrival in 1981?

(c) What was the marginal contribution of Wilma Josephson's income to the total income in the community in 1982? What happened to the average income level in Stamford after Josephson's arrival in 1982?

(d) What was the marginal contribution of Paul Blair's income to the total income in the community in 1983? What happened to the average income level in Stamford after Blair's arrival in 1983?

(e) What general conclusions can you draw about the relationship between marginal income and average income from this example?

CHAPTER 13

Competitive Industry

I. OVERVIEW

The supply curve for a competitive industry can be derived from the supply curves of the individual firms in the industry. A firm in a competitive industry is a price taker. In order to operate efficiently and maximize profits, individual price-taking firms will always produce that level of output at which price equals marginal cost. The price-taking firm's marginal cost curve is its supply curve. More precisely, the upward sloping portion of the marginal cost curve is the firm's supply curve if it is maximizing profits. If the costs of all firms are independent and the number of firms in the industry is fixed, then market supply is obtained by adding up each firm's supply at any given price. Market supply is found by summing the marginal cost (supply) curves of the individual firms parallel to the quantity axis. Since each firm's supply curve is upward sloping, market supply is also upward sloping.

The law of one price (Chapter 6) says that when a market clears, all demanders and suppliers in the market face a single price. When the market is in equilibrium, a single price prevails that equates market supply with market demand. An efficient level of output is being produced at which the marginal valuation (the height of the demand curve) is equal to the marginal opportunity cost (the height of the supply curve). Each individual firm takes the market-clearing price as given and produces the output level at which this price is equal to marginal cost. Since there is only one price that clears the market, each firm produces at the same marginal cost. Each firm produces at its optimum and therefore maximizes its profits. Industry profits are also maximized.

In certain circumstances, the costs of firms in the market will be interdependent. These situations arise when the firms in the industry are all drawing on a common resource or input that is being supplied inelastically to the entire industry. If all firms in the industry expand output together, then costs will rise more than if only a single firm expands output. In this situation, the industry supply curve will be less elastic than the individual marginal cost curves. The industry supply curve will still be upward sloping.

Downward sloping supply curves are theoretically possible. A <u>pecuniary external economy of industry scale</u> will tend to lower the cost of an input as industry output rises. If this effect is strong enough, it can lead to a downward-sloping supply curve for the input. This downward-sloping supply curve affects the supply curves of all products that make use of the input. In the extreme, the cost curve of each firm in the industry might fall rather than rise as output increases, leading to a downward-sloping market supply curve for the output.

If a market supply curve is downward sloping, then the price-mechanism will no longer lead to optimal levels of output. Too little output will be produced by the market. In the presence of such economies of scale, a larger scale of output will lead to cheaper and more efficient production. Government intervention might be argued for in order to increase growth and output in the industry. As a theoretical possibility, such a situation is plausible. Yet, empirical findings shed doubt on the importance of this shortcoming.

SUMMARY OF KEY CONCEPTS

- industry supply
- general equilibrium
- economies of scale
- diseconomies
- case against intervention
- interdependent costs
- partial equilibrium
- pecuniary external economy of industry scale
- case for intervention
- laissez-faire

II. ANSWERS TO "WHAT TO READ FOR"

13.1 INDUSTRY SUPPLY WITH A FIXED NUMBER OF FIRMS AND COSTS INDEPENDENT: OPTIMALITY AND UPWARD SLOPE

1. How is the marginal cost curve for a competitive firm related to its supply curve? The marginal cost curve is the supply curve for a competitive firm.

2. How do the curves of marginal cost for a bunch of individual firms add up to make the supply curve for the industry? The supply curve for a competitive industry is obtained by summing the marginal cost curves of the individual firms parallel to the quantity axis.

3. Why are profits necessary to get the individual firms to produce the efficient amount? If the individual firms maximize profit, then society will be on its production possibility curve.

Each firm maximizes profit by producing the quantity at which marginal cost is equal to marginal benefit. Marginal cost is the same for each firm and is equal to the market price. When each firm is at its profit- maximizing level of output, the market is in equilibrium and the marginal cost of a unit supplied in the market is equal to the marginal valuation of a unit consumed.

4. Would it be good if some of the firms did not pursue profit? If some of the firms did not pursue profit, market price would rise. The marginal costs of production of the individual firms would no longer be equal. Total industry costs therefore rise and society would no longer be on its production possibility curve.

5. Why does the supply curve of the industry always slope upward? The industry supply curve is upward sloping because each firm's supply curve is upward sloping. The industry supply curve is the sum of the individual supply curves.

13.2 INDUSTRY SUPPLY WITH A FIXED NUMBER OF FIRMS BUT COSTS INDEPENDENT: EXTERNALITIES

1. What causes the prices of specialized inputs for the petroleum industry to rise? The prices of specialized inputs for the petroleum industry rise because they are supplied inelastically to the industry as a whole. At the same time the individual firms in the industry all draw on these common specialized inputs. When producers of all petroleum products expand, then the price of the specialized input will rise.

2. Does the increase of production by one firm do it? The increase of production by one firm alone does not cause the price of a specialized input to rise. Producers of all petroleum products must expand output at the same time, while drawing on the common specialized input.

3. How does the simultaneous increase in production by all firms reinforce the law of upward sloping supply? The simultaneous increase in production of all firms will raise costs more than will a similar expansion in just one firm when certain specialized inputs are supplied inelastically to the industry as a whole. This means that the supply curve for the entire industry will be less elastic than the individual marginal cost curves. This reinforces the law of upward sloping supply.

4. What happens when the price of specialized inputs falls as the industry's output rises? When the price of specialized inputs falls as the industry's output rises, pecuniary economies of industry scale are realized. The supply of the specialized input slopes downward, and this may be transmitted to the supply

curve for industry output. The optimality of the market is destroyed. Since the reduction in costs is external to the individual firms, no single firm expands its output to reduce the cost of the input. Too little output is produced in the industry.

5. <u>Can the price fall offset the forces of upward sloping supply?</u> The fall in price of specialized inputs can offset the forces of upward sloping supply of industry output.

6. <u>What is wrong with the idea that the market will fail to exploit the few downward sloping supply curves?</u> Empirical findings indicate that there is doubt about the idea that the market will fail to exploit the few downward sloping supply curves.

III. <u>MULTIPLE CHOICE</u>

1. In a competitive market, the marginal cost is the same for each firm because
   (a) profits cannot be made in a competitive market
   (b) firms equate marginal cost to marginal revenue and marginal revenue is equal to zero at maximum profits
   (c) competitive firms maximize profits by equating marginal cost to market price and there is only one equilibrium market price
   (d) all firms are identical in a competitive market

2. When each competitive firm is as its optimum
   (a) firms are making zero profits
   (b) total industry profits are zero
   (c) marginal cost of a unit of output supplied is equal to the marginal valuation of a unit consumed
   (d) marginal revenue from the last unit supplied is greater than the marginal cost of producing that unit

3. A competitive firm will never produce along the downward sloping portion of its marginal cost curve because
   (a) marginal revenue can never equal marginal cost along the downward sloping portion of the marginal cost curve
   (b) marginal revenue equals marginal cost along the downward sloping portion of the marginal cost curve
   (c) profits are not maximized along the downward sloping portion of the marginal cost curve
   (d) marginal cost is always above average cost along the downward sloping portion of the marginal cost curve

4. In the long run, a firm will only produce along the upward sloping portion of the marginal cost curve
   (a) below minimum average variable cost
   (b) above minimum average variable cost

(c) at minimum average variable cost
(d) above average total cost

5. In the short run, if a firm is not covering its fixed costs, it will
(a) shut down and produce no output
(b) continue to produce if marginal revenue is above average variable cost
(c) continue to produce if marginal revenue is equal to average variable cost
(d) continue to produce only if marginal revenue is equal to marginal cost

6. Pecuniary economies of industry scale
(a) always lead to a downward sloping industry supply curve
(b) always lead to an upward sloping industry supply curve
(c) sometimes lead to a downward sloping industry supply curve
(d) sometimes lead to an upward sloping supply curve of an input

7. When there are pecuniary economies of industry scale
(a) too little is produced and government intervention is needed to encourage balanced growth
(b) too much is produced and government intervention is needed to encourage balanced growth
(c) the optimality of the market is still preserved since individual firms will expand output in order to reduce the cost of the input
(d) all firms will reduce output in order to reduce the cost of the input

8. Reductions in price in rapidly growing industries like the electronics industry are a result of
(a) technological progress that shifts the supply curve outward
(b) economies of scale
(c) either economies of scale or technological progress
(d) upward sloping demand curves

9. If a specialized input is elastically supplied
(a) then as output is expanded by all firms the price of the input is forced up
(b) the downward-sloping supply curve of the input may be transmitted to the industry supply curve for output
(c) pecuniary economies of industry scale are realized
(d) the price of the input remains fixed

10. The equilibrium achieved by a competitive market
(a) is not always consistent with profit maximizing behavior by the individual firms
(b) is consistent with the rule of rational life
(c) might lead to shortages if the industry supply curve is

inelastic

(d) might lead to shortages if the industry supply curve is elastic

IV. EXERCISES

1. Brett Harrington owns a new automobile tire store. He invested $50,000 of his own income in the venture in order to establish himself in the business. $40,000 of this money was used to purchase a new store, furniture for the interior, and the equipment needed for balancing and mounting automobile tires. The remaining $10,000 was used to cover operating expenses as they are incurred.

After being in business for over six months, Brett discovered that the prevailing competitive market price for tires, which is the price he charges, is below his average variable cost. Yet, the price per tire is high enough to cover his average fixed costs. Brett decided to stay in business for another six months and hoped for an improvement in business conditions.

After being in business for over a year, Brett found that the marginal revenue received per tire was below his average total costs. He realized that he was losing money by producing tires, but concluded that if he could increase the volume of tires he sold, he could make up for his losses.

(a) Was Brett Harrington's decision to stay in business after six months of operation the correct decision to make? Why?

(b) Was Brett's rationale for staying in business after one year correct? Why?

2. The Getcha Paper Supply Company is one of many competitive stationary producers in New Jersey. In March 1984, each of the stationary producers in New Jersey had an equal share of the market. But in April, the Getcha Paper Company decided that it wanted to increase its profits and concluded that the best way to do that was to increase its production. What change in profits might one expect for the Getcha Paper Company if it proceeds with this strategy?

3. Tastem Foods is one of several competitive hamburger joints on George Street in New Brunswick, New Jersey. In 1983 the competitive market price for a hamburger was 80 cents. In 1984 the owners of Tastem Foods decided that the hamburger business wasn't as profitable as they would like, so they decided to close

down their store. What effect did this action have on the market for hamburgers on George Street?

PROBLEM

The Competitive Hotel Industry

New Orleans is a city that has rapidly become more competitive in the lodging field. Several major hotels have located in New Orleans, including a Hilton, Sheraton, Hyatt, Holiday Inn, Marriott, Fairmont and Ramada Inn.

The 1982 recession had a big effect on the hotel industry in New Orleans. The number of visitors to the city declined and the hotel industry slumped. Many hotels were forced to reduce their payrolls by firing employees. Others improved and modernized their operations in order to reduce costs. New management techniques were introduced. Many also reduced their room rental rates.

(a) Assume that all of the hotels in New Orleans try to maximize their total profits. Draw a graph showing the number of hotel rooms each hotel would build if each hotel takes the standard room occupancy rate as given in the marketplace. Relate this to a graph showing the market equilibrium for the hotel industry in New Orleans.

(b) When the number of visitors to the city of New Orleans declined in 1982, what would one have expected to happen to the equilibrium rental rate for a standard room? Is this predicition consistent with what actually happened?

(c) Why did hotels try to improve and modernize their operations during the recession? What effect would their success or failure to reduce costs have on their long-run decision about whether to stay in the hotel business?

CHAPTER 14

The Long-Run Supply Curve and the Principle of Entry

I. OVERVIEW

It is important in economic arguments to carefully define the industry about which one is talking. One cannot characterize an industry by the technology that different firms have in common. Two firms that are similar technologically may have different sets of customers because of differences in location, and are therefore in different "industries". In order for firms to comprise an industry, they must all be potentially profitable suppliers of goods to a common set of customers who view the products as close substitutes. This definition of an industry includes all potentially profitable firms, whether or not they are already in existence. The long-run industry supply curve consists of all potential entrants.

The actual number of firms in existence within an industry depends upon the demand for industry output. As demand changes, the equilibrium market price changes. When market price is above the point of minimum average total cost including normal profits, supernormal profits are being earned and new firms enter the industry. When market price is below the point of minimum average total cost, firms leave the industry.

The ability of firms to freely enter or exit in response to changes in market price ensures that long-run profits are zero. Firms can earn profits that exceed normal profits in the short run. But the existence of supernormal profits attracts new firms into the industry and results in a reduction of the market-clearing price. Entry will continue until the equilibrium market price has fallen to the point of minimum average total cost. Similarly, subnormal profits can also be earned in the short run, but not in the long run.

The principle of entry leads to <u>The American Question</u>: "If you're so smart why aren't you rich?" Many individuals claim to see unexploited profit opportunities. (Think about the many stock market analysts who make such claims every day!) But such claims assume that other individuals have not already seen the unexploited profits, entered the market and exploited the profits. The principle of entry and exit makes economists skeptical about the existence of unexploited profit opportunities in the long run.

SUMMARY OF KEY CONCEPTS

- definition of an industry
- normal profit
- quasi-rent
- entry and exit
- economic rent
- rational expectations
- substitutability in consumption
- supernormal profit
- entrepreneurship
- entry price
- Tiebout effect

II. ANSWERS TO "WHAT TO READ FOR"

14.1 THE LONG-RUN SUPPLY CURVE

1. Can an "industry" be defined by the techniques it uses to make its products? An "industry" cannot be defined by the techniques it uses to make its products. Firms that are technologically similar may be in different industries because they serve different groups of customers or because their products are not close substitutes.

2. Are railways "an industry"? Railways are not an industry because the different railway lines are not substitutes. Many railways are separated by large distances and therefore serve different groups of customers.

3. Which suppliers are in it? An industry consists of all potentially profitable firms that share the same set of customers and produce goods or services that are close substitutes.

4. What about potential suppliers? Because of the possibility of entry, potential suppliers are also considered to be part of an industry.

5. What is "normal return"? "Normal return" or "normal profit" is the return to the entrepreneur. It includes the return to the entrepreneur of seeing the business opportunity, knowing the market, and assuming the risk.

6. What is an "entrepreneur"? An "entrepreneur" coordinates all of the factors of production. Entrepreneurship is defined as all inputs that cannot be hired.

7. What is an "entry price"? An "entry price" is the market price at which a new firm has an incentive to enter a market because profit opportunities exist. If price is above the point of minimum average total cost for a particular firm, then the firm will enter the industry at that "entry price."

8. If an entrepreneur is getting a price higher than his entry

price, what is the excess called? If an entrepreneur is getting a price higher than his entry price, the excess is called economic rent. The firm is earning profits that exceed normal profits. If the profits are temporary, then the excess is called quasi-rent.

9. What is "economic rent"? "Economic rent" is the sum of all the excess of actual price over the minimum price necessary to yield various different supplies.

10. What is the "margin of cultivation"? When all firms have the same entry price the industry supply curve is flat. When all firms do not have the same entry price the supply curve is upward sloping. The area above the supply curve and below the market price is producer's surplus. This area represents all the profit in excess of zero profit. This area is known as the "margin of cultivation" and firms inside the margin earn economic rents.

14.2 THE USES OF ENTRY AND EXIT

1. What happens when there is an opportunity to earn supernormal profits? When there is an opportunity to earn supernormal profits in the short run, potentially profitable firms enter the industry.

2. Can supernormal profits be earned in the long run? Supernormal profits cannot be earned in the long run. If supernormal profits are being earned in an industry, new firms will enter the industry and increase the existing market supply. This will result in a fall in the market clearing price. Entry will continue until all supernormal profits have been eliminated. Supernormal profits can be earned in the short run but not in the long run.

3. Do suppliers of expensive goods like diamonds make a lot of money? Suppliers of expensive goods like diamonds can only earn normal profits in the long run if there is free entry into the diamond selling industry.

4. Should cab drivers support higher cab fares, considering that the drivers are hired by cab owners? Cab drivers should not support higher cab fares simply because they are hired by the cab owners. There is free entry into cab driving. The return to cab driving therefore depends upon the return to the drivers in other occupations.

5. What is the "principle of entry"? The "principle of entry" asserts that entry will occur until "profit" is zero. At that point, no more entry is encouraged. The principle says that eventually, in the long run, revenue is equal to cost.

6. <u>What is the "Tiebout effect"?</u> The "Tiebout effect" asserts that people can freely reveal their preferences for public goods by moving from one community to another. People disagree about the amounts of public goods to be provided within communities. Given free entry and exit from communities, these disagreements can be solved by moving the people.

7. <u>Why are many American communities segregated by tastes and income?</u> Many American communities are segregated by tastes and income because in America people are free to enter or exit communities. This type of segregation is a result of the Tiebout effect.

8. <u>What is "The American Question"?</u> The American Question asks: "If you're so smart why aren't you rich?" Economists are skeptical about claims of the existence of unexploited profit opportunities. This is due to their belief in the principle of entry. When a "smart" person claims to see unexploited profit opportunities, economists question why other "smart" individuals haven't also seen these opportunities, entered the relevant markets, exploited them, and eliminated the supernormal profits.

9. <u>Do these ideas apply only to industries, towns, and stock markets?</u> The principle of entry, the Tiebout effect, and the American Question apply to more than just industries, towns and stock markets. They are applicable to every situation in which movement can earn the mover profit.

10. <u>What is the principle of "rational expectations"?</u> When a scientific or economic prediction is announced, it immediately changes the conditions on which the forecast was based. Individuals incorporate these forecasts into their behavior. Forecasts must therefore incorporate the economics of how people acquire and use forecasts. This concept is called rational expectations.

III. <u>MULTIPLE CHOICE</u>

1. New Jersey Bell and Pacific Bell are both telephone companies that provide customers with local telephone service. These two companies
   (a) are geographically far apart but are both in the same telephone industry
   (b) use the identical technologies and are therefore in the same industry
   (c) are not technologically close substitutes for one another and are therefore in different industries
   (d) serve different groups of customers who do not perceive them as close substitutes, and are therefore in different industries

2. Commodore, Coleco and Radio Shack all produce low-priced microcomputers. These three firms are all in the same industry because

(a) the cross price elasticity of demand for their products is low
(b) the cross price elasticity of demand for their products is high
(c) the own price elasticity of demand for their products is high
(d) the own price elasticity of demand for their products is low

3. The Yellowstone Pencil Company is one of many pencil companies in the United States. The pencil industry is a competitive industry. Yellowstone therefore

(a) doesn't earn any profits
(b) doesn't earn any normal profits
(c) doesn't earn any supernormal profits
(d) doesn't earn any losses

4. The fast food hamburger business is very competitive. The supply curve for this industry is

(a) flat because the skills for running this type of business are widespread
(b) upward sloping because each firm earns some economic profits
(c) upward sloping because each firm earns some normal profits
(d) upward sloping because none of the firms earn supernormal profits

5. In a competitive industry

(a) all firms earn economic rent
(b) some firms earn economic rent
(c) all firms earn quasi-rents
(d) no firms can earn long-run supernormal profits

6. The microcomputer market is a rapidly growing market. Many potentially profitable firms have been entering this industry. The existence of entry means

(a) that demand currently exceeds supply
(b) firms can earn supernormal profits in the long run
(c) existing firms are earning supernormal profits
(d) the existing microcomputer manufacturers are really all in different industries

7. A recent law was passed in New Jersey that permitted the state to fine firms that were leaving the state if they did not announce far enough in advance their intentions to leave the state. The effect of this new law will be

(a) to reduce the sizes of firms that already exist in the state
(b) to increase the sizes of firms that already exist in the

state
   (c) to reduce the amount of business in New Jersey
   (d) to increase the amount of business in New Jersey

8. The American Question implies that
   (a) it is impossible to make supernormal profits in the short run
   (b) it is impossible to make supernormal profits in the long run
   (c) entry into industries in which firms are making supernormal profits is not always possible
   (d) exit from industries in which firms are making subnormal profits is not always possible

9. The theory of rational expectations implies that
   (a) meaningful forecasts are not possible
   (b) forecasts must consider the ways in which people acquire and use forecasts
   (c) meaningful forecasts are possible only if they are made before people can react to them
   (d) meaningful forecasts can be made only if their predictions are unexpected by the people who listen to them

10. An entrepreneur
   (a) earns the same return as all other factors of production
   (b) is an input that cannot be hired
   (c) is an input that can be hired
   (d) is independent of all of the other factors of production

IV. EXERCISES

1. The Garden State Parkway in New Jersey is divided in the middle by a concrete divider. On the northbound side are three different gasoline stations that all charge $1.19 per gallon of unleaded gasoline. On the southbound side are three more gasoline stations that all charge $1.25 per gallon of gasoline. If the retail gasoline industry is competitive, how can one explain the differences in prices?

2. In March 1984, an article in the business section of the nationwide newspaper USA Today claimed that lucrative gains could be found in the Japanese stock market. The article said that "Tokyo-listed shares have gone up more than 12% since the beginning of the year...Most GNP (gross national product) growth estimates for the Japanese fiscal year, which ends March 1985, call for an increase of 4% to 4-1/2% after inflation." Andre Sharon of Drexel Burnham Lambert Inc. was quoted as saying, "I'm very bullish on foreign stocks..." Comment on the claims made in

this article.

3. John Thompson is a taxi driver who knows very little about the stock market. John recently read an article in a national business magazine that recommended that its readers purchase several different stocks. The recommendation was based upon a belief that these particular stocks would outperform the rest of the stock market during the next several months. Since John doesn't know too much about the stock market, he called his friend Barry Whitman who is an economist at the local university. John asked Barry for his opinion about the recommended stocks. If Barry is a "smart" economist, what should his response have been to John? Why?

V. PROBLEM

One-Hour Photo Processors

Mini photo labs that offer fast color film processing right on the premises have been around since the early 1970s. Many of these "minilabs" offer to have customers' pictures ready in as little as one hour and therefore compete with other companies that offer next-day processing.

Although minilabs have been around for a decade, they only started to become popular in the early 1980s. In 1980, there were about 600 minilabs in the United States. By 1983, there were 2,700 in operation. The result of the proliferation of these minilabs was to make the entire photo processing business more competitive. The Photo Marketing Association, a trade group in Jackson, Michigan, estimated that minilabs accounted for 10% to 12% of the $3.5 billion photofinishing market in 1984. Many existing camera and photographic equipment stores responded to the new competition by installing their own minilabs. Other companies were hurt by the proliferation of the minilabs. Fotomat Corporation, for example, announced that it would close 1,000 of its 3,700 retail outlets in 1984.

A major factor contributing to the increase in number of minilabs was the lowering of the cost of photo processing equipment. By 1984, Kis S.A., a French firm, was offering minilab machinery for $33,000. This was about one-third of the cost of most equipment that had been sold by the Japanese companies that had previously dominated the minilab-making business.

Eugene Glazer, an analyst at Dean Witter Reynolds Inc. in New York, summarized the evolution of the photo processing market: "By lowering the entry level into the business, Kis is attracting too many entrepreneurial types. So we'll reach saturation, and there will be a shakeout within the next two years."

(a) Assume that photo processing is a competitive industry with free entry and exit. Using a long-run average cost curve, depict the equilibrium situation in which the industry found itself prior to the introduction of minilabs.

(b) What effect did the introduction of Kis minilabs have on the short-run profitability of firms in the industry? Show this with a diagram.

(c) As entry into the industry occurs, a "shakeout" will take place. Depict this shakeout graphically and show the new long-run equilibrium for the industry.

(d) Who benefitted from the introduction of the minilabs?

CHAPTER 15

Taxes

I. OVERVIEW

Taxation is the most common constraint on exchange. Understanding the effects of taxation is therefore important.

An obvious effect of a tax on a good is that it reduces the amount of the good consumed. This is just the law of demand. A tax on any particular good raises the price of the good to demanders and reduces consumption. An interesting question asks by how much consumption is reduced. The answer is that the amount by which consumption falls depends on the elasticity of the demand and supply curves. The First Fundamental Theorem of Taxation says that a tax has little effect on inelastically supplied or demanded goods. If the demand for the good or its supply is elastic, then the change in price has a large effect on the quantities transacted.

The Second Fundamental Theorem of Taxation asserts that taxes cause a deadweight loss. When the government taxes a good, there is a loss in consumers' surplus and producers' surplus. The sum of these two losses is always greater than the revenue gained from the tax. The difference between the revenue gained from the tax and the sum of the losses in consumers' and producers' surpluses is called a deadweight loss. This deadweight loss results from the fact that a tax puts a wedge between the marginal cost of the taxed good (the supply price) and its marginal valuation (the demand price). A tax raises the buying price and lowers the selling price.

The General Theory of Second Best says that the best strategy for a society that is trying to operate efficiently is to impose a tax on goods equal in percentage terms to the existing tax on other goods in order to eliminate the distorting effects of all taxes. If a society has to impose some taxes, distortions will occur in the market. Given that the society cannot attain the first-best position of no taxes at all, its optimal strategy might be to impose more taxes rather than eliminating taxes. This is known as a second-best solution.

The only tax that does not have any costs in efficiency is one that does not alter any incentives to do anything. This type of tax is known as a lump-sum tax. It imposes a fixed cost. The amount collected by the tax is independent of decisions to produce or consume a little more of some good or service. No existing income or excise tax approaches a lump-sum tax.

The <u>Third Fundamental Theorem of Taxation</u> says that taxes fall where they fall, not where lawyers plan to put them. The effects of a tax depend only on the size of the tax and the elasticities of supply and demand. For example, it is often argued that when a state government imposes a corporate income tax, it is avoiding taxing people. But this argument is wrong. The burden of the tax is eventually also borne by people outside of the corporation.

SUMMARY OF KEY CONCEPTS

deadweight loss
lump-sum tax
First Fundamental Theorem of Taxation
Second Fundamental Theorem of Taxation
Third Fundamental Theorem of Taxation
General Theory of Second Best
poll tax

II. ANSWERS TO WHAT TO READ FOR

1. <u>How do taxes constrain exchange?</u> Taxes constrain exchange by reducing the amount consumed of the taxed good.

2. <u>How does the elasticity of demand and supply change the way a tax affects output?</u> A tax has little effect on inelastically supplied or demanded goods. In contrast, a tax has a large effect on elastically supplied or demanded goods.

3. <u>What happens to the revenue from the tax?</u> The government uses the command over resources acquired by taxation to redirect the resources towards other uses. The government spends the revenues that it acquires through taxation. The tax revenues can be turned back to the public in either a neutral or a nonneutral way. A neutral method has no repercussions on the expenditures of the government, the level of alternative taxes, or the size and distribution of income.

4. <u>What is the deadweight loss from a tax, and how is it calculated in a diagram of supply and demand?</u> The difference between the revenue acquired through a tax and the sum of the losses in consumers' surplus and producers' surplus is a deadweight loss. In Figure 15.1, consumers lose consumers' surplus in the amount A+x and suppliers lose producers' surplus in the amount B+y. The sum of the losses in consumers' surplus and producers' surplus is therefore (A+B)+(x+y). But the government gains areas A and B by collecting the taxes. Society therefore loses areas x and y. This is the deadweight loss to society.

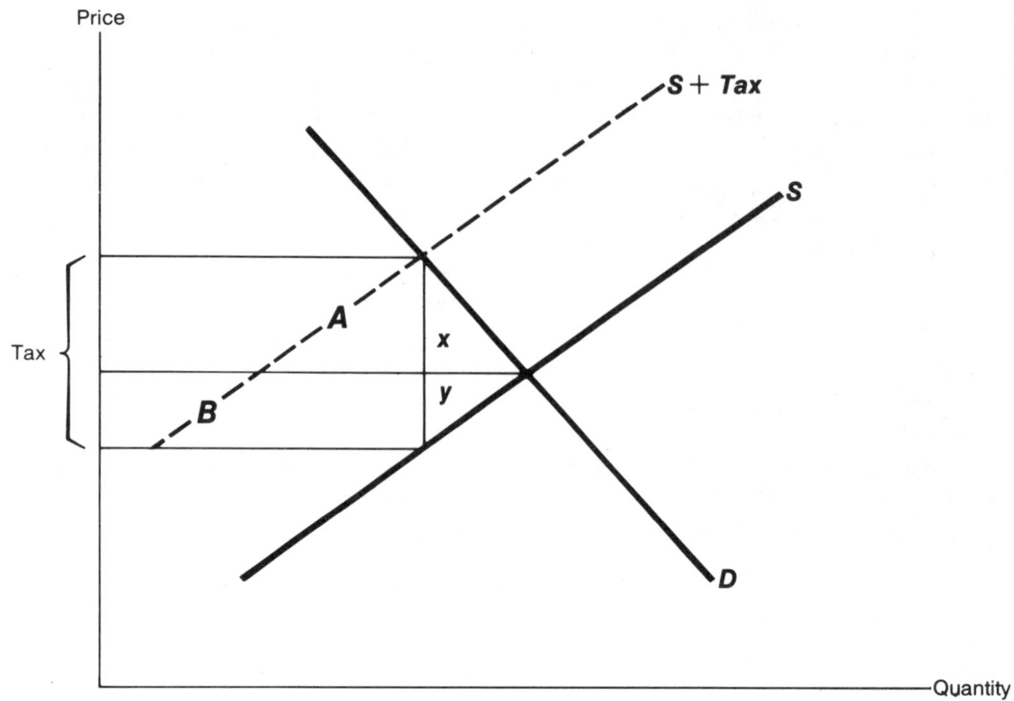

FIGURE 15.1

5. <u>What is the "second-best" argument?</u> A society that must impose some taxes cannot attain a "first-best" position. If the society is trying to operate efficiently, it must resort to a "second-best" solution. The theory of second best asserts that this society should impose a tax on all goods that is equal in percentage to the existing tax on other goods. This strategy eliminates the distorting effects of the taxes.

6. <u>What is a lump-sum tax?</u> A lump-sum tax is equivalent to imposing a fixed cost on producers and consumers. It does not alter any of the incentives or decisions to produce or consume a little more of some commodity.

7. <u>Does a tax stay where it is placed legally?</u> Not necessarily. Taxes fall where they fall. The effects that a tax has on consumption and production depend only on the size of the tax and the elasticities of supply and demand.

III. <u>MULTIPLE CHOICE</u>

1. The less elastic is either the demand or the supply for a commodity, the less will a given tax reduce output because
   (a) taxes increase prices to suppliers and reduce them to demanders
   (b) suppliers and demanders change the amounts they wish to supply or demand a lot when the prices they face change

(c) neither suppliers nor demanders change the amounts they wish to supply or demand very much when the prices they face change
(d) the less elastic is demand or supply, the larger the fall in quantity caused by price changes

2. Suppose the elasticity of supply for apples in the little town of Apple Blossom is very large. The elasticity of demand for apples if 2.5. The local government of Apple Blossom decides that taxing apple sales would generate large revenues for the town, so it imposes a 6.5% sales tax on apples. In this case, the number of apples sold will
(a) rise by 6.5%
(b) fall by 6.5%
(c) fall by 13%
(d) fall by more than 13%

3. The total loss to consumers and producers due to the imposition of a tax is equal to
(a) total tax revenue
(b) consumers' surplus lost
(c) producers' surplus lost
(d) consumers' surplus plus producers' surplus lost

4. Suppose supply and demand are both elastic with respect to price. The sum of what producers and consumers lose from a tax is
(a) less than the revenue from the tax
(b) always equal to the revenue from the tax
(c) at least as large as the revenue from the tax
(d) always greater than the revenue from the tax

5. The deadweight loss from a tax is equal to
(a) the fall in national income
(b) the loss in consumers' surplus
(c) the loss in producers' surplus
(d) the loss in consumers' surplus plus producers' surplus

6. If prices were at their socially optimal values prior to a tax, then
(a) the tax will move society away from the optimum
(b) put society on a lower indifference curve
(c) lower national income
(d) all of the above

7. The only tax without costs in efficiency is
(a) a sales tax
(b) a property tax
(c) a proportional income tax
(d) a poll tax

8. A tax on corporations
(a) may raise the relative price of goods produced in the

corporate sector
(b) will not affect people who are not employed by the corporation
(c) only falls on corporate stockholders
(d) is eventually completely passed on to consumers

9. The shifting of the incidence of a tax or subsidy does not stop until
(a) the marginal suppliers and demanders are back on their supply and demand curves
(b) new incentives have been created to enter or exit the industry
(c) the deadweight loss to society is zero
(d) national income is restored to its original pre-tax level

10. Given the need for taxes, a second-best solution that imposes taxes on all marketed goods in equal percentages
(a) has no losses in efficiency
(b) causes the production possibility curve for marketed goods to expand outward
(c) leaves the production possibility curve among marketed curves unchanged
(d) still shrinks the production possibility curve among marketed goods

IV. EXERCISES

1. During the campaign for the Presidency in 1984, a major issue raised by the candidates was the question of "fairness." The Democratic candidate, Walter Mondale, accused President Reagan of favoring big business and big corporations in his tax programs, at the expense of the middle class in America. The Reagan administration countered with a claim that the President succeeded in reversing a 20-year rise in personal income taxes.

(a) Are private "big business" corporations entities that are truly distinct from middle class America?

(b) Does the reduction in corporate taxes stay where they are initially put; that is, on corporate profits?

(c) What effect might the reduction in corporate taxes have on entry and exit in the corporate sector? What effect might it have on wages and the employment of resources?

(d) Given your answers to questions (a)-(c) above, what can you conclude about the Mondale-Reagan debate about fairness?

2. Suppose the New York state government is contemplating increasing the sales tax on each of the following items:

(a) cigarettes
(b) gasoline
(c) chocolate bars

On which of these would you expect the tax increase to have the greatest effect?

3. Several proposals have been presented in the U.S.Senate to institute a tuition-tax credit to parents of children in parochial and private schools. These measures would provide as much as $300 in tax credits per child.

(a) What effect would such a credit have on the number of children attending parochial schools? (Hint: Is the supply of classroom space in parochial schools infinitely elastic?)

(b) Who would benefit from the tax credit?

V. PROBLEM

National Energy Tax to Control Acid Rain

In December 1983, six governors from the northeastern United States proposed a national tax on electricity that is generated by utilities burning coal or oil. The proposal was made in an attempt to control the emissions that cause acid rain. Acid rain is formed when sulfur dioxide and other pollutants from the electricity-generating plants mix with moisture in the atmosphere. Their contention was that acid rain threatens lakes, forests and wildlife in the northeast and in Canada.

The proposal advocated returning the tax revenues to the electrical utilities to help pay the capital costs of altering the plants to reduce emissions. It was estimated that the tax would raise as much as $1 billion. Polluters would also be required to pay as much as $1 billion through a pollution tax. The taxes would be collected over a six year period.

The governors estimated that as much as $5 billion would be required to reduce sulfur dioxide emissions by the desired 10 million tons by 1995. They agreed that ratepayers would ultimately foot the bill, but the effects of the tax would be minimized by spreading it out nationally.

(a) Is there a deadweight loss to society resulting from

the tax? Will the tax revenue completely offset any losses to society?

(b) What effect will the electricity tax have on the aggregate quantity of electricity demanded in the United States? What effect will the pollution tax have on the aggregate quantity supplied? (Neglect the possible effects of regulation on the decisions of utilities to supply electricity.)

(c) What effect will the electricity and pollution taxes have on entry and exit from the electricity-generating industry?

(d) What will happen to social welfare as a result of the taxes?

CHAPTER 16

Competition for Property Rights

I. OVERVIEW

Governments constrain exchange in many ways. They impose taxes and quotas, provide subsidies, regulate industries, control prices, and even constrain entry into markets. Many of these constraints are attempts by governments to circumvent the market. But the market is irrepressible. Scarce resources must still be allocated amongst unlimited human wants. This allocation will occur through nonexchange competition if governments do not permit allocation through voluntary exchange.

Consider government intervention in foreign trade through the use of either quotas or tariffs. A quota restricts the amount of a particular good that can be imported during a given period of time. A tariff is a tax imposed on an imported good. When a quota is imposed, the government restricts entry into the market by giving a select number of firms a license to import the foreign good. If a quota is effective, it causes the price of the good to rise by an amount equal to the value of the license. A tariff has similar effects to those of a quota. A tariff also causes the price of the imported good to rise. The difference between a tariff and a quota is that a tariff transfers revenue from consumers to the government. A quota transfers revenue from consumers to the owners of the quota rights. The loss from quotas and tariffs is equal to the foregone opportunities for exchange.

Another common form of government intervention is price controls. Governments impose price controls in an effort to locate a "fair" or "just" price for a good or service. For example, rent controls are often imposed to protect tenants from allegedly "unfair" and "exorbitant" rents that might be charged by landlords. The controlled prices are usually lower or higher than the market-clearing price. A controlled price below the equilibrium price is known as a price ceiling. A controlled price above the equilibrium price is known as a price floor. The loss from price controls, as with tariffs and quotas, is equal to the foregone opportunities for exchange.

People often try to avoid or circumvent government regulations. They also try to get for themselves the benefits that the regulations create. Consider licenses. The institution of licensing by the government is equivalent to the creation of valuable property rights. These property rights are controlled by the owners of the licenses and can be bought and sold for an amount equal to the net present value of the <u>economic</u> profits that accrue because of the property rights. People are generally rent seekers, so secondary markets develop as the owners of the licenses attempt to collect rents equal to the value of the licenses.

From an efficiency standpoint, the development of secondary markets is not bad. Evasion of government restrictions puts the property rights into the hands of those individuals who value the rights the most. But sometimes secondary markets cannot form. People want to enter into market exchanges but are unable to do so. A gap therefore develops between what people actually pay for the property rights (that is, for the license to import or the rent controlled apartment) and what the good actually costs. This gap is supernormal profit that is earned by the lucky individuals who get the property rights. Nonmarket competition for the supernormal profits often then develops. Bribes are paid to government officials. Key money is paid to tenants in rent-controlled apartments. Time is spent waiting in queues. These types of nonmarket competition are wasteful. Yet the waste occurs because people continue to compete for scarce resources, either by exchange or nonmarket forms of competition.

The best way to eliminate this waste and inefficiency is to eliminate the regulations that led to the nonmarket competition. More generally, waste and inefficiency can be eliminated by assigning to someone unambiguous property rights to the scarce resource. The assignment of property rights is good. <u>Adam Smith's generalization</u> asserts that if everything is owned and if exchange is costless, then efficient (but not necessarily equitable) outcomes will prevail. The existence of property rights can even eliminate externalities. A well defined and enforced property right often ensures that the privately perceived opportunity cost of using a resource is equal to the social cost.

Markets do sometimes fail however. This occurs when it is too expensive to enforce and sell a property right. Alternatives then exist to the market mechanism. Quotas can be imposed at the source of the externality. Alternatively, a tax can be imposed that brings the marginal private costs into equality with marginal social costs. <u>Coase's Theorem</u> however, says that when there are transaction costs, the location of the tax does matter for efficiency. The technological, legal or moral cause of the externality is not necessarily the place where the tax should be imposed.

Property rights are a part of well-functioning markets. They may be desirable or undesirable. But they are created because it is in someone's self-interest to do so. The fact that many things are scarce provides an incentive for the creation and enforcement of property rights.

SUMMARY OF KEY CONCEPTS

quotas
licenses
nonmarket competition
rationing
transactions costs
key money
external economy
tariffs
price controls
queuing
Adam Smith's Generalization
Coase's Theorem
nonpecuniary externalities

II. ANSWERS TO "WHAT TO READ FOR"

16.1 COMPETITION FOR SUPERNORMAL PROFITS

1. How do quotas mimic and contrast with tariffs? The effects of a quota are in many ways the same as the effects of a tariff. An effective quota will cause the price of the imported good to rise. A tariff that is intended to allow the same quantity of the good to be imported will cause price to rise by the same amount. The difference between a quota and a tariff is in the transfer of revenue from consumers. A quota causes the transfer of revenue from consumers to the owners of the quota rights. A tariff causes a transfer of revenue from consumers to the government.

2. Why are price controls bad? Price controls are bad because they result in a loss equal to the foregone opportunities for voluntary exchange. Price controls do not permit mutually advantageous exchanges to be made between the suppliers and demanders of the price-controlled product.

3. How do price controls, licenses, quotas, and the like produce corruption? Price controls, licenses, and quotas produce corruption because people will try to avoid the government's regulation of exchange. Quotas, price controls, and licenses do not simply stay where they are imposed. Mutually advantageous trades may still exist and rent-seeking individuals will try to exploit them. The market is irrepressible. The problem of allocating scarce resources will be solved, either by nonexchange competition (such as corruption) or by free exchange.

4. How do they produce waste in competition? Price controls, licenses, and quotas may result in wasteful forms of competition. The waste occurs when people want to enter into voluntary exchange for a good but are unable to do so. They are unable to compete with money. A gap results between what people are willing to pay for a good and what they actually must pay. This gap represents supernormal profits. People will compete for the privilege of getting these supernormal profits. Since consumers

cannot compete with money, they will try to circumvent the market. For example, they will spend time standing in long queues in an attempt to obtain a good on a first-come-first-serve basis. They will hire accountants and lawyers to help them evade income taxes. These attempts to circumvent the market regulations reduce national income by the amount of lost exchange plus the amount of wasteful competition. Resources are wasted that could be used in some other productive activity.

5. Does a person standing in a queue pay only the money price? A person standing in a queue does not only pay the money price for the good. Time is money. The time spent standing in the queue is money wasted. A person standing in a queue therefore pays the money price of the good plus the value of the time wasted standing in line.

6. How do ration coupons prevent the waste that is a result of queuing? Ration coupons can eliminate queues. The distribution of ration coupons defines clearly who has the right to exploit the supernormal profits. If the rationing device is effective, then it makes it pointless to join the queue and avoids the loss of queuing.

16.2 UNASSIGNED PROPERTY RIGHTS AND EXTERNAL EFFECTS

1. What is the simplest way of eliminating the waste from price controls? The simplest way to eliminate the waste from price controls is to abandon the price controls.

2. What is Adam Smith's Generalization? Adam Smith's generalization says that when the rights to a resource are unambiguously assigned to someone, so that the rights can be sold for whatever the owner can get for them, the resource will be used efficiently.

3. Is it a good or bad idea to extend private property to whales, lakes, fish, freeways, and buffalo? It is a good idea to extend private property to whales, lakes, fish, freeways, and buffalo if one is concerned about the danger of extinction. In an unconstrained market in which property rights are clearly defined and enforced, the killing of these animals would have a price, and the opportunity to sell the right to kill them and their future offspring would lead their owners to conserve them.

4. What are nonpecuniary externalities? Nonpecuniary externalities are "external" or "neighborhood effects" from an activity that impose losses or gains on people who are not directly involved in that activity. For example, an electric utility that dumps waste into the atmosphere affects people living near the utility who are external to the business of

generating electricity.

5. How would tolls, if set optimally, cause highways to be used efficiently? If a highway is not owned, a driver who is thinking about riding on the road thinks only of the average cost she faces of joining the highway. She does not consider the increase in average cost her trip imposes on other drivers. A toll that maximizes revenue, if set optimally, presents this driver with the full social marginal cost of her decision. It forces the marginal driver to bid the full social cost of the road space that she is taking.

6. What are external economies? External effects that are good can still cause a misallocation of resources. An external economy (as opposed to a diseconomy) is a benefit that accrues from a productive activity to a person who is external to the activity. For example, the owner of an orchard benefits from the placement of a beekeeper next door to her orchard because the bees pollinate her orchard.

7. Is it always best to tax polluters in the amount of the harm from their pollution? It is not always best to tax polluters for the amount of the harm from their pollution. If the costs of making deals is low, the party that could most cheaply avoid the hurt from the pollution could be induced to do so.

8. What is Coase's Theorem? Coase's Theorem says that in the presence of transaction costs, the location of a tax does matter for efficiency.

9. Does it hold in a situation in which deals and bribes are cheap to make? Coase's Theorem does not apply to situations in which deals are cheap to make. It applies to a case of high transaction costs. If transaction costs are low, Adam Smith's generalization will ensure that the tax or liability will find its way to the correct party.

10. Should the person morally responsible for an accident bear the costs, on grounds of efficiency? The moral question is irrelevant to the efficiency of the solution. The person morally responsible for an accident should not necessarily bear the costs, on grounds of efficiency. Efficient arrangements are not necessarily moral, and moral arrangements are not necessarily efficient.

11. Why does private property become private? Private property becomes private because it is in someone's self-interest to make it so. Property rights are created, whether or not they are desirable, because people are rent seekers and it is in someone's interest to create the property rights.

III. MULTIPLE CHOICE

1. If a quota on, say, Japanese cars is to have any effect
   (a) the amount allowed to be imported must be less than the amount that would have been imported without the quota
   (b) the amount allowed to be imported must be equal to the amount that would have been imported without the quota
   (c) the amount allowed to be imported must be more than the amount that would have been imported without the quota
   (d) the amount allowed to be imported must be more than the amount that would have been imported under a tariff system

2. A quota was recently imposed on the number of small Japanese cars that can be imported every year into the United States. The result of this quota is
   (a) to lower the price of imported Japanese cars
   (b) to reduce the demand for small Japanese cars
   (c) to transfer revenue from consumers to the government
   (d) to transfer revenue from consumer's to the American automobile manufacturers

3. The Atlantic Ocean is considered to be "international waters." No single country owns property rights to the Atlantic Ocean beyond a 200 mile limit from its shores. The nonexistence of property rights to the Atlantic Ocean is due to the fact that
   (a) it would be amoral for any one country to own the Atlantic Ocean
   (b) the Atlantic Ocean is not a scarce resource
   (c) ownership of the Atlantic Ocean would impose serious nonpecuniary externalities on other countries
   (d) ownership of the Atlantic Ocean would impose serious percuniary externalities on other countries

4. The Garden State Parkway in New Jersey is usually congested with traffic at 5:00 P.M. on weekdays. Suppose you want to enter the Parkway at 5:00. Prior to your driving onto the Parkway, the trip from Edison to Rahway took 15 minutes to drive. Once you enter the congested Parkway, the trip takes 15 minutes and 0.01 seconds. If there are 6,000 cars on the Parkway at 5:00, then your use of the Parkway results in
   (a) a social cost of 0.01 seconds
   (b) a social cost of 15 minutes
   (c) a social cost of 15 minutes and 0.01 seconds
   (d) a social cost of 16 minutes

5. Coase's Theorem implies that
   (a) taxes imposed on polluters of rivers are never efficient
   (b) taxes imposed on polluters of rivers are irrelevant
   (c) taxes imposed on polluters of rivers are not always efficient
   (d) taxes imposed on polluters of rivers are always efficient

6. Major league baseball and football teams are often sold for millions of dollars. The selling price for these teams appears to be so high because
   (a) entry into the leagues is restricted
   (b) there are huge tax advantages to owning a major league team
   (c) most major league teams are extremely profitable
   (d) most major league teams incur large losses which must be made up for by a high selling price

7. Stuffy university professors hire secretaries to do their typing for them because
   (a) most professors don't know how to type
   (b) secretaries can type faster than professors
   (c) the professors' time is money
   (d) professors have a very low opportunity cost to typing

8. Fred Bernstein and Maureen Golenbock are both assistant professors at Rutgers University. When Fred and Maureen first arrived at Rutgers, the other members of their department made sure that they each were placed in an office that was located next to a senior faculty member's office. This was presumably done because
   (a) there are external economies to being located next to a senior faculty member's office
   (b) there are external diseconomies to being located next to a senior faculty member's office
   (c) there are external economies to being located next to another assistant professor's office
   (d) there are external diseconomies to being located next to another assistant professor's office

9. Residents next to the Three Mile Island nuclear reactor have argued that the plant should be shut down in order to protect them from hazardous nuclear waste that might be emitted into the atmosphere. If transaction costs are low, an alternative proposal that would be economically efficient is
   (a) to force the homeowners to move
   (b) to allow deals to be made between the owners of the power plant and the homeowners
   (c) to force the owners of the power plant to install more expensive equipment to monitor the functioning of the reactor
   (d) to impose a quota on the amount of electricity that the power plant can generate per month

10. In New York City, a quota is imposed on the number of taxis that are allowed to drive on the streets. This quota is created by selling licenses ("medallions") to cab owners. At the same time, the fare that a taxi can charge is set by the city at a level below the market-clearing price. One would therefore expect
   (a) a shortage of taxi service in New York City
   (b) a surplus of taxi service in New York City

(c) a low value to be placed on the licenses
(d) bribes to be paid to city officials

IV. EXERCISES

1. The Littletown Electric Company is contemplating building a substation on a hill above Gates Road. The 10 homeowners on Gates Road are upset because sewage from the Electric Company will seep into the ground and destroy their water wells. The city of Littletown has proposed regulations that would require the Electric Company to install pollution abatement equipment that would cost $500,000 if the sewage continues to pose a problem to the residents.. The Electric Company would rather see the city require the homeowners to pay $250,000 for the installation of new pipes that would run from the Littletown Water Company to the 10 homes on Gates Road. In this way, the Electric Company argues, the homeowners would have fresh water and the Electric Company could continue to dump their sewage. From an efficiency standpoint, under what conditions would each alternative proposal be the best?

2. During the 1973-74 oil embargo of the United States by the OPEC cartel, long queues formed at gasoline stations in many cities around the country. Gasoline stations were unable to raise the per gallon price of gasoline at the pumps because it was regulated by the federal government. In order to eliminate the queues, several politicians argued for a rationing system, under which ration coupons would be distributed to drivers of automobiles according to their specific needs.

(a) Would the ration coupon system be effective in eliminating the long lines at gasoline stations?

(b) Would a rationing system that prohibits the resale of coupons be as efficient as an alternative system that would permit the resale of coupons?

3. Public building inspectors are often bribed by builders of homes to overlook violations of plumbing and electric wiring construction codes. In many of these instances, it is also the case that local laws require that any work on plumbing and electric wiring must be done by licensed and unionized workers who earn a particular minimum wage. Given these circumstances, is it surprising that these cases of bribery occur?

V. PROBLEM

Domestic Price Controls on Natural Gas

The price of natural gas that is produced in the United States is regulated. In November 1983, the Reagan administration presented to the Senate a bill that would have phased out all price controls on natural gas by 1987. The bill also would have eliminated many existing contracts and required producers and pipeline companies to renegotiate contract prices. The Senate defeated the Reagan bill by a 67-28 margin.

At the same time, the Senate rejected another bill that would have rolled back natural gas prices, imposed tighter price controls on natural gas pipelines, and retained controls on several types of gas indefinitely. The Senate's defeat of this bill indicated that it was equally hesitant about rolling back prices in order to keep natural gas prices down.

(a) Suppose that the current controlled price of natural gas is below the equilibrium price. Using the supply and demand curve framework, determine the effect of price controls on the market price and quantity exchanged of natural gas.

(b) Who gains from the price controls? Who incurs a loss from the controls? What is the total loss from price controls on natural gas equal to?

(c) Suppose the Reagan administration bill had been passed. What would have been the effect on the market for natural gas? Who would have gained from passage of the bill? Who would have lost?

(d) Suppose the alternative bill had been passed. What would have been the effect on the market for natural gas?

(e) If there are no price or quantity restrictions on the resale of natural gas, what would one expect to happen over time despite the controls?

PART V. MONOPOLY

CHAPTER 17

The Behavior of Monopoly

I. OVERVIEW

A monopoly is said to exist if there is only one seller in a well-defined market. The fact that there is only one firm in the market does not imply that the monopolist's behavior is unconstrained. The actions of a monopolist are constrained by the indirect competition of all goods for the consumer's dollar, the indirect competition of reasonably adequate substitute goods, and the threat of potential competition if market entry is possible.

Since the monopolist is the only firm in the market, the market demand curve is the monopoly demand curve. The demand curve facing the monopolist will always be negatively sloped. When demand is negatively sloped, the marginal revenue curve is also negatively sloped and below the demand curve. The marginal revenue curve is below and steeper than the demand curve because the monopolist has to lower the price that it charges on <u>all</u> units in order to sell an extra (marginal) unit of output.

A monopolist is a profit maximizer. Like the perfect competitor, the monopolist maximizes profit where the difference between total revenue and total cost is the greatest. Stated differently, the monopolist produces where marginal revenue is equal to marginal cost. A monopolist will maximize profit or minimize loss by producing that output for which marginal revenue is equal to marginal cost. This is just the Rule of Rational Life.

Since a monopolist does not equate price with marginal cost, it is possible for different demand conditions to give rise to the same output, but to different prices. The quantity of output that the monopolist will supply depends upon the shape and location of the demand curve. Different demand curves have different marginal revenue curves, which lead to different combinations of monopoly price and output. It is meaningless to ask what price a monopolist will charge for a given level of output. The answer is not unique. Recall that the perfect competitor's supply curve is exactly her marginal cost curve. The marginal cost curve is not the monopolist's supply curve. "Supply" has a much less precise meaning under monopoly.

Whether the monopolist makes a profit or a loss depends on the relationship between monopoly price and average total cost. In the short run, a monopolist can earn a profit, just like a perfect competitor. If demand is low enough, the monopolist can also incur a loss. But in contrast to perfect competition, pure economic profit is not eliminated in the long run under monopoly. Economic profits can be earned because entry into the market is somehow restricted.

Under perfect competition, production occurs at minimum long-run average cost. In contrast, the monopolist chooses its price and output and then utilizes the plant size capable of producing the monopoly output at the least unit cost. But this plant is not associated with absolute minimum unit cost. Society's scarce resources are used more efficiently under perfect competition. The perfect competitor produces where price is equal to marginal cost. The monopolist produces a level of output at which price is greater than marginal cost. Under monopoly, the marginal social valuation of the monopolist's product by society is greater than the marginal social cost of production. Society would benefit by having more of its scarce resources used in producing the monopolist's output. The monopolist, being a profit maximizer, will not increase its output to the social optimum. Producing where price is equal to marginal cost would eliminate monopoly profits. The monopolist produces output in the least-cost way, but this level of output does not correspond to minimum average total cost.

SUMMARY OF KEY CONCEPTS

barriers to entry
monopoly demand
monopoly supply
patents
price searching
inefficiencies under monopoly
natural monopoly

II. ANSWERS TO WHAT TO READ FOR

17.1 MONOPOLY: THE ELEMENTS

1. Can a monopolist just announce a higher price? A monopolist cannot just announce a higher price. A monopolist is able to restrict quantity, preventing other firms from supplying to its customers. But a profit-maximizing monopolist must still be sensitive to the demand for its product. It cannot arbitrarily charge any price for its product.

2. How do unions, professional associations, and governmental agencies act as monopolies? Unions, professional associations,

and governmental agencies all raise their prices by restricting the output supplied to demanders. For example, the American Medical Association maintains a high price for medical services by limiting output through restrictions on the number of doctors.

3. What is a monopsony? A monopsony is a market with a single buyer (the monopsonist).

4. What is price taking and price searching? A single competitive firm among many is a price taker. A price taker is small in size relative to the rest of the market and takes the market price as given. A monopolist is a price searcher. The monopolist faces an entire demand curve for its product and searches for the best price to charge for its product.

5. How does a higher output spoil the market of a monopolist? The monopolist faces a demand curve for its product rather than a single price. The marginal revenue curve facing the monopolist lies below the demand curve. If the monopolist raises its output by one unit, people are willing to pay less for previous units of output. It is in this sense that higher output spoils the market of a monopolist.

6. What is the algebraic relation between marginal revenue, price, and spoilage? The algebraic relation is $MR = P - Q\Delta P$. This equation says that marginal revenue falls short of price by the amount of spoilage.

7. How do you construct a marginal revenue curve for a straight-line demand curve? The marginal revenue curve is the straight line from the point where the demand curve cuts the price axis to the point midway out to where the demand curve cuts the quantity axis.

8. What areas represent total revenue? The area under the marginal revenue curve out to monopoly output is total revenue.

9. How does a monopolist with no costs follow the Rule of Rational Life? A monopolist with no costs will set price at the point of maximum revenue. At this price and corresponding quantity, marginal revenue is equal to zero.

10. Does a monopolist produce the same output as is socially optimal? A monopolist produces an inefficient amount of output. The monopoly output is less than the social optimum.

11. Does a monopolist ever produce along an inelastic segment of his demand curve? A monopoly will never choose a price at which the demand curve is inelastic. Inelasticity is associated with falling revenues. A monopolist always produces where marginal revenue is equal to marginal cost. This corresponds to a level of output that is lower than the competitive output and lower than the point of unit elasticity. The demand curve at the point

of equilibrium for a monopolist must be elastic.

17.2 ADVANCED APPLICATIONS OF SIMPLE MONOPOLY

1. Does a monopolist always end up exactly where marginal cost equals marginal revenue? The equality of marginal cost and marginal revenue under monopoly is just a tendency. A monopolist, like a perfect competitor, does not know its price and costs perfectly. Even if the monopolist knew its costs and price perfectly, it would have to search for the point of maximum profit through trial and error. The theory of monopoly and the equality of marginal cost and marginal revenue are merely approximations.

2. How does the output and price of a monopolist change if the monopolist has a price ceiling imposed on him? The monopolist facing a price ceiling will produce where marginal cost is equal to marginal revenue. If the price ceiling is below the monopoly price, the monopolist is induced to produce more output at a lower price. In the extreme, if the price ceiling is set at the competitive equilibrium, the profit-maximizing monopolist would offer exactly the competitive output, where price is equal to marginal cost.

3. How can this idea be used to undermine cartels? A cartel can be undermined by imposing a ceiling on the cartel's price. This will affect the cartel's marginal revenue and induce it to supply more of its product.

4. Are monopolies always bad? Monopolies are not always bad. One must look at the causes of the monopoly to begin to judge its goodness or badness. For example, a monopoly might have marketing advantages that reduce its costs. If these advantages are eliminated, the industry's costs might be higher. A monopoly might also have technological advantages which also reduce costs.

5. Are patents, which are monopolies, always bad? Patents are not always bad simply because price does not equal the marginal of production if the production process is patenable. Marginal cost may be lower because of the patented invention. The invention is produced because it is patenable. Without patents, the knowledge would not be produced and costs might be higher.

III. MULTIPLE CHOICE

1. Monopolies often exist because
   (a) entry into the market is restricted

(b) other goods do not compete for the consumer's dollar
(c) consumers have no choice but to consume the monopolist's product
(d) firms often choose to restrict their output

2. Since the demand curve facing a monopolist is the same as the market demand curve
(a) the monopolist takes the market price as given
(b) the monopolist is a price searcher
(c) the monopolist does not maximize profits by producing the level of output at which marginal revenue is equal to marginal cost
(d) the monopolist always produces where marginal revenue is greater than marginal cost

3. Under monopoly, marginal revenue falls short of price by the amount of spoilage because
(a) the monopolist has to raise the price that it charges on some units in order to sell an extra unit
(b) the monopolist has to raise the price that it charges on all units in order to sell an extra unit
(c) the monopolist has to lower the price that it charges on some units in order to sell an extra unit
(d) the monopolist has to lower the price that it charges on all units in order to sell an extra unit

4. If a firm is a monopolist in an input market, then
(a) the price of the input will depend on the purchases of this firm
(b) the firm must be a price taker in the input market
(c) the firm cannot be a monopolist in the market for its output
(d) the firm does not likely require any specialized inputs

5. The monopolist's supply curve
(a) is its marginal cost curve
(b) is the same as the demand curve it faces
(c) is the same as the marginal revenue curve it faces
(d) does not exist

6. If a firm is a multiplant monopolist, it maximizes monopoly profits where
(a) marginal revenue is equal to marginal cost in each individual plant
(b) total revenue is maximized in each plant
(c) marginal revenue is maximized in each plant
(d) plant marginal cost is equal to monopoly marginal cost, which in turn is equal to marginal revenue

7. In the short run, a monopolist can
(a) earn positive economic profits
(b) break even
(c) incur a loss

(d) earn positive profits, break even, or incur a loss

8. Under monopoly
   (a) social welfare is being maximized
   (b) society's resources are being used efficiently
   (c) the marginal social valuation of the monopolist's output is less than the marginal social cost of production
   (d) the monopolist is producing its output in the least-cost way

9. A monopolist always produces
   (a) along the elastic portion of the demand curve
   (b) at the point of unitary elasticity on the demand curve
   (c) along the inelastic portion of the demand curve
   (d) at the point on the demand curve where marginal revenue is rising

10. The Rule of Rational Life
   (a) does not apply to a monopolist because it does not use society's resources efficiently
   (b) does not apply to a monopolist because it always produces at the point of unitary elasticity on the demand curve
   (c) does not apply to a monopolist because social welfare is not maximized
   (d) also applies to a monopolist

IV. EXERCISES

1. Consider Figure 17.1.

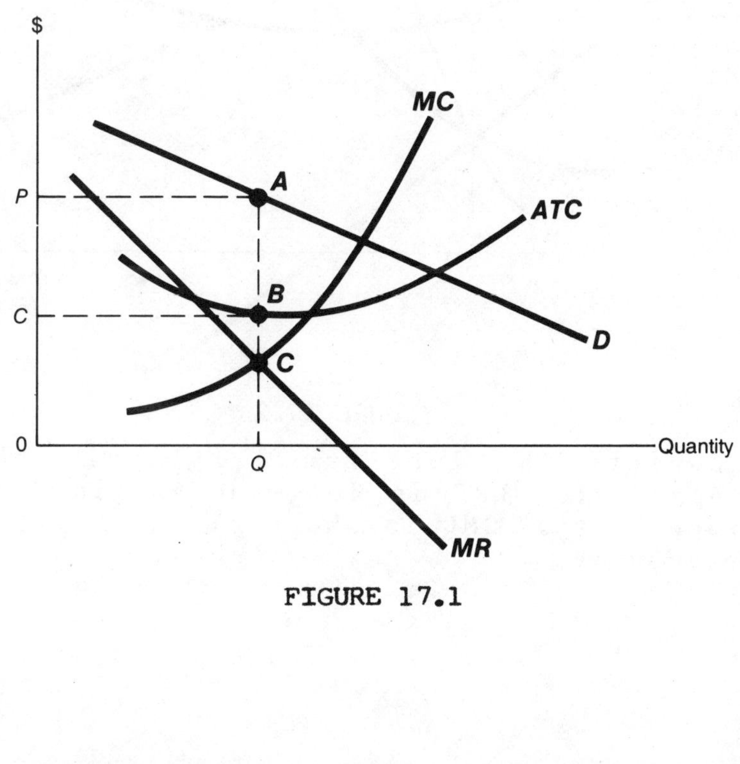

FIGURE 17.1

This figure shows one possible short-run situation that a monopolist might find herself in. MC is the marginal cost curve, D is market demand, MR is marginal revenue, and ATC is average total cost. Assume that the monopolist is a profit maximizer.

(a) Given the existing market demand, what price will the monopolist charge to maximize profits? Why?

(b) At the monopoly price, how much output will be bought and sold in the marketplace?

(c) At the profit-maximizing output level, what are the monopolist's average total costs? What are total costs?

(d) What are short-run monopoly profits? Are they positive, negative, or zero? Discuss the significance for monopoly profits of the market demand curve.

(e) Depict this profit-maximization problem in terms of the monopolist's total revenue and total cost curves.

2. Consider Figure 17.2.

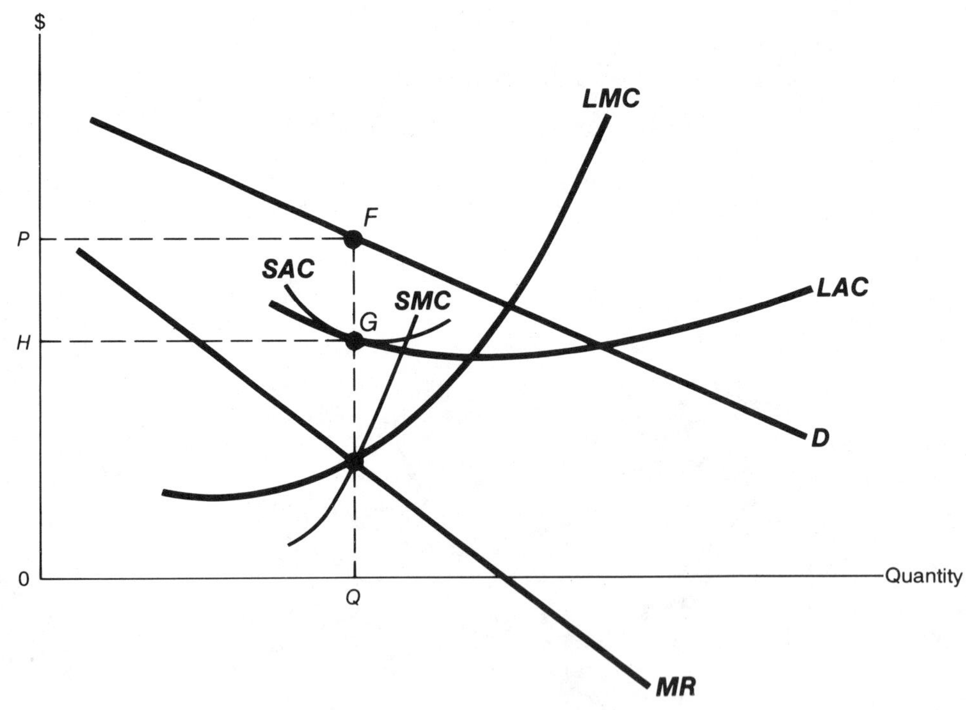

FIGURE 17.2

Figure 17.2 depicts the long-run equilibrium for a profit-maximizing monopolist. LMC is long-run marginal costs. LAC is long-run average costs. SMC is short-run marginal costs. SAC is short run average costs.

(a) At what price and output levels does a profit-maximizing monopolist produce in the long run?

(b) What are the per unit costs in the long run? What are total costs?

(c) What are the maximum long-run monopoly profits in this scenario?

(d) What is the optimal plant size that the monopolist will use to produce the long-run monopoly output? Why? Is this the plant size associated with absolute minimum per unit cost?

(e) What conclusions can you draw about the efficiency of monopoly as compared to perfectly competitive markets?

V. PROBLEM

Multiplant Monopoly

It is possible for a monopolist to produce with more than one plant. Consider the case of a monopolist producing electric cars in two different states. One production plant is in Michigan and one is in Alabama. Because of regional differences in labor and capital costs, the cost conditions differ between the two plants. The following table describes the production technologies of the two plants by giving their respective cost schedules:

Output	Price	MR	MC_1	MC_2	Monopoly MC
1	10,000		1,000	1,900	
2	8,500		1,500	3,000	
3	8,000		2,001	3,100	
4	7,500		2,100	3,200	
5	7,000		3,000	3,500	
6	6,500		3,500	4,000	
7	6,000		4,000	4,500	
8	5,500		4,500	5,000	

(a) Complete the marginal revenue schedule and the monopoly marginal cost schedule in the table above.

(b) Explain the derivation of the monopoly marginal cost schedule.

(c) Assume that the monopolist is a profit maximizer. At what level of output will profits be maximized? Why?

(d) How will the monopoly output be allocated between the two different plants?

CHAPTER 18

Measuring Monopoly

I. OVERVIEW

Monopoly theory has taught us that there are several significant differences between monopolies and competitive industries. If monopolies are common, then the level of output that is produced in the economy is not socially optimal. There would be reason to argue for policies that would change the existing level of output. It is therefore important for economists to derive reasonable measures of monopoly power. But the problem of measuring monopoly is not a simple one. Several different measures exist, each with its own problems.

One possible way to measure monopoly power is to look at the level of profits being earned by the firm. The argument for this measure is that monopolies earn above-normal profits which should distinguish it from other firms. This measure is not reliable. Firms that are not monopolies can still earn quasi-rents that are not monopoly rents. It may be impossible to empirically distinguish quasi-rents from monopoly rents.

A second possible measure is the height of the barrier to entry that permits the existence of the monopoly. A barrier to entry that has been a very controversial measure of monopoly is advertising. Proponents of this measure argue that the very fact that firms spend a lot of money on advertising indicates that they face downward-sloping demand curves. Advertising is an attempt to move out their marginal revenue curves. Opponents of this measure claim that advertising is primarily informative in nature, not argumentative, and therefore is not a large barrier to entry. The argument is an important one because if the barrier to entry is high, there are large monopoly distortions.

A third measure of monopoly is the number of firms in the industry. If there is one firm in the industry, then it is a monopoly. If there are many firms in the industry, then it is competitive. The problem with this measure is that it ignores the existence of firms waiting on the fringe. These firms are potential entrants into the market. A few firms may have a large share of a market, but the market price may still be close to the competitive price if the fringe firms will enter whenever the price only slightly rises above the competitive level.

A fourth measure of monopoly power looks at the divergence of price from marginal cost. Monopoly theory tells us that a monopoly will set its price above marginal cost. If it is possible to measure this difference, then economists would have a reasonable measure of monopoly power. The Fundamental Equation of Monopoly provides such a means by relating the elasticity of demand facing the monopolist to the ratio of marginal cost and monopoly price.

It is important to understand the significance of the price elasticity of demand facing the monopolist. When the elasticities of demand differ between groups of customers, the monopolist can price discriminate. The Rule of Rational Life leads the monopolist to shift outputs among various markets until marginal revenues in all markets are equal to each other and equal to the common marginal cost. This type of behavior will often result in unequal prices being charged in different markets, even though costs are the same. The Fundamental Equation of Discriminatory Monopoly relates the price and elasticity of demand in one market to the price and elasticity of demand in another market.

Price discrimination takes on many forms. Firms often charge one price at home and a different price in foreign markets. Firms charge retailers a different price than they charge commercial customers. The phone companies charge businesses different fees for phone installation than they charge households. The electric company charges large users of electricity less per unit than it charges smaller users.

Whether or not monopolies are common is clearly an important question. The answer to this question however, is still uncertain.

SUMMARY OF KEY CONCEPTS

barriers to entry	advertising
concentration ratio	Fundamental Equation of Monopoly
ratio of marginal cost to monopoly price	elasticity of demand facing a monopolist
price discrimination	Fundamental Equation of Discriminatory Monopoly
multipart pricing	

II. ANSWERS TO WHAT TO READ FOR

1. Why does it matter how common monopoly is? If monopoly is common, then there is reason to be unhappy with the amount of output produced in the economy. A case could be made to change

the level of output so that it is closer to the (higher) competitive level.

2. Is profit a good measure of its commonness? Since monopolies make above-normal profits, profit is a good measure of how common monopoly is. But this technique has its problems. If all firms are monopolies, then it would be difficult for the profits of any one monopolist to stand out as being unusually profitable. Furthermore, it is possible for firms to earn rents without being monopolists. Only some rents are monopoly rents. It is difficult to discern which rents are monopoly rents.

3. Does the purchaser of an existing monopoly make monopoly profits on his purchase? No. For the secondhand owner of a monopoly, the monopoly profit is a cost. For a person who buys the right to a monopoly from a previous holder, the monopoly profits are normal costs because she must compete with many others for the monopoly right.

4. What is dissipation of rents and how does medical education show it? Monopoly rights are valuable. A monopolist is willing to spend resources to acquire and protect her monopoly rights. These resources, or monopoly rents, are wasted and dissipated. The monopoly profits are buried in costs so that the monopolist does not earn above-normal returns. Consider the case of medical education. Doctors spend many years in school gaining the required amount of medical education. This schooling is expensive. Even though doctors' fees are often cited as being very high, the individual doctor might only earn a normal return on her large initial investment in medical education. In this sense, her monopoly profits are dissipated in costs required to acquire the medical education.

5. Is advertising an indication of monopoly? The size of a barrier to entry that leads to a monopoly is a measure of the monopoly. The significance of expenditures on advertising as a barrier to entry is however, controversial in economics. Some economists believe that the barrier is high and leads to large monopoly distortions. Other economists dispute this claim. The proponents of the argument claim that the large advertising budgets that many firms have indicate that these companies face downward-sloping demand curves and are trying to move out their marginal revenue curves. Other economists dispute this argument and claim that most advertising is of an informative nature; that "you can bring a horse to water but you can't make him drink."

6. Is the number of firms in an industry a good measure of monopoly power? The number of competitors in an industry is easy to measure. If there is one firm in the industry, then it is a monopoly. If there are many firms, then it is competitive. The problem with this measure is that it neglects the existence of potential entrants into the market.

7. <u>On what does the elasticity of demand facing one firm depend?</u> The elasticity of demand facing one firm depends on the elasticity of market demand, the elasticity of market supply, and the firm's share of the entire market.

8. <u>What is the Fundamental Equation of Monopoly?</u> The Fundamental Equation of Monopoly relates the elasticity of demand facing the monopolist to the ratio of marginal cost to the price charged by the monopolist. It is useful for using the elasticity of demand as a measure of monopoly power and the divergence of the price charged by the monopolist from marginal cost.

9. <u>How can one measure the marginal cost in the Fundamental Equation?</u> The solution is to find a second market in which the monopolist is a competitor. In the competitive market, the monopolist will set its price equal to marginal cost. In this way, the monopolist reveals its marginal cost.

10. <u>At what price does a monopolist at home sell in foreign, competitive markets?</u> If a firm is a monopolist at home and a competitor abroad, it will set the marginal cost of output equal to the marginal revenue in both markets. It is setting both marginal revenues equal to each other. (This is just the Rule of Rational Life again.) In the foreign market, price is equal to marginal revenue. This price therefore drives the model. The firm will sell in foreign, competitive markets as long as the foreign price is high enough relative to marginal costs.

11. <u>What is the Rule of Rational Life for a monopolist in two markets?</u> The Rule of Rational Life says that the monopolist must shift outputs among the various markets it is in until the marginal revenues in all markets are equal to each other and equal to the common marginal cost.

12. <u>What is the Fundamental Equation of Discriminatory Monopoly?</u> The behavior of a monopolist who is obeying the Rule of Rational Life will often lead to unequal prices in different markets that cannot be explained by unequal (marginal) costs. The prices are unequal because of differences in the price elasticities of demand in the different markets. The Fundamental Equation relates the price and elasticity of demand in one market to the price and elasticity of demand in another market.

13. <u>Are scholarships examples of price discrimination?</u> Yes. Giving college scholarships that depend on a student's income level is an example of price discrimination. A scholarship is a discount that a college is offering to a student with an elastic demand curve.

14. <u>Can a monopolist price discriminate if the customers can resell the product?</u> No. If two consumers with different elasticities of demand can trade, then the monopolist's practice of price discrimination will break down.

15. <u>What is multipart pricing?</u> Multipart pricing is a practice used by some monopolists to price discriminate. Under this scheme, the monopolist charges lower prices per unit to those customers who buy a larger quantity of the product.

16. <u>Does charging different prices to different customers always indicate monopoly?</u> No. The presence of quantity discounts does not always indicate monopoly. The products sold at different prices may, in fact, have different costs of production. For example, it is conceivable that it is possible for the firm to produce larger quantities of its product more cheaply than small quantities.

III. <u>MULTIPLE CHOICE</u>

1. Suppose the price elasticity of demand in a monopoly is equal to 500. The Fundamental Equation of Monopoly indicates that the ratio of marginal cost to the price charged by the monopolist is
   (a) extremely large
   (b) zero
   (c) one
   (d) -1

2. Price discrimination by a monopolist is possible because of
   (a) differences in the price elasticities of demand
   (b) differences in the price elasticities of supply
   (c) differences in marginal cost
   (d) quotas on foreign trade

3. If high-volume customers have higher elasticities than do low-volume customers, then it is rational for a monopoly that can prevent resale to
   (a) charge the high-volume customers more
   (b) charge the high-volume customers less
   (c) charge all customers the same price in order to equate marginal costs
   (d) charge all customers the same price in order to equate marginal revenues

4. In 1920, before the advent of road trucking, the railroads faced two markets: low-elasticity customers shipping general merchandise and high-elasticity customers shipping bulk freight. Assume that the marginal cost per ton-mile was the same in both markets. A typical railroad maximized profit by
   (a) setting prices equal in both markets
   (b) shifting output to the bulk freight market so that marginal revenue in bulk freight was larger than marginal revenue in general merchandise shipping
   (c) charging the customers with elastic demands higher prices

(d) charging the customers with inelastic demands higher prices

5. Consider the case of the German steel cartel in 1890. The cartel supplied the entire domestic market in Germany and exported to the world market. Its monopoly power at home can be measured by

(a) the ratio of its marginal cost in the world market to its marginal cost in the domestic market
(b) the ratio of the world price divided by the domestic price
(c) the difference between the world price and the domestic price
(d) the difference between its marginal cost and the world price

IV. EXERCISES

1. Book clubs that sell popular hard-covered books at discounted prices are common. Many people who prefer to purchase hard-covered books for their personal libraries join these book clubs. At the same time, it is observed that other people are willing to pay the full retail prices for hard-covered books at local bookstores, even though these same books are available from the book clubs. Suppose it is observed that the price elasticity of demand for a typical book club member is 2, and the price elasticity of demand for a typical retail buyer is 1.5.

(a) Do these observed price elasticities of demand make sense?

(b) Given these elasticities of demand, how much more than a book club member is a buyer of books at retail willing to pay for the same book?

2. A popular computer program makes it possible to transfer computer diskettes between different types of computers. This program, known as Trancomp, is produced by the Trancomp Computer Corporation of America and sells for $99.95. This program is recognized by the computer industry as being the best program available on the market. At the same time, Trancomp has sold licenses to Mediacomp Software Company that permits it to sell the Trancomp program under the name Compfile for the low price of $25. Under the terms of the agreement, Mediacomp must pay Trancomp $5 per program that it sells. Mediacomp is also forbidden from advertising that Compfile is the same program as Trancomp. Is this licensing agreement rational for Trancomp Computer Corporation if it is trying to maximize its annual profits?

3. Steve White and Dorothy Perkins are public activists. They both work for an organization that lobbies for legislation that is considered to be socially desirable.

During a recent meeting of the organization, Steve and Dorothy reported on a study they did of the generic aspirin industry. Their study found that although there are over five hundred independent manufacturers of aspirin, the typical firm was making over $25,000 in annual profits. Steve argued that the existence of such exorbitant profits proves that the aspirin market is not competitive. Dorothy argued that the existence of such a large number of firms in the industry proved that it had to be competitive, but she wasn't sure why the typical firm earns positive profits.

(a) Is it possible for firms in the generic aspirin market to earn positive profits if the market is perfectly competitive, or must the firms in the market have monopoly power? Explain.

(b) Does the existence of a large number of firms necessarily prove that the market is perfectly competitive?

V. PROBLEM

Patented Solar-Powered Food Blenders

The Solar Beater Food Company is a maker of solar-powered food blenders. Solar Beater has a patent for their product and is the only maker of this product in the country. The price of a solar-powered blender is $250 per blender. Given the existing market demand for solar-powered blenders, Solar Beater has been earning substantial economic profits from the production of their product during the past two years.

A local New York television station interviewed people walking on Fifth Avenue in a random survey. These people were asked if they felt that Solar Beater is charging a "fair price" for their product. The results of these interviews indicated that the typical pedestrian felt that Solar Beater was taking unfair advantage of consumers and was charging an exorbitant price for their product. One pedestrian was even quoted as saying, "There is absolutely nothing constraining Solar Beater from charging anything it wants for its product."

(a) What type of market structure best describes the market for solar-powered blenders? Why does this type of market structure exist?

(b) Would a market concentration ratio be a good measure of

Solar Beater's market power? Why?

(c) Is it true that there are absolutely no constraints on the behavior of the Solar Beater Company and the price that they can charge for their product? Explain.

(d) Whether or not there are any constraints on Solar Beater's behavior, the company's managers somehow must make a decision about how many solar-powered blenders to make. How will this decision be made. Draw a graph to help illustrate your answer.

(e) What does the supply curve for solar-powered blenders look like for the Solar Beater Company?

(f) An investigative reporter for a New York newspaper discovered that Solar Beater is charging different prices for its product in several different regions of the country. After extensive study, he concluded that the price differences were not due to differences in transportation costs. If transportation costs do not explain the price differences, what other explanations might there be? Is Solar Beater rational in its decision to charge different prices in different geographic regions?

(g) U.S. Senator Sam Helpman decided to introduce a bill into Congress after seeing the television report about Solar Beater. Senator Helpman concluded that Solar Beater was taking unfair advantage of consumers and had to be restrained from charging unfair prices. He argued that the price of solar-powered blenders and the quantity supplied by Solar Beater should be regulated by the federal government. From society's point of view, is this type of regulation desirable?

(h) Senator Ralph Pickins introduced an alternative bill into the Congress. He argued that Solar Beater's patent should simply be revoked. If this bill is passed by the Congress, what will the long-run equilibrium for this market look like? Draw a graph to help illustrate your answer.

CHAPTER 19

The Welfare Economics of Monopoly

I. OVERVIEW

The theory of monopoly developed in chapter 17 led to the conclusion that monopoly is socially inefficient. Simple monopoly reduces output. It leaves mutually beneficial opportunities for exchange between the monopoly and other parties unexploited. But monopoly still has its defenders. Monopoly is sometimes justified on the grounds that it subsidizes certain activities that might not otherwise be provided. For example, the U.S. postal service is a monopoly. Its existence as a monopoly is justified on the grounds that it can provide mail service to regions of the country that are unprofitable to service. Another less conclusive argument is that monopoly provides incentives for innovation. If a person knows that her invention will be protected by a patent, she will have a greater incentive to innovate. But even the proponent of this argument, Joseph Schumpeter, recognized that it was inconclusive. He recognized that monopoly might also thwart progress. This problem cannot be resolved in static economic theory.

It is curious that monopoly leaves mutually beneficial opportunities for exchange between the monopoly and its victims unexploited. The explanation is that transaction costs of making agreements is the cause of simple (single-price) monopoly and its inefficiencies. For example, if a monopoly is allowed to perfectly price discriminate, then an efficient outcome would prevail. The monopoly's utility is maximized and the victim's utility is no lower than it was at the start. But the costs of such price discrimination are high. Price discrimination is expensive and difficult to maintain.

Are the efficiency losses from simple monopoly large or small? Opportunities for exchange are left unexploited. The opportunities are a cost. If one knows the shape of the monopolist's marginal cost curve and the shape of the demand curve, then it is a straightforward exercise to measure the social loss. When this is done, the social loss appears to be small. But appearances are deceiving. This approach fails to take into consideration the resources that are wasted by individuals seeking the supernormal profits that prevail under monopoly. The social loss from these wasted resources must be added to the social loss from sacrificed exchanges. And the loss from wasted resources might well be substantial.

SUMMARY OF KEY CONCEPTS

infant industry tariff
unexploited exchange
perfect price discrimination
monopoly and innovation
efficiency loss from monopoly
transaction costs and inefficiency

II. ANSWERS TO WHAT TO READ FOR

1. What social purposes are used to defend monopolies? It is sometimes argued that monopolies are justified because they subsidize some socially desirable activity that might otherwise not occur. For example, the postal service is a monopoly. Its existence is often justified on the grounds that it subsidizes delivery of mail to unprofitable customers.

2. What is the infant industry tariff? The infant industry tariff is a very high tax imposed by the government on imported goods in order to protect a young domestic industry from foreign competition while it is still growing.

3. Can static economic theory decide whether or not monopoly is good for technical innovation? No. Joseeph Schumpeter argued that monopoly protects the rewards of innovation and therefore might provide incentives for innovation. But he also admitted that monopoly might "sabotage all progress." From a theoretical point of view, it is unclear whether or not monopoly is good for technical innovation.

4. How is a monopoly's behavior represented in an Edgeworth box? An Edgeworth box can be drawn with the monopoly at one origin and the party with which it trades at the other origin. The monopolist will maximize its utility subject to the other party's offer curve. At the point where the monopoly is exercising its monopoly power, one of the monopolist's indifference curves is tangent to the other party's offer curve. The monopolist's indifference curve will not be tangent to the other party's indifference curve. The result will be a lens-shaped area of mutually advantageous exchange that is left unexploited.

5. Can the monopoly itself be made better off by exchange beyond the monopoly point? Yes. The lens-shaped area that exists inside the Edgeworth box indicates possible points of mutually advantageous exchange. Even the monopolist would be made better off by exchange beyond the monopoly point.

6. What does the cost of making agreements have to do with the efficiency of a monopoly? Transaction costs, such as the cost of making agreements, are the cause of inefficiency. The cost of making agreements is the cause of single-price monopoly and its

inefficiencies. Consider the result that the monopoly itself would be made better off by exchange beyond the monopoly point in the Edgeworth box. This exchange does not occur however, because it is too costly to make agreements.

7. Is a perfectly discriminatory monopoly inefficient? No. Perfect price discrimination is efficient. Multiprice monopoly is efficient. If a monopolist is able to perfectly discriminate, then it will be able to trade to its best point, and the utility of the other party will be no lower than it was to start.

8. Is the loss from sacrificed exchanges in simple monopoly large? It is possible to calculate the loss from sacrificed exchanges in simple monopoly if one knows the shape of the monopoly's marginal cost curve and the shape of the demand curve. When calculated this way, it appears that the social loss is small.

9. Is this loss the largest loss attributable to monopoly? No. The appearance that the social loss is small is deceiving. The reason the losses are larger than they appear is that under monopoly, supernormal profits are earned. People seek these returns. Resources are therefore spent seeking monopoly profits. The resources are wasted. This loss is in addition to the loss from sacrificed exchanges under simple monopoly.

III. MULTIPLE CHOICE

1. Which of the following is not a possible justification for monopoly?
   (a) transaction costs
   (b) incentives to innovate
   (c) subsidization of desirable activities
   (d) an infant industry

2. The high tax imposed on foreign cotton textile goods in the nineteenth century was a
   (a) lum sum tax
   (b) quota
   (c) regressive tax
   (d) infant industry tax

3. It is incorrect to argue that a monopolist has no incentives to keep costs down because
   (a) monopolists are profit maximizers
   (b) high costs would lead to entry
   (c) monopoly is inconsistent with high costs
   (d) monopolists experience diminishing returns to scale

4. When a monopoly maximizes its happiness, the constraint on

its behavior is that
(a) it stay on its victim's offer curve
(b) it stay at a point on its indifference curve tangent to its victim's indifference curve
(c) it achieve a Pareto optimal allocation
(d) it stay on the production possibility frontier

5. A price discriminating monopolist cannot leave its victims any worse off than they were to start with because
(a) the outcome would not be Pareto optimal
(b) the outcome would not be on the contract curve
(c) the victims can refuse to trade
(d) there are transaction costs to making agreements

6. Under perfect price discrimination and perfect competition
(a) mutually beneficial exchanges are left unexploited
(b) incentives to innovate are at a maximum
(c) the distribution of income is the same
(d) marginal cost is equal to marginal valuation

7. The perfect discriminating monopolist
(a) maximizes consumers' surplus
(b) earns all the gains from trade
(c) minimizes producers' surplus
(d) has no efficiency costs

8. The perfect discriminating monopolist
(a) earns supernormal profits
(b) does not waste any resources
(c) would never offer an all-or-nothing deal to its victims
(d) is never able to completely extract the consumers' surplus

9. Restricting entry to medical school
(a) improves medical care
(b) may improve the average quality of doctors
(c) allows doctors to perfectly price discriminate
(d) leaves society on the contract curve

10. If the victims of OPEC were to pay a stated sum of money to OPEC in exchange for an agreement by OPEC to sell its oil competitively
(a) the new equilibrium would be on the contract curve
(b) the new equilibrium would be off the contract curve
(c) society ends up outside the lens-shaped area of mutually advantageous exchange in the Edgeworth box
(d) an inefficient outcome prevails

IV. EXERCISES

1. It is often argued that college football teams serve the same

purpose as a minor league for professional football teams. The argument continues that professional football teams should therefore subsidize colleges to help support their football teams. Is the perceived "minor league" status of many college football teams a compelling argument for subsidization?

2. Many people have argued that it is possible to construct a crash-proof automobile that would also be so durable that it would never wear out. It is further argued that the automobile companies would never want to produce such a car because it would eventually put them out of business. Do yo agree with such an assessment?

V. PROBLEM

The Breakup of AT&T

In January 1984, AT&T was required by the courts to divest itself of all of its local subsidiary phone companies. A major question that has arisen about the court order is whether the courts went further than was necessary to introduce the desired degree of competition into the telecommunications industry.

The principle argument for the breakup of AT&T was that communications technology had become too vast of a field to be controlled by a regulated monopoly. It was believed, for example, that the possibilities for improvements in data transmission would be best exploited in a competitive market. Other types of communications services would also become more efficient. It was widely recognized that long-distance phone rates would be forced down by increased competition. But it was also understood that the end of AT&T's subsidization of more costly local phone service would cause many local rates to rise.

In 1983, Republican Senator Packwood and Democratic Congressmen Wirth and Dingell introduced legislation into the U.S. Congress that would have subsidized local phone service again with revenues received from long-distance phone service. This legislation was eventually defeated by the Congress.

(a) Was the argument for the breakup of AT&T on the grounds that a competitive environment would be more innovative correct?

(b) What benefits that existed under the old AT&T might be lost under the new system?

(c) Is subsidization of local phone service with revenues from long-distance service desirable?

CHAPTER 20

Monopolistic Competition and the Economics of Location

I. OVERVIEW

Do the theories of perfect competition and monopoly provide a sufficient basis for predictions about price and market behavior in real economies? The models of perfect competition and monopoly provide useful insights into the problems of profit maximization, cost minimization, market entry and exit, barriers to entry, the maximization of social welfare, and productive efficiency. But many economists feel that there is a need for better, more "realistic" models of the economy.

Monopoly and perfect competition are two extreme cases that do not describe much of the American economy. It is possible to observe many industries in which there are numerous firms that depart from some of the conditions of perfect competition. For example, there are very few industries in which products are entirely homogeneous among producers. It is also possible to observe many industries with only one or a few firms that depart from the conditions of monopoly. For these reasons, economists turned their attention to a form of market structure that is intermediate between monopoly and perfect competition. This type of market structure is known as monopolistic competition.

As its name implies, monopolistic competition takes on some of the characteristics of perfect competition and some of the characteristics of monopoly. Like perfect competition, monopolistic competition is characterized by many firms that have the freedom to enter and exit the industry. Like monopoly, each firm within the industry has some power over the price it charges for its output. Each firm has this limited "monopoly" power because each sells a product that is <u>differentiated</u> from the output of other firms in the industry. Product differentiation implies that each firm has a certain degree of monopoly power over its own product. It is interesting to note that product differentiation characterizes most American markets.

Since each monopolistic competitor has some monopoly power over its own differentiated product, it is not a price taker. Rather, like a pure monopolist, each firm faces a downward-sloping demand curve for its product. In contrast to monopoly, the demand curve facing each monopolistic competitor is usually elastic because of the existence of close substitutes. Downward sloping demand is significant because it allows monopoly profits to be earned in the short run.

Monopolistic competition is also characterized by freedom of entry and exit. This characteristic, which is similar to perfect competition, forces profits supernormal to zero in the long run.

Productive efficiency is not achieved under monopolistic competition. Like monopoly, firms do not produce at their least attainable cost. But one must ask whether productive efficiency is desirable in monopolistically competitive markets. One must consider the characteristics and reasons for the existence of this form of market structure. Differentiated products exist because people have different tastes. Some consumers prefer one differentiated product to the other. There is a trade-off between producing more products to satisfy these diverse tastes and producing any output at the lowest possible cost. Given the empirical observation that differentiated products exist, the conclusion that must be drawn is that consumer satisfaction is not maximized by increasing production of each differentiated product until it is produced in the least-cost way. Social welfare is maximized under monopolistic competition.

SUMMARY OF KEY CONCEPTS

- transport costs
- product differentiation
- local monopolies
- Hotelling model of two-part competition
- downward-sloping demand
- elastic demand
- satisfaction of diverse tastes
- bid rent curves

II. ANSWERS TO WHAT TO READ FOR

20.1 MONOPOLISTIC COMPETITION AS COMPETITION AMONG LOCAL MONOPOLIES

1. What are the desirable features of a competitive equilibrium? There are two desirable features of a competitive equilibrium. First, marginal valuation is equal to marginal opportunity cost. Second, no firm earns supernormal profits.

2. How does monopolistic competition violate them? Optimality breaks down under monopolistic competition because there are transport costs. When there are transport costs, there are local monopolies. Supernormal profits can be earned in the short run. The industry is not at the competitive point on the bottom of the

U-shaped average cost curve.

3. <u>How do you construct the demand curve facing a local store?</u> A certain price at the local store will attract a certain number of customers in all directions around the store. How many depends on what the neighboring stores are doing. The quantity sold at any particular local store will depend on several factors: (a) the price charged at the local store; (b) the total cost, including transport costs, to customers at the local store (given by the local stores's "price line"); (c) the prices charged to customers of neighboring stores (given by the neighboring stores' price lines); (d) the density of customers between the stores; and (e) the fact that customers choose the cheaper delivered price. The local store can sell to customers that are located out to the point where its price line intersects the price lines of neighboring stores. In order to construct the demand curve facing the local store, a vertical axis is drawn above the local store. A "tent" is then drawn over the local store's location. The top of the tent is equal to the sum of transport costs and the neighboring stores' price lines. The demand curve for the local store is a line that begins at the peak of the tent above the location of the local store. It is drawn so that it is equidistant from the vertical axis and the neighboring stores' price lines. (See Figure 20.1 in the text.)

4. <u>What do you have to assume about how neighboring stores react to various different prices set at the store?</u> Each store chooses quantity such that marginal cost is equal to marginal revenue, each store charges the same price, and the territory is divided equally between the stores. The price levels at neighboring stores are given and assumed to be fixed at the levels they would attain in equilibrium. Each firm ignores its interaction with any other firm.

5. <u>How does the demand curve shift as more firms enter?</u> As more firms enter, stores become located closer together, their individual price lines are lowered, and the demand curve each firm faces is lowered. Entry shifts the demand curve inward at any given price.

6. <u>Why do they enter?</u> New firms enter because supernormal profits are being earned in the short run. The firms enter in pursuit of these profits.

7. <u>What is the long-run equilibrium?</u> In the presence of transport costs, the long-run equilibrium is characterized by zero supernormal profits, and a large number of firms producing at less than full capacity and at a price above the competitive price. The industry does not end up at the competitive point on the bottom of the U-shaped average cost curve.

8. <u>What is product differentiation?</u> Product differentiation is a term used by economists to describe the methods used by a firm

to persuade customers that its product is somehow different and better than its competitors. It has come to be another word for advertising.

9. What are the three objections to the theory of monopolistic competition? The objections to the model of monopolistic competition are that it results in (i) many small, pointlessly differentiated firms characteristic of competition, that (ii) produce low levels of output characteristic of monopoly, and (iii) are all supported by advertising at the customer's expense.

10. Is product differentiation always bad? No. Product differentiation exists because consumers have differing tastes.

11. Is the assumption about how neighboring stores react a reasonable one? The assumption is dubious. It is doubtful, as Chamberlin asserted, "that any adjustment of price or of 'product' by a single producer spreads its influence over so many of his competitors that the impact felt by any one is negligible and does not lead him to any readjustment of his own situation."

12. Has the theory of monopolistic competition been rich in application? No. It has been argued that the model of monopolistic competition is a better description of reality than either of the models of perfect competition or monopoly. But the model also fails to present any significant proposition about how such industries behave.

20.2 THE THEORY OF LOCATION

1. How can the theory of location be applied to politics? The theory of location can be used to view the political arena as a market that can be subdivided into regions within which each seller (or political party) is in a quasi-monopolistic position.

2. Why do American political parties look so similar? There are two major American political parties: the Democratic Party and the Republican Party. Suppose the Democratic Party starts at the left end of the political spectrum and the Republican Party starts at the right end. The Democratic Party knows that if it moves towards the middle of the road, they will continue to capture all voters to their left, but will capture additional voters to their right. The Republican Party has a similar incentive to move to the left. Since both parties make these moves, the moves cancel each other out and they end up sitting slightly to either side of the middle of the road.

3. How does transport cost to a central city determine land rent away from the city? Because of transport costs, locations away from the city are valued less than locations near the city.

4. What is a bid-rent curve? A bid-rent curve is an equation that tells how much one would be willing to bid to rent land at various distances from some central location.

III. MULTIPLE CHOICE

1. In the short run, monopolistic competition is most likely to have which of the following characteristics?
   (a) many large firms earning supernormal profits and operating at full capacity
   (b) many large firms earning supernormal profits and operating at less than full capacity
   (c) many small firms earning supernormal profits and operating at full capacity
   (d) many small firms earning supernormal profits and operating at less than full capacity

2. In the long run, monopolistic competition is most likely to be characterized by which of the following?
   (a) many large firms earning no supernormal profits and operating at full capacity
   (b) many small firms earning no supernormal profits and operating at full capacity
   (c) many small firms earning no supernormal profits and operating at less than full capacity
   (d) many small firms earning supernormal profits and operating at less than full capacity

3. Full capacity means that the firm is
   (a) employing as much capital as it possibly can
   (b) producing output at the highest possible unit cost
   (c) producing output at the lowest possible cost
   (d) earning zero normal profits

4. In the model of monopolistic competition, each firm is a local monopoly because
   (a) of transport costs
   (b) of different production technologies
   (c) different average costs
   (d) different marginal costs

5. Chamberlin asserted that
   (a) each firm can ignore its interaction with any one other firm
   (b) the price facing the local monopoly becomes fixed by competition and the analysis reduced to perfect competition
   (c) spatial distances between monopolistic competitors makes the impact felt by any one firm negligible and the analysis reduces to perfect monopoly
   (d) the taking of the neighboring prices as fixed for

purposes of analysis is false

6. Middle-of-the-road third parties in the United States have been short lived because
   (a) the difference in nearness for any voter between the third party and the traditional parties has been negligible
   (b) the difference in nearness for any voter between the third party and the traditional parties has been too extreme
   (c) the third parties in general failed to move to an extreme left or extreme right position
   (d) transport costs for the third parties were too high

7. Which of the following is <u>not</u> a characteristic of monopolistic competition?
   (a) barriers to entry
   (b) many firms
   (c) differentiated products
   (d) supernormal profits in the short run

8. The demand curve facing a monopolistic competitor is
   (a) inelastic because its product is differentiated
   (b) inelastic because of the existence of close substitutes
   (c) elastic because its product is differentiated
   (d) elastic because of the existence of close substitutes

9. In a long-run equilibrium, each monopolistic competitor produces
   (a) where its demand curve is tangent to its average total cost curve
   (b) where its demand curve is above its average total cost curve
   (c) at the minimum point of its average total cost curve
   (d) at a point to the right of the minimum point on its average total cost curve

10. In a long-run equilibrium, each monopolistic competitor produces
   (a) less output than the one for which its long-run average total cost curve reaches its minimum point
   (b) the output level at which its long-run average total cost curve reaches its minimum
   (c) more output than the one for which its long-run average total cost curve reaches its minimum
   (d) at the point of tangency of its demand curve and minimum long-run average total cost

11. The long-run equilibrium in a model of monopolistic competition is
   (a) efficient
   (b) inefficient
   (c) unstable because of entry

(d) characterized by supernormal profits

12. The long-run equilibrium in a model of monopolistic competition is a trade off between
   (a) producing more products to satisfy diverse tastes and producing any given set of products to the left of minimum long-run average total cost
   (b) producing more products to satisfy diverse tastes and producing any given set of products inefficiently
   (c) producing more products to satisfy diverse tastes and producing any given set of products at lowest possible cost
   (d) producing more products to satisfy diverse tastes and operating at less than full capacity

13. Suppose a new highway is built in Israel between the port city of Haifa and the desert city of Revivim in the Negev. The construction of the highway reduces the cost of sending imported goods from Haifa to Revivim. The result of the construction of the highway will be to
   (a) decrease the profitability of land in Haifa
   (b) decrease the profitability of land in Revivim
   (c) increase the profitability of land in Revivim
   (d) equate land rents in Haifa and Revivim

14. The area under the bid rent curve is
   (a) the rent of all land at various distances
   (b) total rent earned by all land at a particular location
   (c) total transport costs
   (d) marginal transport costs

15. In the short run, a monopolistic competitor picks output at
   (a) its price line bisects its demand curve
   (b) zero supernormal profits
   (c) opportunity costs are zero
   (d) the point where marginal revenue equals marginal cost

IV. EXERCISES

1. Dr. Igor Sternovsky is a Russian economist who is visiting the United States. His host is Professor Stan Stymie from the Department of Economics at Podonk University. Sternovsky and Stymie are having a discussion about the lack of product diversity in the Soviet Union and the abundance of diversified products in the U.S. Sternovsky is arguing that the product diversification in the U.S. is not consistent with productive efficiency and is therefore not socially desirable. Stymie disagrees. He thinks product diversification within particular industries is good.

(a) What type of market structure best describes industries in which many heterogeneous products exist?

(b) Is Sternovsky correct in saying that markets like this are not consistent with productive efficiency? Explain.

(c) Why does product diversification within U.S. industries exist? Is product diversification necessarily bad?

(d) Does a stable market equilibrium exist for U.S. markets like this?

2. The Excess Capacity Theorem of Monopolistic Competition states that social welfare is not maximized by increasing production of each product until it is produced at its least-cost point. Rather, social welfare is maximized under monopolistic competition when the number of differentiated products is increased until the marginal gain from adding one more product is equal to the marginal cost of having to produce each existing product at a higher cost than under perfect competition.

(a) Is productive efficiency achieved under monopolistic competition? Why?

(b) Draw a graph to illustrate your answer to part (a).

(c) Is productive efficiency desirable? What is the justification for the Excess Capacity Theorem?

(d) Under monopolistic competition, are resources being wasted in society?

V. PROBLEM

Product Diversity in the American Automobile Industry

Alfred Sloan, the former chairman of General Motors Corporation, once declared that his firm would build a car "for every purse and purpose." In pursuit of that goal, American automobile manufacturers have during the past twenty years nearly doubled the number of different models of cars they produce. Lloyd Reuss, the general manager of GM's Buick division, was quoted as saying, "You can't stay in this business just by making black sedans."

A recent study of the American automobile industry determined that this approach to the domestic automobile market has added over $1,000 to the cost of the average car. The

American car manufacturers have had to develop sophisticated factories that are capable of producing many different types of automobiles. The study suggested that American manufacturers might be losing more customers than they gain by offering this extensive product diversity. The costs of this extreme product differentiation might outweigh the price consumers are willing to pay for the product diversity.

In contrast to the American approach, Japanese car manufacturers have limited the number of different models of cars they have introduced into the American market. This approach results from the fact that the Japanese are contrained by having to ship their cars across the Pacific. The Japanese manufacturers' strategy has been to conduct market studies of American consumer preferences and target the design of their products to these tastes. The Japanese companies have also been able to offer their cars for sale at lower prices.

(a) What was Alfred Sloan's objective when he committed GM to building a car "for every purse and purpose?"

(b) What are the implications of Lloyd Reuss' comment for product differentiation and the structure of the American automobile market?

(c) What is "overhead"? What effect does the addition of $1,000 to the overhead cost of the average car have on GM's average total cost of production?

(d) Who bears the cost and burden of the product differentiation? Is the product differentiation necessarily bad?

(e) If the recent study is correct about average costs, what implications does it have for GM's "optimal" point of production?

(f) What does the Japanese experience suggest about where on the long-run average cost curve American manufacturers currently are?

(g) Is the Japanese strategy of conducting market studies a good one?

(h) What cost advantages accrue to the Japanese firms due to the fact that they do not offer as diverse a selection of automobiles?

(i) Is it surprising that the prices of comparable Japanese cars are lower?

CHAPTER 21

Competition Among the Few

I. OVERVIEW

Three models of industry structure have been presented: perfect competition, pure monopoly, and monopolistic competition. We now turn our attention to the market structure of oligopoly. Oligopoly is a market in which only a few firms exist. Each firm constitutes a substantial share of the market.

Recall that in the models of perfect competition and monopolistic competition, each firm took the behavior of other firms as fixed when it made its output choice. This characteristic was justified by the assumption that each firm constituted a relatively small part of the industry. Under perfect competition, firms are price takers. Under oligopoly, firms are price (or quantity) setters. An oligopolist sets its price by conscious decision. This does not mean that market demand and supply do not affect this price. An oligopolist must always consider demand, costs, and the prices of competing products when it sets its price. Once the oligopoly price is set, a change in demand is signalled to the firm by a change in its sales at the set price. (In contrast, a change in demand was signalled to the perfect competitor by a change in the prevailing market price.)

A major difficulty in modeling the behavior of oligopolists arises because of the many alternative reactions the firms might have to each other's actions. One possibility is that the oligopolists will cooperate with each other. Cooperation enables the oligopolists to produce the monopoly output, charge the monopoly price, and reap monopoly profits. Cooperation is desirable because the monopoly profits are the maximum profits the industry can possibly earn. But firms often have an incentive to cheat on such agreements, complicating the analysis. The forms of behavior that are alternative to cooperation are numerous.

One alternative is the Bertrand assumption. This model assumes that each firm makes its pricing decision while assuming that the other firms will keep their prices fixed. The "dual" to the Bertrand assumption is the Cournot assumption. The Cournot model is a model of duopoly; that is, it models an industry containing only two firms. both firms sell an identical product. Each firm chooses its profit-maximizing output level on the assumption that the other firm will hold its output constant. The result of this assumption is that after a series of output choices in which each firm adjusts its output to the other firm's previous decision, a stable equilibrium is reached. The market is divided between the two firms in a definite way. Each firm charges the same price, which is greater than the competitive price and less than the monopoly price.

A particularly interesting problem in oligopoly theory is the problem of collusion. Any oligopolist has an incentive to cooperate with its rivals to maximize their joint profits. When an oligopolist chooses its price or output, it recognizes the interdependence of all oligopolists. All of the oligopolists face downward-sloping demand curves. Joint profits depend on the price that each of them charges. Their incentive is to charge the same price that a pure monopoly would charge. But in conflict with the incentive to collude is the oligopolist's desire to receive as large a share of the profits as possible. Each firm has an incentive to cut its own price below the monopoly price in order to gain a larger market share. If other firms follow this behavior, then total industry profits fall and the agreement to collude breaks down. Each firm must therefore balance what it hopes to gain in the form of a larger market share against the losses it will incur due to smaller joint industry profits.

The tendency toward joint profit maximization is greater when there is only a small number of sellers. When there are fewer firms, it is easier for the industry to coordinate its policies. The incentive to collude is also greater when the firms are producing similar products, rather than differentiated products. When firms produce very similar products, the competition for customers is greater. The tendency toward collusion is also greater in a growing industry. In a contracting industry, firms have excess capacity and want to compete for the existing market demand.

Other impediments to collusion exist. The desire to increase its market share will lead to nonprice competition between the oligopolists. Firms will try to increase their market share through advertising, product differentiation, and product improvements.

SUMMARY OF KEY CONCEPTS

duopoly	Cournot assumption
Bertrand assumption	joint profit maximization
collusion	incentives to cheat
prisoner's dilemma	cartels
cocktail party problem	game theory

II. ANSWERS TO WHAT TO READ FOR

21.1 SIMPLE SOLUTIONS: BERTRAND AND COURNOT

1. How do two sellers alone in a market behave? There are many possibilities. One possibility is that they will cooperate. The two sellers can agree to charge the monopoly price and then divide up the monopoly profits equally. But there is a reasonable possibility that the two sellers will cheat on their agreement. The alternatives to cooperation are numerous. One is the possibility of a price war between the two sellers. The two sellers might make the Bertrand assumption that the other will keep its price constant. Alternatively, they might make the Cournot assumption that the other firm will keep its quantity constant. Either of these assumptions leads away from the monopoly solution.

2. What if they cooperate fully? If the two sellers (duopolists) cooperate fully, then the duopoly reduces to monopoly.

3. What if they maximize selfishly and assume the other will keep his price constant? This is the Bertrand assumption. Each duopolist maximizes selfishly with the assumption that the other firm will keep its price constant. In this case, the price will fall to the competitive level.

4. What if they assume the other will keep his quantity constant? This is the Cournot assumption. Each firm maximizes selfishly with the assumption that the other firm will keep its output constant. In this case, the quantity will rise toward the competitive level. It will stop well short of the competitive level for two sellers.

5. What are the Bertrand and Cournot solutions? The Bertrand and Cournot solutions are two main solutions to the oligopoly problem. In the Bertrand solution, each duopolist takes the other's price as given. In the Cournot solution, each duopolist takes the other's quantity as given.

6. How do you prove the Cournot solution diagrammatically? Each duopolist has a belief curve that is based on the assumption that the other duopolist will not change his output. Regardless of what the duopolist believes he faces however, he actually faces one half of market demand. The reality curve divides the market between the duopolists. (Recall that in equilibrium, identical duopolists must have the same price and output.) The equilibrium point is one which lies on both the belief curves and the reality curve. The midpoint of the belief curve is always chosen since it is the point of maximum revenue. The reality curve must therefore bisect the belief curve.

7. <u>How do you apply it, or its "dual," to the case of end-to-end railroads?</u> One can set up the problem of end-to-end railroads in the form of a Cournot problem by assuming that there are two railroads with no costs, no competitors, and no other trade except for a particular route. Further assume that the demand for railroad services along the route is a straight line. Suppose that the two railroads were merged into one company. In this case, the monopoly situation would prevail. Next suppose that the two railroads are separate and take each other's price as given. The analysis shows that the case of end-to-end railroads leads to an even higher price than does a monopoly. The combined profits of the two railroads are less than monopoly profits.

21.2 THE IRRATIONALITY OF SIMPLE SOLUTIONS TO THE PROBLEM OF FEWNESS

1. <u>What is wrong with the Cournot assumption?</u> The problem with the Cournot assumption is that when the number of firms gets small, it is no longer reasonable for each firm to believe that its actions will have a trivial impact on the other firms. The Cournot assumption becomes an assumption of foolish behavior.

2. <u>Why is pure bargaining relevant to what is wrong with it?</u> Duopolists do depend on each other by the very nature of their fewness. It would be foolish not to recognize their interdependence. Duopolists are placed in an environment of pure bargaining.

3. <u>What is a reaction function?</u> A reaction function is a curve that shows the reaction of a duopolist to the actions of the other duopolist.

4. <u>How is it related to the Cournot assumption?</u> The reaction function embodies the Cournot assumption. Each duopolist assumes that the other duopolist will keep his output fixed. Each duopolist never learns that the other duopolist has a reaction function.

5. <u>Can it be used as a full representation of the arms race?</u> No. It can only be used as a crude, first-step representation of the arms race. One problem is that the Americans and the Soviets never learn that the other has a reaction function. Further, it is possible to construct the problem so that there is no point of equilibrium. The fundamental problem though, is that both countries would be irraitonal to react so predictably to the behavior of the other.

6. <u>Could Mokyr do better if he knew Hughes was making the Cournot assumption?</u> Of course. This is the principle of

outsmarting. If Mokyr knew Hughes was making the Cournot assumption, then by using this superior knowledge he can do at least as well as if he behaved in a Cournot fashion.

7. <u>What does the principle of outsmarting have to do with the Cournot assumption?</u> According to the principle of outsmarting, the analysis is unfinished if there is still an opportunity for one of the duopolists to improve its situation. The Cournot solution leaves open such an opportunity. The Cournot solution violates the principle of outsmarting because it is possible to think of a feasible way in which a Cournot duopolist could improve its situation.

8. <u>Should you believe stock market advice?</u> Of course not. If the advisers are so smart, why aren't they rich? Since they are not rich (at least not from taking their own advice), it must be false that they can predict fluctuations in the stock market.

21.3 CARTELS AND GAME THEORY AS SOLUTIONS TO THE OLIGOPOLY PROBLEM

1. <u>What are the advantages of a successful cartel and the disadvantages of its collapse?</u> The advantage of a successful cartel is that oligopolists can stop competing with each other and form a monopoly. But agreements to collude are difficult and expensive to enforce. Collusion has a price. Further, the oligopolists often have an incentive to cheat on the agreement. A successful cheater can do better for himself than under the terms of the agreement. If all the members of the cartel cheat on the agreement, then the cartel will collapse and the members will be worse off than they would have been if they had cooperated.

2. <u>What is the prisoner's dilemma?</u> The prisoner's dilemma is a matrix of payoffs from cooperation with, and defection from, a collusive agreement. This matrix shows that it is always desirable to defect from the collusive agreement.

3. <u>How does it suggest cartels will work out?</u> The prisoner's dilemma suggests that cartels must ultimately collapse. When every participant in a cartel cheats, each participant ends up at the competitive point.

4. <u>What is the Cocktail Party Problem?</u> The Cocktail PArty Problem is an example of the prisoner's dilemma. Everybody at a cocktail party would like to be heard over the voices of the other people who are talking. If everybody cooperated, then each person would speak softly and everybody could be heard. But in fact, everybody generally ends up shouting. Shouting is the equilibrium of a prisoner's dilemma.

5. <u>How can the payoff matrix be altered by punishment to bring about cooperation?</u> In order to solve the prisoner's dilemma, some form of punishment must be imposed on cheaters or defectors. By imposing penalties for defection, the matrix of payoffs that a participant faces changes. This change can make it worth the participant's while to cooperate rather than to defect.

6. <u>Will a small group able to communicate be able to avoid the prisoner's dilemma?</u> Yes. The smaller the group, the larger is the chance of being caught. When one is caught, one is shamed or punished.

7. <u>What is game theory?</u> Game theory discusses the situation of intelligent people facing other intelligent people in games. Oligopolists play a game of cooperation and defection that may or may not have monopoly as its outcome.

8. <u>Does it solve the oligopoly problem?</u> No. Game theory does not solve the oligopoly problem. Its main use in economics has been metaphorical -- like the theory of monopolistic competition.

III. MULTIPLE CHOICE

1. Enforcement of collusion is difficult because it is always in the interest of one firm
   (a) to charge the monopoly price
   (b) to charge the competitive price
   (c) to increase its own production if it believes the other firm will hold its production constant
   (d) to decrease its own production if it believes the other firm will hold its production constant

2. Oligopoly is a form of market structure in which
   (a) there are relatively few firms that have enough market power to be price takers
   (b) there are relatively few firms that have enough market power to be price setters
   (c) there are relatively few firms that have enough market power to be quantity takers
   (d) there are many firms that still have enough market power to be regarded as quantity takers

3. It is very common for firms to be faced with a prisoner's dilemma in which of the following market structures?
   (a) perfect competition
   (b) monopoly
   (c) cartel
   (d) monopolistic competition

4. The principle of outsmarting in game theory is the same as

(a) the principle of increasing marginal product
(b) the principle of opportunity costs
(c) the principle of sunk costs in utility theory
(d) the principle of entry in the analysis of the firm

5. When price rather than quantity is the object of choice and belief, the Cournot model leads to
(a) a higher price under duopoly than under monopoly
(b) a lower price under duopoly than under monopoly
(c) the same price under duopoly as under monopoly
(d) the same price under duopoly as under perfect competition

IV. EXERCISES

1. Consider the case of duopoly. Each of the two firms is a profit maximizer. Let X be the output of firm 1 and Y be the output of firm 2. Assume that each firm takes its competitor's supply as fixed. Further suppose that the two firms have identical cost structures, given by the cost function $C(\cdot)$.

(a) What is the aggregate supply in this market?

(b) What is firm 1's total revenue function? What is its profit function?

(c) What is firm 2's total revenue function? What is its profit function?

(d) Under what circumstances will the actions of the two firms be consistent?

(e) Draw a graph to illustrate the Cournot equilibrium for this problem.

2. Consider the case of a duopoly. Assume that each firm takes its competitor's output as fixed. Let X be the output of firm 1 and Y be the output of firm 2.

Suppose firm 1's reaction function is

$X = a+Y$, where a is a positive constant.

Suppose firm 2's reaction function is

$Y = b-X$, where b is a positive constant.

Find the Cournot equilibrium for this market.

3. Consider the case of a duopoly. Both firms in the market are profit maximizers. Let X be the output of firm 1 and Y be the output of firm 2. Suppose that firm 1 has the reaction function C=C(Y). That is, firm 1's output decision depends on the output of firm 2. Firm 1 assumes that the output of firm 2 is fixed. Firm 2 however, is a bit smarter than firm 1. Firm 2 knows that firm 1 has a reaction function and knows the form of the reaction function. Firm 2 takes firm 1's reactions as given when it makes its output decisions.

Firm 1 has the cost function $C_1=C_1(X)$. Firm 2 has the cost function $C_2=C_2(Y)$.

(a) What is firm 1's profit function that it is trying to maximize?

(b) What is firm 2's profit function that it is trying to maximize?

(c) Interpret the behavior of firm 1 and firm 2. (Hint: Is one firm "leading" the other firm?)

(d) In general, should a firm be a "follower" or a "leader" of another firm?

V. PROBLEM

The European Community and Price Controls for Steel Products

In November 1983, the Common Market Commission of the European Community imposed minimum prices on steel products within the community. The goal of the action was to help Europe's ailing steel industry. Etienne Davignon, the steel industry commissioner, indicated that floor prices were being set on steel products in order to end a price war among European Community makers of steel. He also noted that weak demand had caused steel-product prices to fall below the target levels set a year earlier. He threatened financial sanctions against any companies that failed to abide by the new price regulations.

(a) What is the Common Market Commission of the European Community?

(b) What are the minimum prices that are set by the Commission? (Hint: Are these the competitive prices?)

(c) Why did it become necessary to set new price floors?

(d) The members of the industry Commission agreed to the new price floors in 1983. Would you expect the agreement to survive, given the existing market conditions?

(e) What is the purpose of the financial sanctions?

PART VI. LABOR, CAPITAL, AND DISTRIBUTION

CHAPTER 22

Marginal Productivity and the Demand for Labor: The Fundamentals

I. OVERVIEW

The analysis so far has dealt with consumer theory, the theory of the firm, and different types of market structure in the goods market. In order to complete the analysis of the economy, the market for the services of factors of production must be considered. Of special interest is the market for labor services because the income that workers earn by selling their labor services is the income that is spent on commodities.

The supply and demand theory that was developed in earlier chapters can be applied to labor markets. The concepts of demand and supply elasticities, shifts in the supply and demand functions, and the existence of a market equilibrium that clears the market can all be applied to labor theory.

The demand for labor is known as derived demand. This phrase simply indicates that labor is not demanded directly by consumers. Rather, it is the firm that demands labor services in order to satisfy the demands of consumers for its product. The firm's demand for labor services is derived from the demand for the firm's output. Firms do not hire labor on the basis of any tastes that they might have for certain kinds of labor. Firms do not have tastes to indulge in the same sense that consumers have tastes for particular products. The profits that the firm earns indirectly from the workers' labors is the primary determinant of the firm's derived demand for labor services. Firms hire labor and other factors of production in order to satisfy the consumers' tastes for their products.

Labor is therefore a commodity. The labor market equilibrium occurs at the point of intersection of the labor supply curve and the labor demand curve. At the equilibrium wage rate, the quantity of labor demanded by firms is exactly equal to the quantity of labor supplied by the work force.

The derivation of the labor demand curve is straightforward. The firm's problem of how much labor to employ is analogous to its problem of deciding how much output to produce to maximize profits. Since the production of output depends on the quantity of inputs employed, the firm's choice can be characterized as either a choice of output or a choice of inputs. In order to concentrate on the demand for labor, assume that the quantities of all nonlabor inputs are fixed and constant. Output depends only on the quantity of labor used. The total product curve shows the relationship between the amount of labor employed per unit of time and the quantity of output produced per unit of time. It is possible to derive the total revenue product curve from the total product curve by simply multiplying the price of output by total product. Total revenue product is the revenue that the firm earns when it employs a particular amount of labor. The difference between total revenue and total cost (the amount of labor times the wage rate) is the profit earned by the firm. Profits are maximized if labor is employed at the point where the slope of the total revenue product curve is equal to the total cost curve. The marginal revenue product of labor curve is a plot of the slopes of the total revenue product curve. Profits are therefore maximized at the point of labor employment where marginal revenue product (the slope of the total revenue product curve) is equal to marginal cost (the slope of the total cost curve). This is, once again, the Rule of Rational Life as applied to labor demand theory. The firm's demand curve for labor is just the downward sloping portion of the marginal revenue product curve.

The concept of marginal productivity is extremely useful for determining the distribution of income among the labor and nonlabor factors of production. The theory of marginal productivity asserts that a firm is willing to pay as a wage to labor at most the dollar value of the marginal product due to the hiring of one additional worker. The hourly wage paid to labor is determined at the margin. Formally, profits will be at a maximum when output price times the marginal physical product of labor is equal to the wage rate. The firm hires labor up to the point where the wage rate is equal to the value of the marginal product of labor. The difference between total product and the income paid to labor is equal to the income paid to nonlabor factors of production.

SUMMARY OF KEY CONCEPTS

- factors of production
- discrimination in the labor market
- labor demand curve
- marginal revenue product of labor curve
- derived demand
- distribution of income among factors
- total revenue product curve
- the minimum wage

II. ANSWERS TO WHAT TO READ FOR

22.1 LABOR AS A COMMODITY

1. In what market do consumers earn the income they spend on goods? Consumers earn the income that they spend on goods in the market for factors of production.

2. What is derived demand? The demand for factors of production is a demand by firms, not by consumers. The firms use the factors of production to satisfy the demands of consumers. The demand for the factors of production is derived from the demand for whatever the firm makes. The demand for factors of production is therefore called derived demand.

3. Do firms hire labor for what the labor can do or for who it is? Firms do not have tastes for labor in the same sense that consumers have tastes for particular products. Firms hire labor for what the labor can do and for the indirect profit from the laborers' work.

4. How does one portray racial discrimination in the labor market? Labor is viewed as a commodity. If employers prefer to hire white workers rather than black workers, then a rise in the proportion of blacks to whites in the labor market will cause the relative wage paid to black workers to fall. A firm that discriminates against black workers will pay more for labor than a firm that takes advantage of the lower wage for blacks. Firms that discriminate a lot will be driven out of the market until all firms have the lowest level of discrimination available among the class of existing employers.

5. Does the minimum wage make people better off? The minimum wage causes unemployment. Workers whose value to employers is less than the minimum wage are not employed. The minimum wage forces employers up their demand curves for labor and the low-value workers are not hired.

22.2 MARGINAL PRODUCTIVITY AS THE DEMAND FOR LABOR BY THE FIRM

1. Does the firm choose its level of output or its level of input? The production of output depends on the input. It does not matter whether the firm is viewed as choosing its level of output or choosing its level of input. The demand for labor by a profit-maximizing firm is related to the production function of the firm. The production function indicates how much of each input is required to produce the profit-maximizing level of output.

2. What is the total product of labor curve? The total product of labor curve is a slice of the production function. It relates the amount of output per unit of time to the amount of labor employed per unit of time.

3. The total revenue product of labor? The total revenue product shows how the firm's revenue varies with the amount of labor employed.

4. The marginal revenue product of labor? The marginal revenue product of labor curve is a plot of the slopes of the total revenue product curve.

5. The demand curve for labor? The demand curve for labor shows the amount of labor demanded at various different prices for labor (wages).

6. Does the amount a firm is willing to pay for labor depend on the total, average, or marginal product of labor? The amount a firm is willing to pay for labor depends on the marginal product of labor. The falling portion of the marginal revenue product curve is the demand curve for labor.

7. How does marginal productivity give a theory of the distribution of income among factors of production? The theory of marginal productivity asserts that a firm is willing to pay at most the dollar value of the marginal increment to product due to the hiring of one more unit of labor. The hourly wage of labor is determined at the margin. Also consider the marginal revenue product curve for labor. The entire area under the curve out to the equilibrium amount of labor employed is the total product. Subtract out the rectangle of income to labor. The triangular area that is left is the income of nonlabor factors. In this way, marginal productivity shows how income is divided between different factors of production.

8. What is the analogy with consumer's surplus? The triangular area under the marginal revenue product of labor curve that represents the income of nonlabor factors is equivalent to consumer's surplus. The nonlabor factors of production can be thought of as profit, which the firm is trying to maximize. The triangular area therefore gives the total gains from trade to the firm. This is analogous to consumer's surplus, which gives the total gains from trade to the consumer.

9. How does marginal productivity show the desirability of free immigration? Free immigration causes the existing supply of labor to increase. The increase causes the real wage to fall. Firms are enriched at the expense of workers. The triangular area under the marginal revenue product of labor curve that represents the income of nonlabor factors of production gets larger in area.

III. MULTIPLE CHOICE

1. Suppose all nonlabor factors of production are taken as fixed. The prevailing wage for labor in the United states in 1985 will be determined by
   (a) the marginal product of the labor force in 1985
   (b) the average product of the labor force in 1985
   (c) the total product of the labor force in 1985
   (d) the share of labor in total output in 1985

2. Some employers have a distaste for hiring female workers rather than male workers at the same wage. Suppose the proportion of females to males in the labor force rises. A perfectly functioning labor market will
   (a) drive all such discriminatory employers out of the market
   (b) drive some of these employers out of the market
   (c) result in a rise in the relative wages of females
   (d) result in a fall in the relative wages of males

3. It is often argued that illegal immigration into the United States is a major cause of unemployment in certain geographic regions. This argument ignores the fact that
   (a) marginal productivity is diminishing
   (b) the supply of labor is inelastic
   (c) if immigration is permitted, the wage will fall to induce more employment
   (d) jobs are slots

4. Many economists argue that the minimum wage causes unemployment. A counterargument would be that
   (a) the marginal product of labor never falls below the minimum wage
   (b) working conditions for the employed tend to improve
   (c) the minimum wage encourages improvement in the quality of labor
   (d) the minimum wage encourages improvement in the quality of capital

5. The marginal physical product of labor is
   (a) the amount that an additional worker would produce
   (b) the revenue from the output that an additional worker would produce
   (c) equal to the wage rate
   (d) equal to the firm's profit

IV. EXERCISES

1. Ray Ryan is a pilot for a major passenger airline. Ray earns

the prevailing wage of $50,000 per year. He flies one of the airline's routes three times a week. Ray knows that the airline earns $15,000 in profits every time a flight is flown. He argues that all pilots should be paid much more than the prevailing wage because, in his words, "our true value is much higher than the wage indicates. Those planes could never fly without us." Is Ray Ryan correct in his assessment of a pilot's true value to the airline?

2. The Atlanta Braves baseball team has been an active participant in the free-agent baseball market during the past several years. After the 1978 baseball season, the Braves sought free-agent Pete Rose and overwhelmed all other bidders with their offer. (Rose signed with the Philadelphia Phillies.) After the 1980 season, the Braves pursued Dave Winfield. Ted Turner, the owner of the Braves, invited Winfield to Atlanta as his guest. He took Winfield to parties, Atlanta Hawks basketball games and business meetings, and offered him a lucrative contract. (Winfield signed with the New York Yankees.) After the 1983 season, the Braves sought Rich Gossage. They offered him a five-year, $5.5 million contract. (Gossage signed with the San Diego Padres.)

(a) <u>True or False:</u> The Atlanta Braves are irrational to pursue these high-priced free agents and to offer them such lucrative contracts.

(b) Does the fact that other baseball teams also offered these players lucrative contracts necessarily justify the Braves' strategy?

V. PROBLEM

Marginal Productivity and The Three Stages of Production

Consider Figure 22.1 below. This figure depicts three different stages of production for a competitive firm. Stage one corresponds to the employment of labor to the left of the maximum average product of labor. Stage two corresponds to the employment of labor between maximum average product and zero marginal product. Stage three corresponds to the employment of labor at all points where the marginal product of labor is negative.

Using your knowledge of production theory, cost theory, and the theory of marginal productivity, determine in which stage efficient production occurs.

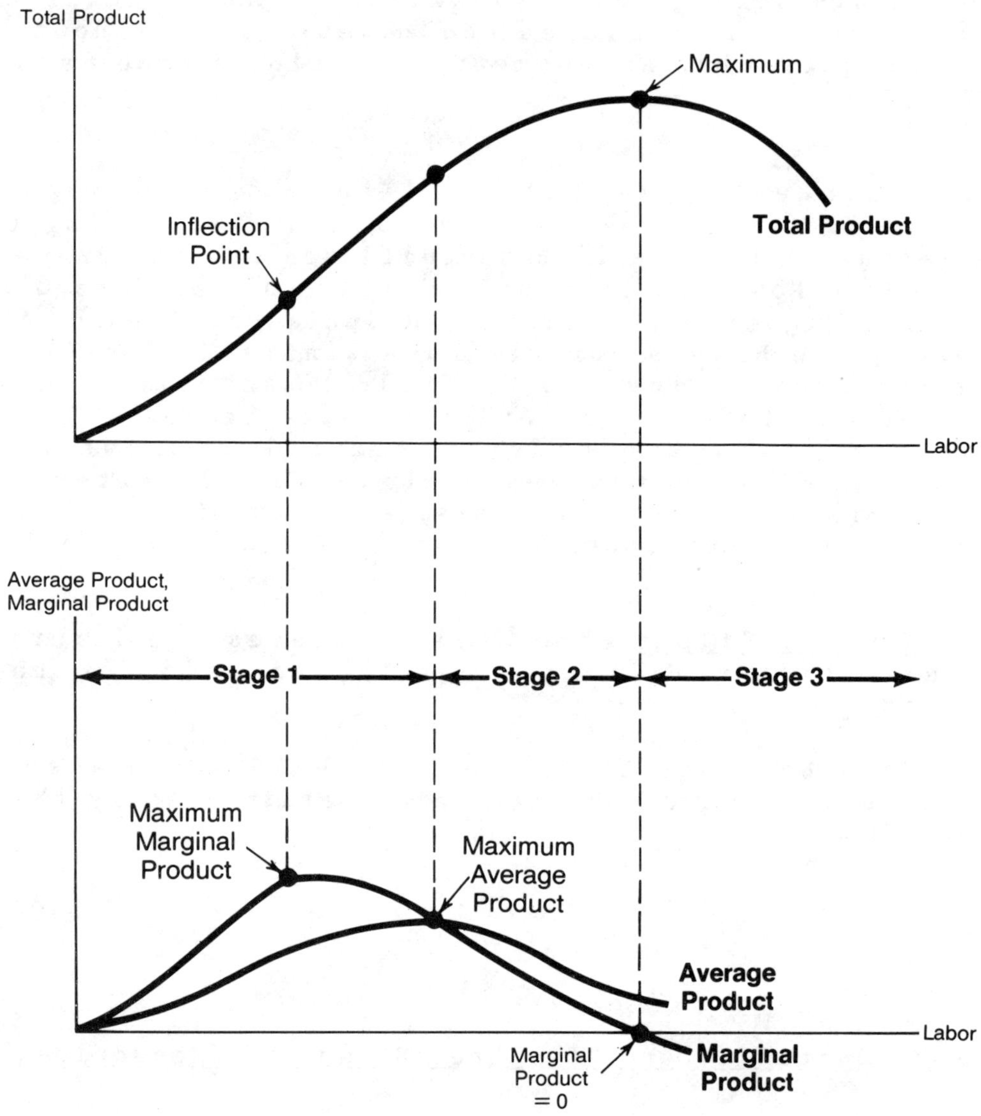

Total Product
Maximum
Inflection Point
Total Product
Labor
Average Product, Marginal Product
Stage 1
Stage 2
Stage 3
Maximum Marginal Product
Maximum Average Product
Average Product
Labor
Marginal Product = 0
Marginal Product

FIGURE 22.1

CHAPTER 23

Marginal Productivity in Theory and Use

I. OVERVIEW

It is possible to extend the theory of marginal productivity to more than one factor of production. It has already been shown that a profit-maximizing firm that uses one factor of production will employ that factor up until the point where marginal revenue product is equal to the price of the factor. A firm that employs several different factors of production will want to apply this rule to each of the factors. The firm will simultaneously satisfy each of the marginal revenue product conditions.

The difficulty with the generalization of this procedure to several factors of production is that if all factors are paid their marginal products, there is no reason why total product will be exactly exhausted. This problem, known as the <u>problem of the exhaustion of the product</u>, is related to the type of returns to scale exhibited by the production function. If a production function exhibits constant returns to scale, then the total product will be exactly exhausted by paying all factors their marginal product. But if a production function exhibits either increasing or decreasing returns to scale, it is not true that total product will be exactly exhausted.

This result about constant returns to scale production functions leads to another important problem. Recall that a firm experiencing constant returns to scale faces a flat marginal cost curve. Under perfect competition, if a price-taking firm faces a flat marginal cost curve, then it will expand output indefinitely or contract output to zero. The question therefore arises as to how a competitive firm can have constant returns to scale. The solution to this problem is to introduce another factor of production called <u>entrepreneurship</u>. Consider that at a competitive equilibrium, the average costs of each firm just exhaust its revenues. This suggests constant returns to scale. In order to ensure that a firm is at the minimum point of long-run average cost, the factor called entrepreneurship is introduced. Any rents that a firm earns in equilibrium can be considered as payments to this new factor of production. Profits are therefore zero in competitive equilibrium, the product is exactly exhausted, and the production function exhibits constant returns to scale.

A useful application of the idea of constant returns to scale is to the problem of measuring the rate at which a production function changes. Under constant returns to scale, the sum of all factor shares of output must exactly equal total output. One can empirically measure the contribution of the rise in each factor of production to the change in total output. The difference between the actual change in output and the sum of the contributions of the factor inputs is the amount by which the production function has shifted. This difference is also known as the <u>residual</u>, <u>total factor productivity change</u>, <u>technical change</u>, or <u>a measure of our ignorance</u>.

<u>SUMMARY OF KEY CONCEPTS</u>

- returns to scale
- exhaustion of the product
- technological change
- Fundamental theorem of marginal productivity
- Euler's theorem
- Cobb-Douglas production function
- total factor productivity

II. <u>ANSWERS TO WHAT TO READ FOR</u>

23.1 MANY INPUTS, CONSTANT RETURNS TO SCALE, AND THE FUNDAMENTAL THEOREM

1. <u>How does a firm decide how much of several factors of production to hire?</u> The firm decides how much of each factor of production to employ by equating the marginal revenue product with the price of the factor. But the marginal revenue product (MRP) curves for each input are related to each other. This is expressed algebraically by saying that the MRP is some function of all of the factors of production. From this MRP function, each of the marginal conditions for the factors of production can be derived. The firm simultaneously solves the equations for all of the marginal conditions.

2. <u>What is the problem of the exhaustion of the product?</u> The problem of the exhaustion of the product is that there does not seem to be any reason why the simultaneous satisfaction of all of the marginal conditions would ensure that exactly the amount of money that came into the firm would be spent.

3. <u>What geometrical device generates a constant-returns-to-scale production function?</u> Consider the case of two inputs. Imagine a production function rising out of the corner of a room. One horizontal edge of the floor is the labor axis, the other horizontal edge of the floor is the capital axis, and the vertical edge of the walls is the output axis. Stick a straight

rod through the origin (the corner where all the edges meet). Rotate the rod around the room in any way whatsoever, while keeping the end of the rod at the origin. Every place through which the rod passed is a point on the surface of the production hill. The surface that has been generated exhibits constant returns to scale.

4. <u>What is the Cobb-Douglas production function?</u> The Cobb-Douglas production function is a particular form for a production surface. The general algebraic form for this function is

$$Q = AK^aL^b$$

where a and b are positive constants, and A is a constant representing the height of the production function.

5. <u>Does the Cobb-Douglas production function always exhibit constant returns to scale?</u> No. It exhibits constant returns to scale whenever the exponents a and b sum to one. If a+b is greater than one, then the production function exhibits increasing returns to scale. If a+b is less than one, the production function exhibits decreasing returns to scale.

6. <u>How can a competitive firm have constant returns to scale?</u> If the production function exhibits constant returns to scale, then payments to factors by marginal products just exhausts the product. The firm would have a flat marginal cost curve. But if a competitive firm has a flat marginal cost curve, then it will expand indefinitely or shrink to a zero output. This problem can be reconciled by supposing all firms are identical but do not have production functions that exhibit constant returns to scale. In a full competitive equilibrium, the entire industry has a cost curve that looks like it arose from a constant returns to scale production function. Each firm finds itself at the bottom of its average cost curve. The average costs of each firm just exhaust its revenues. If the firms are not identical, some will be earning positive rents in equilibrium. But this problem can also be reconciled by introducing another factor called entrepreneurship. The positive profits then simply become payments to this new factor of production.

7. <u>What is the Fundamental Theorem of Marginal Productivity?</u> The Fundamental Theorem asserts that the share of costs paid to labor in a competitive industry that exhibits constant returns to scale is the elasticity of output with respect to labor. A similar assertion can be made about all other factors of production.

23.2 CHANGES IN THE PRODUCTION FUNCTION

1. What is a rising production function? Rising production functions are cases in which more output is obtained from the same factor inputs.

2. A unit isoquant? Suppose the production function exhibits constant returns to scale. The production function can then be represented by a single isoquant. This isoquant is the isoquant for a single unit of output. It is known as the unit isoquant.

3. Is a country with higher output per man always on a higher production function? No. It is difficult to discern whether two observed points are on different production functions (one of which is higher), or simply on different points of the same production function. A higher output per man does not necessarily indicate that one country is on a higher production function, because there are other factors of production that must be considered. That one country has a higher output per man may be indicative of the fact that the other country has a different endowment of the various factors of production.

4. What is total factor productivity change? The residual? Total factor productivity change is a measure of the change in height of a production surface. Consider a constant returns to scale production function. If all factors of production increased 5% during a certain period of time, one would expect that output also increased by 5%. But suppose output in the economy actually went up by 8%. Then for some unexplained reason, the production function rose an extra 3%. This 3% rise in the production function is known as total factor productivity change. It is also known as the residual.

5. How can it be used to find out how much invention and war affected the American economy? Let Q' be the rate of change of output, L' the rate of change of labor supply, and T' the rate of change of the supply of land. Let S_1 be labor's share in output and S_t be land's share in output. The difference between the actual increase in output Q' and the entire rise in inputs $S_1L + S_tT$ is the residual measure of how much productivity has risen. By applying this formula to historical data, one can determine how much invention and war have affected the American economy.

6. Can productivity be measured by prices? Absolutely. Productivity affects the ratio of prices as well as the ratio of quantities. A rise in productivity will reduce the competitive price of output relative to the prices of inputs. The measure of productivity change using prices is a "dual" measure to the measure of productivity change using quantities of inputs and output.

7. <u>Would there be any productivity change if new knowledge were the result of methodical investment?</u> As Griliches and Jorgenson have argued, if invention itself and methodical investment in new knowledge is an economic activity expected to earn normal returns, then there would be no productivity change. All larger output would then be attributable to larger input.

8. <u>Is a country with relatively expensive labor more likely to save labor?</u> Not necessarily. If inventive activity is free, then a labor dollar saved is no different than a capital or land dollar saved.

9. <u>Why is knowledge itself difficult to analyze economically?</u> Knowledge is a scarce resource. But knowledge is also a public good. It is difficult to analyze economically because it is an externality and expensive to make private.

III. MULTIPLE CHOICE

1. Which of the following asserts that exhaustion of products is guaranteed for production functions that are homogeneous of degree one?
   (a) Euler's theorem on homogeneous functions
   (b) The fundamental theorem of marginal productivity
   (c) Constant average product
   (d) Constant marginal product

2. After the American Civil War, total agricultural output in the South fell by about one third. This fall can be accounted for by
   (a) destruction of agricultural land
   (b) a fall in inputs
   (c) productivity regression
   (d) a fall in inputs and productivity regression

3. The fundamental theorem of marginal productivity is valid for a competitive industry experiencing
   (a) decreasing returns to scale
   (b) constant returns to scale
   (c) increasing returns to scale
   (c) any type of returns to scale

4. Which of the following describes the general version of the Cobb-Douglas production function?
   (a) decreasing returns to scale
   (b) constant returns to scale
   (c) increasing returns to scale
   (d) any type of returns to scale

5. In the Cobb-Douglas production function Q=AKL, the A is

(a) a measure of the returns to scale
(b) indicative of constant returns to scale
(c) a measure of the height of the production function
(d) a function of output

6. Which of the following does <u>not</u> characterize the production function Q=KL?
(a) it exhibits increasing returns to scale
(b) rewarding factors by marginal product never exhausts the product
(c) the marginal product of K is always equal to L
(d) it is a proportional equation in L

7. With constant returns to scale, a production function can be represented completely by
(a) the value of marginal product
(b) Euler's theorem
(c) any Cobb-Douglas production function
(d) the unit isoquant

8. The optimal price for the use of knowledge once it is produced is
(a) what the holder of the patent or copyright can extract
(b) its opportunity cost
(c) zero
(d) a sunk cost

9. In a competitive industry experiencing constant returns to scale, the share of each factor input in total costs is equal to
(a) its marginal product
(b) its average product
(c) the elasticity of output with respect to the input
(d) the elasticity of substitution

10. The question of whether the technology of one country was superior to the technology of another country reduces to the question of
(a) how much higher one production function is over the other
(b) which production function exhibits increasing returns to scale
(c) which country had the higher output per person
(d) where on the unit isoquant each country is

IV. EXERCISES

1. Consider the linear homogeneous Cobb-Douglas production function

$$Q = f(K,L) = AK^{a}L^{1-a}$$

where A and a are positive constants, and $0<a<1$. Prove that the average product function depends only upon the ratio in which the inputs are combined.

2. Given the Cobb-Douglas production function

$$Q = AK^aL^b$$

show that $a+b>1$ implies increasing returns to scale.

V. PROBLEM

The Theory of Technical Change

In 1957, Robert Solow wrote an article entitled, "Technical Change and the Aggregate Production Function." The objective of the paper was to develop a method for separating changes in output due to technical change from those due to changes in the availability of capital. He used this method to estimate an "aggregate production function" for the United States. The purpose of this problem is to introduce you to the method of measuring technical change that Solow developed.

Let Q=output, K=capital, and L=labor, where capital and labor are measured in "physical" units. Express the aggregate production function as $Q=F(K,L;t)$, where t is time and a proxy for technical change. Define technical change as any kind of shift in the production function. Assume the special case of Hicks neutral technical change:

$$K' = A(t)K$$
$$L' = A(t)L$$

K' is "effective" capital and L' is "effective" labor; that is, capital and labor after technical change. (Shifts in the production function are neutral if they leave the marginal rates of technical substitution unchanged. They simply increase or decrease the output attainable from given inputs.)

(a) Express the production function in terms of effective capital and effective labor. (Hint: Substitute the expressions for K' and L' in place of K and L, respectively.)

The production function derived in part (a) is a function of A, K and L. A(t) measures the cumulated effect of technical shifts over time. The object of the rest of this exercise is to obtain an expression for A(t) in terms of market observable variables.

(b) Differentiate totally the production function from part (a) and divide this expression by Q. The result should be an expression for the rate of change of output.

(c) Let w_k be the relative share of capital in output and w_l be the relative share of labor. Express the equation derived in part (b) in terms of these relative shares. The result will be an expression for the rate of change of output in terms of the relative shares, and the rates of change of A, K and L.

(d) If all factors are classified as either K or L, then what must be true about the sum of the factor shares?

(e) If one assumes that factors are paid their marginal products, what must be true about the returns to scale exhibited by this production function?

(f) Let $q=Q/L$, $k=K/L$, and $w_l=1-w_k$. Rewrite the equation derived in part (c) in terms of the rates of change of q, k and A.

(g) What conclusion can you draw about how one can obtain A(t) from empirical data?

CHAPTER 24

Misallocation and Monopoly in Factor Markets

I. OVERVIEW

The price of labor determines through the marginal revenue product curve the amount of labor purchased by the firm. The real wage rate is determined by the amount of labor hired through the marginal physical product curve. If factor markets are functioning properly, workers with comparable skills will earn the same wage in all industries. If a wage differential exists between industries, workers will shift into the industry with the higher wage rate until the values of the marginal products of labor, and therefore the wage rates, are equalized. This is another manifestation of the rule of rational life.

The idea that the values of the marginal products of labor must be equalized across industries is useful for solving many different problems. It can be used to analyze the effects of a technological improvement in a particular industry or location. For example, a technological improvement in word processors might raise the marginal product for labor. The wage rate for typists using word processors will rise, since the typists are worth more. Output will also rise since their productivity is higher. The value of the marginal product of typists has risen. This will cause a migration of labor into the specialized typing profession until wage rates across industries are equalized again.

The idea can also be used to understand why bad allocations of the labor force sometimes occur. One such application is to the fisheries problem. The problem, also known as the common pool problem, is that overfishing occurs because the sea is not owned by anyone. The fish in the sea are a scarce resource, but since no landlords own the sea, no rents are charged for the scarce resource. If rents could be charged, then labor in fishing would earn only its marginal product. The remainder of output would go to the landlords in the form of rents. But since rents are not charged, labor in fishing earns its average product, leaving no remainder of output. Fishermen will keep fishing until the average product of labor in fishing is equal to the marginal product of labor in other industries. A misallocation of labor occurs.

The fisheries problem illustrates that one source of misallocation of factors of production is the absence of property rights. Another important cause of misallocation of resources is the exploitation of bigness. A big firm that is a monopoly or a monopsony will participate in fewer exchanges of labor than is socially optimal. Recall that a monopoly recognizes that it faces a downward sloping demand curve and therefore a marginal revenue lower than price. In its decision to hire labor, it must be concerned with the problem of spoilage. It views its benefits from labor as the marginal revenue product, not the value of marginal product. (Marginal revenue product is the additional revenue that an extra unit of labor produces, allowing for spoilage. The value of marginal product is the additional revenue that an extra unit of labor produces, not allowing for spoilage.) A firm with monopsony power will also be faced with the spoilage problem. Both a monopoly and a monopsony set the marginal revenue product of labor equal to the marginal cost of labor.

The degree to which a firm can exercise its monopoly power depends on the elasticity of demand for its product. Similarly, the degree to which a firm can exercise its monopsony power depends on the elasticity of supply of the factor input. Since these elasticities are observable, the algebra of monopoly and monopsony can be used to measure the degree of monopoly power and monopsony power that a firm has. Simple monopoly and monopsony are both inefficient. But like discriminatory monopoly, a monopsonist that can discriminate perfectly can achieve an efficient outcome. The equilibrium for perfectly discriminatory monopsony is the same as the equilibrium for perfect competition.

SUMMARY OF KEY CONCEPTS

marginal value product	value of marginal product
the fisheries problem	equalization of marginal product
the common pool problem	sharecropping
the algebra of monopsony	discriminatory monopsony
octopus effect	

II. ANSWERS TO WHAT TO READ FOR

24.1 GOOD AND BAD ALLOCATION

1. Is the value of the marginal product of labor higher in capital-intensive industries? It is meaningless to say that the value of the marginal product of labor is higher in an industry simply because it chooses a capital-intensive point. What matters is the marginal value product. If the marginal value product is higher in one industry, then the higher wage would

attract workers out of other industries and into that industry. Workers would continue to shift into the industry with the higher marginal value product until the values of the marginal products and the wages in all industries were equal.

2. <u>How is the value of marginal product used to think about who benefits from technological improvements?</u> A technological improvement will cause the wage rate to rise, since the labor in the industry is worth more. Output rises because productivity has risen. The value of the marginal product of labor rises because its marginal physical product has risen. The higher wage will cause labor to flow into the industry from other industries. This flow will continue until the values of the marginal products of labor and the wages are equalized again across all industries.

3. <u>Why is overfishing bad?</u> Overfishing is bad because the fish in the sea are not treated as though they are scarce resources. Misallocation of resources occurs.

4. <u>Will fisheries that are not owned by someone be used correctly?</u> No. Labor can farm either the land or the sea. Labor that farms the land earns only its marginal product. A remainder of output is earned as rents by the owners of the land. But if fisheries are not owned by someone, then no landlord can charge rent on the use of the sea. All of the fish that are caught therefore go to labor. Labor in fishing earns its average product. There is no remainder of output left for landlords. The fish are not treated as a scarce resource.

5. <u>In what way is sharecropping like a tax?</u> Under a sharecropping agreement, the landlord gets a share of the crop that is farmed by the laborer. Suppose that the landlord and the laborer agree that the landlord will receive 40% of the crop. If the worker's marginal product is $x worth of the crop, then she would be allowed to keep only .6($x). This is very similar to a tax on labor in agriculture.

6. <u>What feature of the contract prevents it from having the efficiency effects of a tax?</u> One is tempted to conclude from the tax analogy that sharecropping is a bad system because it discourages the laborer from working the crop to the point where her full marginal product is equal to the wage she can earn elsewhere. But this conclusion is false. It is false because the landlord is not a tax collector. A tax collector cannot force a laborer to work out to the point where her full marginal product is equal to the wage she can earn elsewhere. But a landlord can include in the sharecropping agreement a condition that the laborer work the same number of hours as she would in the absence of any agreement, regardless of whether her share of the $x marginal product equals her alternative wage.

24.2 MONOPOLY IN FACTOR MARKETS

1. How does monopoly or monopsony affect the markets for factors? A firm with monopoly or monopsony power sets the marginal revenue product equal to the marginal cost. If a firm has monopoly power in the market for its output, then in the hiring of some factor input, it will view its benefits as the marginal revenue product, not the value of marginal product. If the firm has monopsony power in an input market such as labor, then the marginal cost of the factor is not equal to the average cost (the wage). The marginal cost is higher by the higher wage the firm will have to pay to existing workers in the course of attracting more workers to the firm.

2. What is the difference between the value of marginal product and the marginal value product? The value of the marginal product of labor is the price of the product multiplied by the marginal physical product. Marginal value product is the price of the product multiplied by the amount of output produced per hour.

3. What is the difference between average and marginal factor costs? Average cost is equal to the total cost of the factor divided by the amount of the factor input employed. Marginal cost is the additional cost incurred by hiring one more unit of the factor input. For example, the average cost of labor is equal to the total labor cost divided by the amount of labor employed. The marginal cost of labor is the additional cost that would be incurred by hiring one more unit (hour) of labor.

4. How does one measure the monopsony power of the owners of baseball teams? One can use the algebra of monopsony to measure the monopsony power of the owners of baseball teams. Recall the equation that describes the behavior of a monopsonist:

Marginal revenue product
= (Price of the product) x (Marginal physical product of labor) x (1-1/elasticity of demand for the product)

= (wage rate)(1+1/elasticity of supply of labor)

= marginal labor cost

The equilibrium condition for a baseball owner is to set his hiring such that the marginal revenue product equals the wage times the value of (1 + 1/elasticity of supply of labor). It is possible to observe the percentage of their marginal revenue product that baseball players are paid. The equilibrium condition can then be solved to yield the elasticity of supply of labor.

5. What is the octopus effect? The octopus effect is a

tendency for a monopoly in a factor market to extend its "tentacles" forward into the product market. It is another indication that monopoly is inefficient, unless the monopoly is perfectly discriminatory.

III. MULTIPLE CHOICE

1. Suppose a technological innovation is introduced into a small farming village. This technological innovation raises the value of marginal product of labor. Suppose nonlabor inputs are supplied inelastically to the village. The net gain in output due to this technological innovation becomes
   (a) income to labor
   (b) income to nonlabor factors of production
   (c) income to both labor and nonlabor factors of production
   (b) a social gain not realized by the village

2. A system of sharecropping is often compared to a system of taxation. One would expect after studying empirical data that the analogy is false because
   (a) sharecropping and rented land have identical outputs
   (b) sharecropping does not characterize any rich agricultural regions
   (c) sharecropping and renting do not coexist
   (d) output per acre is lower under sharecropping

3. The common pool problem is similar to
   (a) a tax on labor
   (b) sharecropping
   (c) perfect competition in factor markets
   (d) a prisoner's dilemma

4. If factor markets are functioning properly, then workers of the same quality will receive the same wage in all industries. This fact is another manifestation of
   (a) monopoly power in factor markets
   (b) monopsony power in factor markets
   (c) the rule of rational life
   (d) barriers to entry

5. The marginal physical product of labor is equal to
   (a) the value of the marginal product of labor
   (b) the additional revenue, allowing for spoilage, that another unit of labor produces
   (c) marginal revenue product
   (d) the amount that an extra unit of labor produces

6. The equilibrium for perfectly discriminating monopsony is the same as
   (a) the equilibrium for monopoly
   (b) the equilibrium for perfect competition

(c) the equilibrium for oligopoly
(d) labor monopoly

7. Suppose that the Teamsters Union has a monopoly on truck-driving labor. The Teamsters will set the wage to a competitive trucking company that has a downward-sloping demand for labor at
(a) a high monopoly wage
(b) the competitive wage
(c) the wage that minimizes labor income
(d) the wage that minimizes expenditures on labor

8. A monopoly in a factor market facing a derived demand has an incentive to buy out its victims because
(a) the monopoly point will maximize its profits
(b) the curve of marginal revenue to the labor monopoly is always downward sloping
(c) there are still unexploited opportunities for mutually advantageous exchange
(d) the octopus effect is inefficient

9. The fisheries problem occurs because
(a) of a failure to charge rent and a good allocation of the labor force
(b) of a failure to charge rent and a bad allocation of the labor force
(c) labor earns only its marginal product
(d) the fish in the sea are viewed as a scarce resource

10. Suppose a technological innovation is introduced into a small farming village. This technological innovation raises the value of marginal product of labor. Further suppose that labor from other regions and industries is not allowed to enter the village. The result will be
(a) a fall in the wage rate in the village
(b) a fall in the wage rate outside of the village
(c) a higher level of national income
(d) a lower level of national income

IV. EXERCISES

1. Does a monopolist use inputs efficiently? Consider the case of a monopolist employing two inputs, capital and labor. Explain your answer.

2. If a firm is a monopolist in an input market, the price of the input will depend upon the purchases of this firm. If the monopolist in the output market is a monopolist in the input market, then this firm's individual input demand is the market input demand as well.

(a) Suppose there is a positively sloped supply curve for a factor input. What will input price be a function of?

(b) When a firm is a perfect competitor, it can purchase as much of an input as it desires without affecting the input price. What then is input price equal to?

(c) Define the marginal expense of an input as the addition to total variable cost that is attributable to the addition of one more unit of the input to the production process. Complete the following table for the monopolist:

Price	Quantity Supplied	Marginal Expense of Input
$1	10	
3	11	
5	13	
7	15	
9	17	
11	19	
13	21	

(d) What do columns 1 and 2 in the table represent?

(e) What does column 3 represent?

PROBLEM

The U.S. Postal Service and Multiple-Unit Mail Boxes

For many years, small companies made most of the mail boxes installed in housing developments. Hundreds of distributors purchased the multiple-unit mail boxes from these companies and sold them to thousands of contractors and building owners.

Beginning in 1980, the United States Postal Service became the dominant buyer of multiple-unit mail boxes. The boxes purchased by the post office are "cluster boxes," which are large groups of mail boxes that are placed at a central point of a housing complex. It prefers this type of box because it helps to save on delivery time, fuel and money. The Postal Service admitted that its objective is to provide the boxes to contractors and to maintain them free of charge,

The Postal Service has bought as many as 131,000 multiple-unit mail boxes in a single year, at a cost of $23 million. After its entry into the market in 1980, the post office became the only buyer of these units. Many of the manufacturers of cluster mail boxes have now begun to move into other markets. In response to complaints from some of these manufacturers, the Postal Service responded, "It is an uncomfortable fact of economic life that the workings of any market will not produce equally cheerful results for all producers or sellers."

(a) Prior to the Postal Service's entry into the market for multiple-unit mail boxes, what type of market structure would you expect to have prevailed for this industry?

(b) After the post office entered the cluster mail box market in 1980, what did it become relative to the entire market?

(c) With the post office's entry into the market, what would you expect to have happened to the prices of cluster mail boxes?

(d) Why did many manufacturers of cluster mail boxes leave the industry after the entry of the Postal Service?

CHAPTER 25

The Supply of Labor

I. OVERVIEW

The discussion so far has dealt with the demand for factors of production. We now turn our attention to the supply of the factors. The <u>principle of compensating differentials</u> characterizes the way in which factors of production are supplied to any job. The principle asserts that a worker's pay in any job must equal her pay in any other job. The term "pay" includes compensation in the form of money, working conditions, and happiness. The principle is an equilibrium condition. If it is not satisfied, then workers will shift between jobs until the condition is re-established.

The theory of equalizing differentials can be expressed in terms of indifference curve theory. Workers have preferences for different types of jobs. The different jobs can be viewed as different commodities amongst which the worker must choose. An indifference map represents the worker's preferences for the different jobs. A budget line gives the terms of exchange between the two jobs. The budget line indicates which job is a better way of earning commodities. The point of tangency between the budget line and an indifference curve is the point of maximum utility for the worker. It shows which job is the better way of earning commodities (for any given hour worked).

The equilibrium point shows the allocation of the worker's time between the different jobs that will maximize her happiness. But people usually specialize in only one job. The worker must be paid a compensating differential in order to specialize in one particular job. For example, suppose a consumer is faced with a choice between working as an airline pilot or as a waitress. Her preference is to work as an airline pilot. In order to induce her to specialize in waitressing, she would have to be paid more per hour than as an airline pilot. She would be paid a positive compensating differential. The size of the compensating differential can be determined by drawing a 45-degree indifference curve. A 45-degree indifference curve would represent a consumer who did not care which job she had. The two jobs are perfect substitutes. The divergence between the 45-degree line and the true budget line at the point of equilibrium is the compensating differential.

The problem of labor supply can be extended to an analysis of the worker's choice between labor and leisure. Leisure includes all uses of time other than working for wages. The worker has preferences for work and play, which are represented by an indifference map. The worker is also endowed with 24 hours per day, which must be allocated between labor and leisure. This 24-hour constraint is represented by a budget line whose slope is the real wage rate. The equilibrium point occurs at the tangency between the budget line and an indifference curve. The tangency shows the number of hours allocated to both labor and leisure.

The equilibrium allocation of a worker's time between labor and leisure depends crucially on the shape of the worker's indifference curves. The worker's response to any change in the wage rate will consist of an income effect and a substitution effect. If leisure is a normal good (as would be expected) and the substitution effect dominates, then a rise in the wage rate will cause the quantity of labor supplied to rise. But if the income effect dominates, then the unusual situation arises that the quantity of labor supplied declines as the wage rate increases. This phenomenon is depicted by a backward-bending labor supply curve.

SUMMARY OF KEY CONCEPTS

compensating differentials
the labor-leisure choice
income subsidies
shadow wage
backward-bending supply
negative income tax

II. ANSWERS TO WHAT TO READ FOR

25.1 THE LEADING IDEA IN LABOR SUPPLY: COMPENSATING DIFFERENTIALS

1. What is the principle of compensating differentials? The principle says that a person's pay in one job must equal her pay in another. More precisely, the pay of the marginal worker who is indifferent between the two jobs must be equal in the two jobs.

2. How are compensating differentials determined in the market? The principle of compensating differentials is an equilibrium condition. If it is not satisfied, then workers will move around between jobs until it is re-established. The whole pay that a worker can earn in any job is determined by the amount of competition the worker faces.

3. <u>If most people dislike jobs as pipefitters relative to jobs as professors, which profession will earn a compensating differential?</u> If most people dislike jobs as pipefitters relative to jobs as professors, then pipefitters will earn a compensating differential. Pipefitters will earn more per hour in order to compensate them for their general distaste for the job relative to professing.

25.2 THE CHOICE BETWEEN WORK AND LEISURE

1. <u>What is the economist's definition of leisure?</u> Economists define leisure as all uses of time other than working for wages.

2. <u>Should its value be included in the national income?</u> Absolutely. Much of leisure time is spent in activities such as growing home vegetable gardens, repairing one's own family car, and repairing things around the house. All of these nonmarket activities raise the income of the nation. The problem is that the shadow wages for these activities are difficult to measure. But this difficulty is not a justification for excluding the value of these activities from national income measures.

3. <u>What is the analogy between the theory of consumption and the theory of the supply of labor?</u> The theory of the supply of labor is analogous to consumption theory with one commodity. The commodity is leisure. A worker who is allocating hours of her time to leisure and labor faces a budget constraint. The slope of the budget constraint is the real wage. Both leisure and the commodities earned through labor are goods. The worker's indifference curves between the two therefore have the usual smooth and convex shape.

4. <u>How can supply curves slope backwards?</u> The response of labor supply to changes in the wage rate consist of an income effect and a substitution effect. Consider a rise in the wage rate. An increase in the wage rate will cause the worker's total income to rise. If leisure is a normal good, then an increase in total income will cause the number of hours spent in leisure to rise. The substitution effect is due to the increase of the relative price of leisure to other commodities. The income effect depends upon the shape of the worker's indifference curve. If the income effect is large enough so that it outweighs the substitution effect, then the worker will supply less labor as the wage rate increases.

5. <u>Does an income subsidy reduce work?</u> <u>How?</u> An income subsidy with no strings attached will cause the recipient to work less. The income subsidy puts the recipient on a higher budget line. Leisure is a normal good. The worker will supply less labor at the given wage rate.

6. <u>What is a negative income tax?</u> Society's desires to encourage people to work while at the same time helping them to maintain some minimum level of income are inconsistent. An income subsidy provides the recipient with an incentive to work less. An income subsidy that requires the worker to give back a dollar of subsidy if she goes out and earns another dollar at work causes the workers to work even less. The negative income tax is a scheme that moderates this disincentive to work. The scheme is a simple one. It allows the recipient of the income subsidy to keep some of the extra money she earns at work. Rather than requiring the worker to return one dollar of subsidy for each dollar earned at work, the negative income tax requires the worker to return an amount less than one dollar for each dollar earned at work.

25.3 THE CHOICE OF SCHEMES OF PAYMENT

1. <u>Where do the budget lines facing a supplier of labor come from?</u> The budget lines that firms offer to their workers are those budget lines that make the most money for the firm. But since both the workers and the firms must agree on the budget lines, both must be made better off by them.

2. <u>How does overtime induce workers to work more for less?</u> A payment mechanism that allows for overtime is a two-part pay scheme. Two-part pay schemes are schemes for allowing price discrimination by the firm. Recall that a firm can do better if it can price discriminate.

3. <u>Is a piece rate always better than payment by the hour in getting workers to work?</u> To pay someone by piece is to pay them by how much they produce. The (fallacious) idea behind the piece-rate mechanism is that it will induce someone to always put in the last ounce of effort. Under the piece-rate scheme, the employer gives the worker a schedule of payments and lets the worker choose her output. Under a salary mechanism, the employer assigns the level of output to the worker and at the same time agrees on the total pay for the job. This total pay is based on market competition. If the worker does not produce the required level of output, she will be fired. Both systems end up at the same levels of output and pay.

4. <u>How can the leisure/commodity diagram be modified to show punishment as well as pay?</u> Punishment and pay are symmetric ways of dealing with workers. The worker's indifference curve between work and leisure determines the amount of punishment (in terms of commodities taken away) that is necessary to induce the laborer to work a certain amount of time. This amount of punishment is symmetric to the size of the bribe that is necessary to compel the worker to work. The bribe is the one of

perfect wage discrimination.

III. MULTIPLE CHOICE

1. The principle of compensating differentials says that a person's whole pay in one job must equal her pay in another. This means that in all jobs her
(a) levels of happiness must be equal
(b) her money income must be equal
(c) working conditions must be the same
(d) happiness plus money income plus working conditions must be equal

2. Richard Reichart is an assistant professor of economics. Reichart earns $20,000 per year as an academic. He knows that if he worked instead in New York as a corporate executive he could earn $50,000, but he still chooses to be an academic. This means that
(a) Reichart is not maximizing his utility
(b) he would have to be paid a positive compensating differential to work in the corporate world
(c) the corporate world offers him a riskier occupation
(d) the academic profession offers him a riskier occupation

3. A compensating differential is determined through
(a) competition
(b) government regulation
(c) riskiness of occupations
(d) minimum wages

4. Bob Connors works at the Tennis Pro Camp during his summer vacation from college. At the end of every summer, Bob and the other tennis instructors steal the tennis balls and take them back to college. The management of the camp is aware of this theft but choose not to do anything about it. The management takes this attitude because
(a) it knows that it would be impossible to enforce any regulations against stealing tennis balls
(b) it allows them to set compensating differentials equal to zero
(c) it allows them to pay the marginal worker a higher wage rate
(d) it views the tennis balls as part of the counselors' whole wage

5. A 45-degree indifference curve indicates that the consumer views two jobs as
(a) inferior goods
(b) perfect complements
(c) perfect substitutes
(d) independent goods

6. Indifference curves for most jobs have the shape that yields corner solutions because
   (a) workers often perform secondary jobs at home
   (b) workers usually specialize in only one job
   (c) workers often work overtime
   (d) shadow wages are usually zero

7. Mildred Winger is a recent graduate of UCLA. Her degree was awarded by the Economics Department at UCLA. Mildred is anxious to become a management trainee for a major corporation in Los Angeles. Mildred loves living in big cities. After spending three months job hunting, Mildred has received two job offers. One job offer from a major corporation in Los Angeles is for $11,000 per year. The other offer is for a $35,000 job as an administrative assistant for a public utility commission in Kansas. The corporation in Los Angeles has refused to match the dollar amount of the Kansas offer. This is not surprising because the corporate management knows that relative to the Kansas offer
   (a) they can pay Mildred a negative compensating differential because of her preferences
   (b) they can pay Mildred a zero compensating differential because of her preferences
   (c) they can pay Mildred a positive compensating differential because of her preferences
   (d) they can pay Mildred a positive shadow price

8. The opportunity cost of leisure is
   (a) the wage rate
   (b) the income effect
   (c) the substitution effect
   (d) often negative

9. A shadow wage is
   (a) a dollar value for what is produced in a market activity
   (b) a dollar value for what is produced in a nonmarket activity
   (c) a compensating differential
   (d) not relevant to national income measures

10. A worker supplying labor faces a budget constraint in allocating her hours between labor and leisure. The slope of the budget constraint is equal to
   (a) a negative shadow wage
   (b) the compensating differential
   (c) the real wage rate
   (d) the elasticity of substitution

IV. EXERCISES

1. The phenomenon of a backward-bending labor supply curve is well-known in economic theory. Consider Figure 25.1 which depicts a labor demand (l_d) and labor supply (l_s) situation.

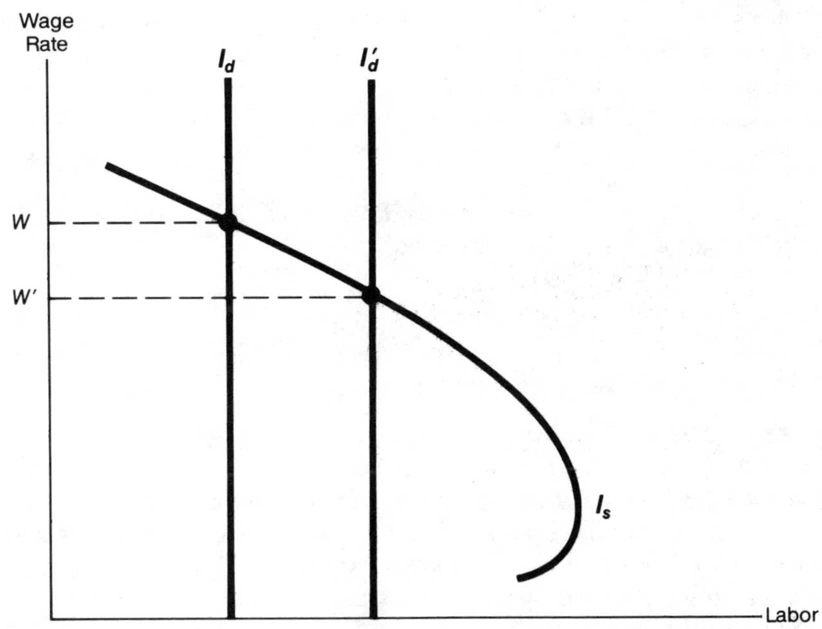

FIGURE 25.1

Suppose labor demand increases from l_d to l_d'. The prediction from neoclassical comparative statics is that wages will rise. But in the situation depicted in Figure 25.1, wages will fall rather than rise.

(a) Explain this seeming contradiction with standard supply-demand analysis.

(b) Assume there are no barriers to entry of new workers into this market. What affect will the movement of workers between markets have on the outcome of the increase in labor demand?

(c) What conclusion can you draw about the backward-bending labor supply curve?

2. At the start of the 1984 football season, the Pittsburgh Steelers cut running back Franco Harris from their team. Harris, who had been a star with the team for many years, was holding out for a larger salary increase. The Steelers had offered to increase his salary from \$385,000 per year to \$600,000 per year.

Harris was asking for $1.25 million for two years on a guaranteed contract. At the time he was cut, Franco Harris was within 363 yards of Jim Brown's all-time career rushing record. No other teams signed Harris to a contract prior to the start of the season.

(a) What was Franco Harris worth to the Pittsburgh Steelers at the time they cut him from the team? Was the $600,000 offer that the Steeler's made to Harris "exorbitant"?

(b) Was the Steeler's decision to finally cut Harris from the team inconsistent with their earlier valuation of his worth?

(c) How can one use observations of the market for football players to ascertain Harris' worth?

V. PROBLEM

Overtime Pay For Overtime Work

Most union-management contracts require overtime pay for overtime work. An important question that management faces is how much overtime work a worker will choose (if she could). Assume that the overtime wage rate is higher than the regular wage rate. Determine the effects of overtime wages on a worker's choice between work and leisure by using the labor-leisure framework of analysis.

CHAPTER 26

Capital's Supply and Demand

I. OVERVIEW

A dollar today is worth more than a dollar tomorrow. A dollar that is earned today can be invested at the market rate of interest. The dollar earned tomorrow is a dollar without interest. There is an opportunity cost to waiting for the dollar. The opportunity cost is the interest foregone.

The idea that a dollar today is different from a dollar tomorrow has important implications for investment analysis. Suppose a firm (or government agency) is considering investing in a project. The project will over time yield monetary returns to the firm. But the money that the firm might invest in the project can also be spent on alternative investments, or placed in a bank where it will earn the prevailing market rate of interest. The firm must compare the cost of the project to the potential future stream of income from the project. Its decision about whether to invest in the project will depend greatly on the market rate of interest.

Suppose the firm knows the future yield from the project. It can use the <u>general discounting formula</u> to determine the price it should pay for the expected future stream of income. This downward valuation of the future income stream, based on the market rate of interest, is known as <u>discounting</u>. If the real interest rate is high, then a project with prospects in the distant future is worth little today. If the real interest rate is low, then a project with distant prospects is worth more. Alternatively, the firm can calculate the sum of money today that would earn the projected stream of income if the sum were invested in a bank at the prevailing rate of interest. This sum of money is called the <u>present value</u> of the stream of income. If the price of the project is greater than the present value of the stream of income, the firm should not invest in the project. If the price of the project is less than the present value of the stream of income, the firm should invest in the project. But the firm must always be aware of the fact that the future returns on any project are <u>expected</u> returns. The price of any project or asset embodies expectations about the future.

Investment in capital implies a trade-off between consumption today and consumption tomorrow. Future consumption requires savings and investment today. Some present consumption must be sacrificed. If the sacrifice is made for consumption tomorrow, then the present value of production should be maximized in order to make the opportunities for consumption as large as possible. Firms attempt to maximize present value in order to maximize their wealth. Workers also maximize their present value by investing in the improvement of their own skills; that is, by investing in human capital.

SUMMARY OF KEY CONCEPTS

- cost of capital
- nominal rate of return
- capital gains
- present value
- annuity
- capitalization
- separation theorem
- real rate of return
- depreciation
- discounting
- perpetuity
- general discounting formula
- internal rate of return

II. ANSWERS TO WHAT TO READ FOR

26.1 THE INTEREST RATE

1. Why is a dollar later worth less than a dollar now? A dollar later is worth less than a dollar now because there is a positive rate of interest. A dollar that is earned now begins to earn interest now. By waiting for a dollar later, one foregoes the interest that the dollar could have been earning. There is an opportunity cost to waiting.

2. What is the full rental rate of capital? The full rental rate of capital is $(i+\delta-P^*)P_k$. The first term is the interest lost by spending money on capital, the second term is the whole depreciation of the capital, and the third term is the capital gain due to changes in the price of capital over time.

3. What is the difference between nominal and real interest rates? Nominal interest rates include the rate of inflation. Real interest rates are adjusted for inflation. A nominal interest rate equals the real rate plus the rate of inflation.

4. What are discounting, present value, perpetuities, and the general discounting formula? A dollar tomorrow is worth less than a dollar today. A person would be willing to pay less than a dollar today for the privilege of getting the dollar tomorrow. The amount less than a dollar that one would be willing to pay

depends on the rate of interest. This downward valuation of future income is called discounting.

An asset today earns a stream of income in the future. The price of an asset today must be equal to the sum of money that could earn the stream of income if invested in a bank at the going rate of interest. This sum of money is called the present value of the stream of income.

A perpetuity is an annual stream of income that is paid forever. The principal is never repaid.

The general discounting formula is:

$$P = [R_1/(1+i)] + [R_2/(1+i)^2] + \dots + [R_n/(1+i)^n]$$

where P is the present value of an asset, R_j is the stream of income in year j, i is the interest rate, and N is the total number of years.

5. <u>How does the expected future return affect asset prices now?</u> Expected returns are capitalized into the value of the asset earning them. Expected returns are made into a capital sum that can be bought and sold today. The price of any asset in this way embodies expectations about the future.

26.2 SUPPLY AND DEMAND CURVES

1. <u>How do markets fix the price of the last factor of production, capital?</u> A controversial assertion in economics is that capital has a demand curve and that the interest rate is related to its price.

2. <u>How is the choice between present and future consumption represented diagramatically?</u> The choice is represented on a diagram with present consumption plotted on one axis and future consumption plotted on the second axis. Plotted on the axes is the production possibility curve and future/present indifference curves. The point of tangency between the production possibility curve and one of the indifference curves is the equilibrium between present and future consumption.

3. <u>What is the separation theorem?</u> The separation theorem says that the slope of the market line of borrowing and lending (in the diagram of present/future consumption) determines the point

of production and the point of consumption. The production decision and the consumption decision are independent of each other.

4. What is the internal rate of return? Businesses often make decisions about whether certain projects should be undertaken. The criterion they follow is that a project should be done if it adds to the firm's wealth. The internal rate of return is the interest rate that brings the present value of the stream of benefits into equality with the present value of the stream of costs.

5. What is human capital? Just as businesses invest in capital equipment, people invest in themselves. Investment in human skills is known as investment in human capital.

III. MULTIPLE CHOICE

1. The whole cost of capital is
   (a) the nominal rate of return
   (b) the real rate of return
   (c) depreciation plus the internal rate of return
   (d) the interest foregone plus depreciation plus the capital gain

2. The sum of money now that could earn a particular stream of income tomorrow is known as
   (a) the present value
   (b) the perpetuity
   (c) the annuity
   (d) the real intrest rate

3. The downward valuation of future income in the presence of an interest rate is called
   (a) the present value
   (b) discounting
   (c) an annuity
   (d) capitalization

4. The inclusion of expected returns into the value of the asset earning them is called
   (a) discounting
   (b) an annuity
   (c) capitalization
   (d) a perpetuity

5. The slope of the production possibility curve in the diagram of present/future consumption is
   (a) the rate of time discount
   (b) the marginal product of capital

(c) the internal rate of return
(d) the present value

6. The slope of the future/present indifference curve is
(a) the rate of time discount
(b) the marginal product of capital
(c) the internal rate of return
(d) the present value

7. A machine should be built if
(a) its present value is positive
(b) its discounted value is positive
(c) its capitalized value is positive
(d) its marginal product is greater than its opportunity cost

8. The best way of making the sacrifice of present consumption is by
(a) maximizing the present value of production
(b) maximizing the future value of production
(c) maximizing the present value of consumption
(d) minimizing savings and investment

9. The internal rate of return
(a) equates the present value of the stream of benefits from a project with the discounted value of the stream of costs
(b) equates the present value of the stream of benefits from a project with the present value of the stream of costs
(c) equates the discounted value of the stream of benefits from a project with the discounted value of the stream of costs
(d) equates the discounted value of the stream of benefits from a project with the present value of the stream of costs

10. A farmer makes her decision about how much to invest by choosing the production plan that
(a) maximizes the present value of her farm at the going interest rate
(b) maximizing the capitalized value of her farm at the going interest rate
(c) minimizing the capitalized value of her farm at the going interest rate
(d) maximizing the discounted value of her farm at the going interest rate

IV. EXERCISES

1. Tommy Ryan has been an expert pilot with a major commercial airline for the past five years. His annual salary is $50,000. Ryan recently decided to return to college to get his undergraduate degree in engineering. Attending college will cost him $5,000 per year. His friends cannot understand why Ryan would give up his lucrative career to attend school, especially when he will have to pay to go to college.

(a) What is the opportunity cost to Tommy Ryan of attending college?

(b) How can Ryan justify his actions?

2. A major commercial airline recently advertised a $218 round-trip air fare from New York to Dallas, Texas. The advertisement appeared during the month of August. Roberta Shell is planning on attending a conference in Dallas during the last week of December. Roberta knows that the normal round-trip air fare to Dallas is $280. She is concerned that if she doesn't purchase her ticket by September 1, all of the discount tickets will be sold out before she buys her ticket. But she is also aware of the fact that if she spends $218 on the ticket ahead of time, she will have to forego the interest that she would have earned on the money during the four months prior to the conference. Assume that at the prevailing market rate of interest, Roberta would earn 3% interest during the four month period. Should Roberta purchase the discount ticket?

V. PROBLEM

Investment in Solar Panels

Solar Ray Inc. is a small firm that produces solar panels for private homes. A recent advertisement by Solar Ray announced that a family could purchase a solar panel for only $250. The advertisement further claimed that a solar panel will yield savings of $100 per year for three years on heating bills for a typical family. "Spend $250 and save $300," the advertisement proclaimed. If the market rate of interest is 10%, should the typical family purchase a solar panel?

ANSWER KEY

CHAPTER 1

III. MULTIPLE-CHOICE

1 - d
2 - b
3 - c
4 - a
5 - b
6 - c
7 - d
8 - b
9 - b
10 - a

IV. EXERCISES

1. State funds are scarce. State funds are also fungible. It is meaningless to think of revenues coming from any particular source as being "crucial for" any specific use. It is therefore meaningless to say that revenues from the state lottery system are being "earmarked" for higher education. These revenues, revenues from other sources, and the funds that are already being allocated to higher education are fungible. A clever politician could also (fallaciously) argue that the revenues from the state lottery are, in fact, being used for higher education, but the funds previously allocated to education have been diverted elsewhere. Both arguments are meaningless. The general public is therefore incorrect in its belief that revenues from the state lottery are being diverted to other uses.

2. Bonus coupons are like dollar bills. They are fungible. It makes no difference whether Mary pays for the development and printing of the next roll of film with her bonus coupons or hard earned money.

3. Consider Figure 1.1. The rise in disposable personal income

is represented by a parallel shift outward in the budget line. The number of attainable consumption opportunities for consumers in the United States increased from November to December.

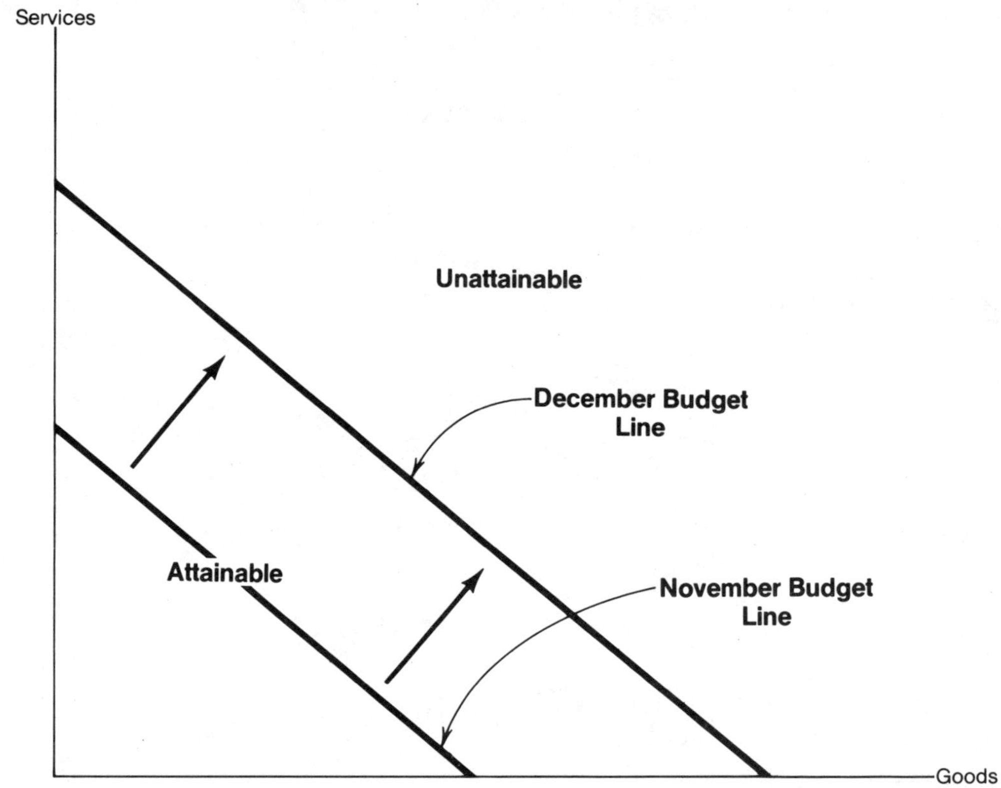

FIGURE 1.1

4. Hogan's behavior violates the Weak Axiom of Revealed Preference. Stone's behavior is consistent with it. Prior to the price change, Hogan chose bundle A and revealed a preference for it over bundle B, which was also affordable. After the price change, bundle A was still affordable but he chose bundle B. The Weak Axiom is violated and his behavior is not consistent with the law of demand.

Stone chose bundle A prior to the price change. Since bundle B was not attainable given his money income and the prices he faced, he did not reveal a preference for A over B. After the price change, he chose bundle B. But under the new price regime, bundle A is no longer affordable. Once again, he has not revealed a preference for B over A. The Weak Axiom is not violated and his behavior is consistent with the law of demand.

5. (a) \$3000 = \$500(C) + \$25(B) where C=number of computers, B=number of textbooks.

(b) The relative price of a computer in terms of textbooks is simply the relative price ratio = \$500/\$25 = 20. This relative price ratio is the slope of the budget line.

(c) The opportunity cost to John of purchasing one more textbook is the number of computers he would have to forego in order to purchase the textbook. This is equal to $25/$500 = .05.

(d) The maximum number of books that he can possibly purchase is equal to his total stipend divided by the price of a textbook = $3000/$25 = 120 books. This number is the intercept of the budget line on the book axis.

6. Consider Figure 1.2. If the tax on gasoline is passed, the price of gasoline relative to all other goods will rise. This is represented by a change in the slope of the budget. The intercept on the gasoline axis changes. The intercept on the All Other Goods axis stays the same, since the maximum amount of other goods that are attainable has not changed.

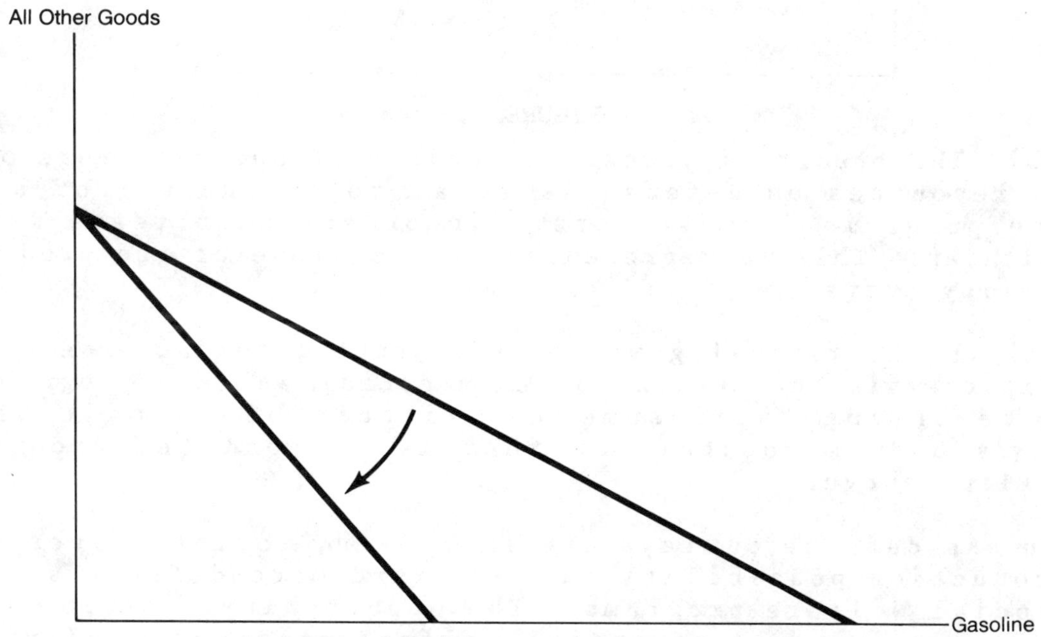

FIGURE 1.2

7. It makes no difference to Eleanor Reynolds whether the government provides her with a cash transfer or the food stamps, as long as she can resell the unused stamps. She is as well off under the food stamp program as if the government had simply given her a cash transfer. (This assumes, of course, that the reselling of food stamps is both easy and legal.)

V. PROBLEM

(a)

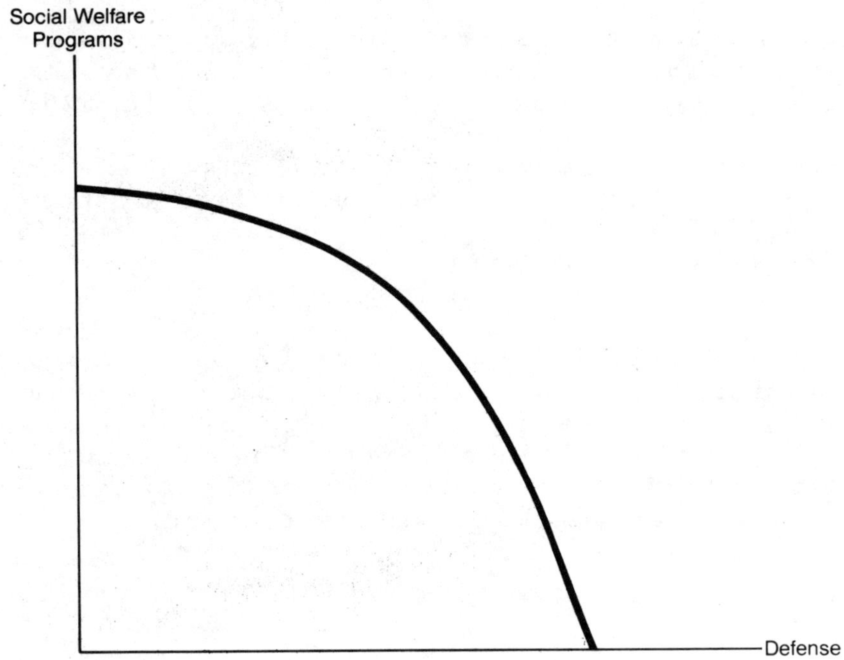

FIGURE 1.3

(b) The opportunity cost to society of spending more of its scarce resources on defense is equal to the number of social welfare programs it must forego in order to increase defense expenditures. This is represented by the slope of the production possibility curve.

(c) If the federal government attempted to increase defense expenditures without cutting back on social welfare programs, it would be trying to consume an unattainable bundle beyond society's budget constraint; that is, beyond the production possibility curve.

(d) As defense outlays are increased, society moves along the production possibility curve toward more defense and away from social welfare programs. The opportunity cost of defense expenditures in terms of social welfare programs will rise as more is spent on defense.

(e) If a major technological breakthrough occurs that lowers the price of existing military equipment, the intercept of the production possibility curve on the defense axis will move to the right. In other words, society will be able to afford more defense, more social welfare programs, or both, given its scarce resources.

(f) Advancing technology that leads to increased productivity in the economy will result in a shift outward (a bulging outward) in the production frontier.

CHAPTER 2

III. MULTIPLE CHOICE

1 - b
2 - c
3 - b
4 - c
5 - d
6 - a
7 - b
8 - b
9 - a
10 - b

IV. EXERCISES

1. Another possible utility function is U=5X+5Y. To convince yourself of this, consider the following bundles that Hilda might consume:

	food	clothing
Bundle A:	10	10
Bundle B:	5	15
Bundle C:	5	5

Given the utility function U=X+Y, bundle A yields 20 joys, bundle B yields 20 joys, and bundle C yields 10 joys. Thus, Hilda is indifferent between bundles A and B, and prefers both of them to bundle C. Given the alternative utility function U=5X+5Y, bundle A yields 100 joys, bundle B yields 100 joys, and bundle C yields 50 joys. The order of preference is preserved.

2. (a) If U=X+Y is the utility function, then the indifference map is given by X+Y=constant.

(b) An alternative indifference map is 5X+5Y=constant. To convince yourself of this, consider the indifference map X+Y=5 joys. Some of the bundles of food and clothing on this indifference curve are (3 ounces food, 2 pieces clothing), (4 ounces food, 1 piece clothing), and (2 ounces food, 3 pieces clothing). The same bundles lie on the indifference curve 5X+5Y=25 joys.

3. The utility-maximizing bundle is independent of the choice of utility function used to represent Hilda's preferences.

4. If all prices and income are multiplied by the same positive constant, the optimal choice is left unchanged. Consider the equation for Hilda's budget line: $P_fF + P_cC = I$, where F is food, C is clothing, P_f is the price of food, P_c is the price of clothing, and I is money income. If P_f, P_c and I are all multiplied by the same positive constant k, then the budget constraint becomes $kP_fF + kP_cC = kI$. Dividing by k one again obtains the original budget constraint.

5. (a) Since a consumer can always compare any bundles, there must be an indifference curve through each point in the commodity space.

(b) Suppose indifference curves can intersect (Figure 2.1).

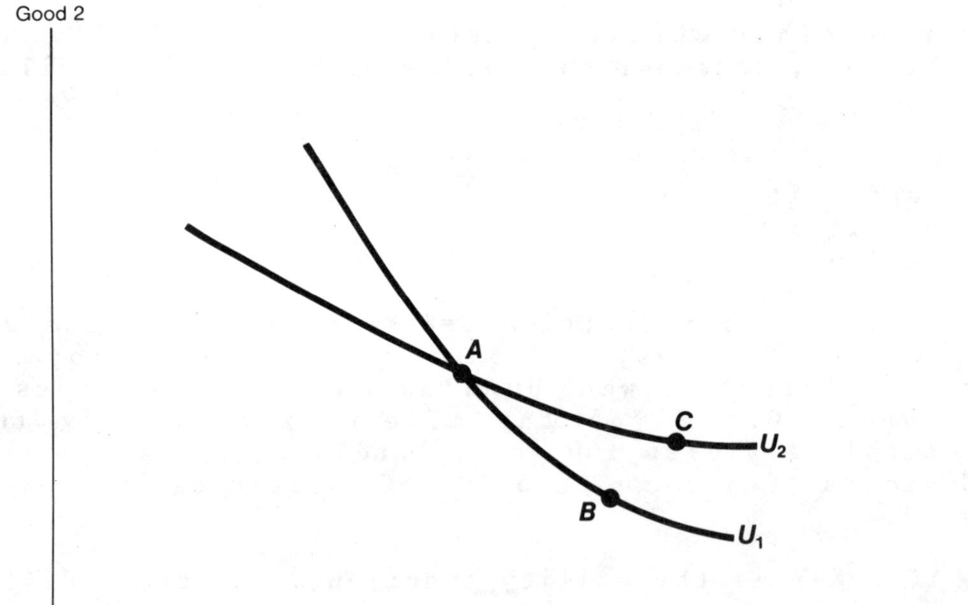

FIGURE 2.1

Either bundle C is preferred to bundle B or bundle B is preferred to bundle C. Suppose bundle C is preferred to bundle B. Bundle A is indifferent to bundle C. By transitivity, bundle A is preferred to bundle B. But bundle A and bundle B are on the same indifference curve. This is a contradiction. Therefore it must be true that indifference curves cannot intersect.

(c) There cannot be a "bliss" point. There is no peak to the hill of utility.

6. The combination of 10 IBM shares and 20 AT&T shares is not an optimal choice for Ted. Recall that the relative price ratio shows the rate at which the consumer is <u>able to substitute</u> one good for another. The consumer's marginal valuation of one good in terms of the other is the rate at which the consumer is <u>willing to substitute</u> one good for the other. In Ted's particular case, the relative price ratio is 2 but his marginal valuation of IBM stock in terms of AT&T stock is 4. Ted is willing to give up as much as 4 shares of AT&T stock in order to get 1 more share of IBM stock, but given the prevailing market prices, he only has to give up 2 shares of AT&T stock in order to get 1 more share of IBM stock. He will therefore give up shares of AT&T stock to get more IBM stock until his marginal valuation of IBM stock in terms of AT&T stock is equal to the relative price ratio.

<u>PROBLEM</u>

(a) Consider Figure 2.2.

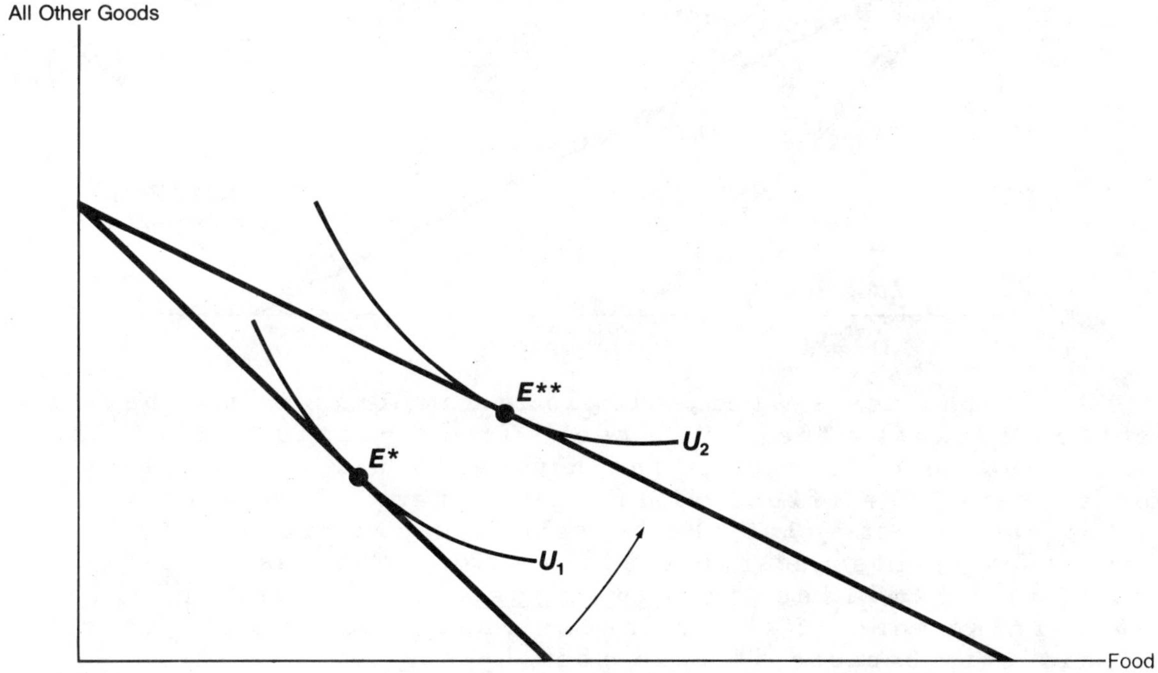

FIGURE 2.2

During the Nixon administration, the method of allocation of food stamps was equivalent to a price subsidy. This is represented by a rotation of the budget line. The optimal choice of food and all other goods changes from the old equilibrium E^* to the new equilibrium E^{**}.

(b) Eligible households may have failed to participate in the food stamp program because they did not wish to spend so much of their income on food even when the price was subsidized. Some households may also have decided not to participate because of the stigma attached to being a food stamp recipient.

(c) With the institution of the changes in the program in 1977, the effect of food stamp allotments to less poor families became similar to cash transfers (Figure 2.3).

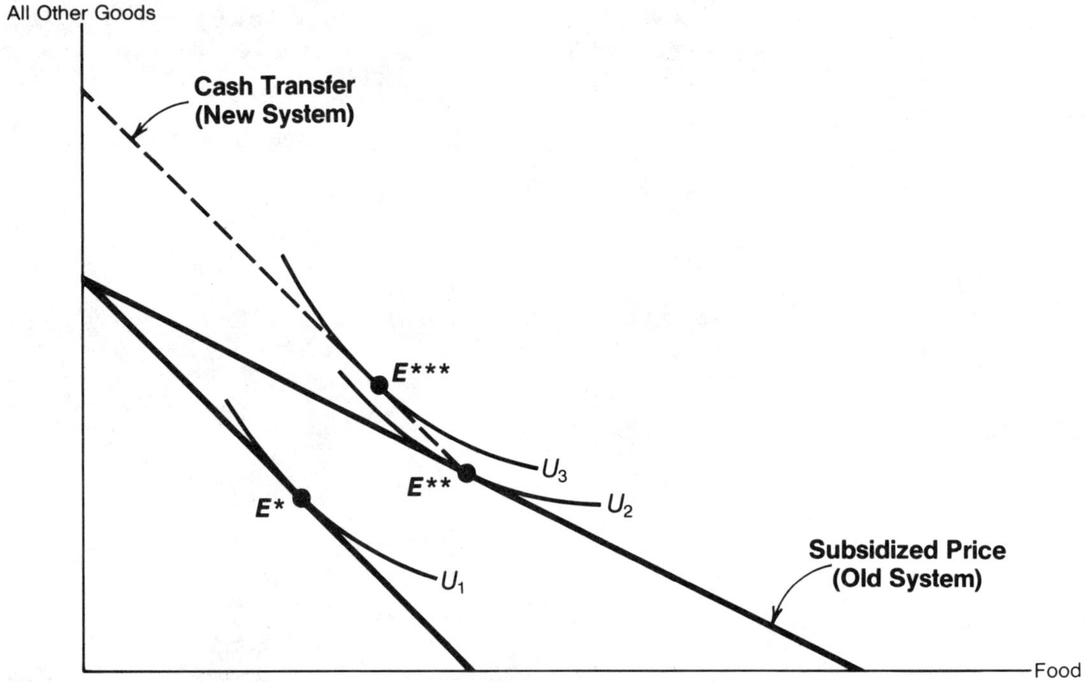

FIGURE 2.3

Under the new system, eligible families do not have to buy the food stamps. They are free. It is possible that the free food stamps were less than the household had planned to spend on food anyway. The effect of the food stamp allotment is then to free up cash income that the household would previously have used to buy food stamps under the old system. The result is that some less poor families freely chose to become hungrier by transferring some of their income from food to all other goods. They did this because it made them happier.

CHAPTER 3

III. MULTIPLE CHOICE

1 - d
2 - d
3 - d
4 - b
5 - c

IV. EXERCISES

1. (a) The amount of money that each driver expects to lose on average from taking a gamble depends upon the probability of an accident occurring (1 in 100) and the loss that the driver would incur if sued ($100,000). The income she would expect to lose on average from taking a gamble is $100,000(1/100) + $0(99/100) = $1,000.

(b) Absolutely. A smart gambler takes a gamble for money when she thinks that the money she will end up with on average is greater than the money she started with. The insurance policy has an annual premium of $700. The driver expects to lose on average $1,000 from taking a gamble of not carrying any insurance. The money the driver will lose on average ($1,000) is greater than the money she will end up paying the insurance company in order to not take a gamble ($700). The insurance policy is therefore fair in a technical sense.

(c) If the typical motorist was risk neutral, the insurance policy would still be fair for the reasons given in (b).

2. (a) Car owners who illegaly drive cars without owning any insurance may be behaving perfectly rationally. If the insurance is not fair in a technical sense, then it might not pay for drivers to purchase the insurance. It might pay for them to take the gamble of having an accident or being caught by a law enforcement official. Whether an individual driver decides that the gamble is worth taking or not depends upon her preference for risk. Drivers who decide to purchase the insurance are not irrational. They are just sufficiently risk averse to choose the insurance policy.

Alternatively, the insurance may be fair, but the uninsured drivers may be extremely risk prone. A sufficiently risk-prone driver may find the prospect of taking the gamble sufficiently attractive so that she will accept a gamble that will leave her, on average, with a lower income than if the gamble had not been taken.

(b) The uninsured motorist problem is more prevalent in some states than in others because the regulation of insurance companies is not uniform across states. Insurance policies therefore differ between states. Insurance policies in Oregon might be fair in a technical sense, while policies in New Jersey are not. Furthermore, the preference for risk among drivers likely differs from state to state. The severity of punishments for being caught without car insurance also differs between states.

3. Not necessarily. Morton's shift in investment strategy could have been due to a change in risk preference. But it is also possible that his preference for risk remained the same, while the money he expected to end up with on average by investing in a risky money market fund went up. (In fact, interest rates on money market accounts rose dramatically during the late 1970s and early 1980s.)

V. <u>PROBLEM</u>

(a) Not necessarily. As with Carl Morton in Exercise #3 above, it is possible that the increase in premiums reflected a change in risk preference on the part of the insurance companies. Insurance companies are gamblers. They gamble on the possibility of having to pay out money to their insured customers. Insurance companies also want to behave like smart gamblers. They will take a gamble (that is, write an insurance policy) only when they think that the money they will end up with on average is greater than the money they start with. If the insurance companies suddenly became more risk averse, then they would require that the insured parties pay higher premiums in order to make the insurance policies a fair bet for the insurance companies.

(b) The premiums rose after the satellite failures in early 1983 because of a change in the perceived probabilities of failure. Because of the more frequent failures, insurance companies changed their perceptions of the probabilitiy of failure. The loss to insurance companies, on average, rose. This resulted in the need for the insurers to raise their premiums.

(c) If premiums did not rise, one would expect owners of

satellites to increase their purchases of insurance policies. It is possible that they also perceived the probability of failure, as well as their loss on average, as rising. This might lead them to increase their demand for insurance.

(d) Not surprisingly, insurers demanded a say over new space technology that they thought was too risky. The perceived riskiness of the space projects affects the desirability of writing insurance policies. If the projects are too risky, then insurance companies will eventually exit from the industry. In order to stay in the business of insuring space payloads, many insurers attempted to reduce the riskiness of the projects by controlling the technologies used in the projects.

CHAPTER 4

III. MULTIPLE CHOICE

1 - c
2 - c
3 - a
4 - d
5 - a

IV. EXERCISES

1. (a) Consider Figure 4.1.

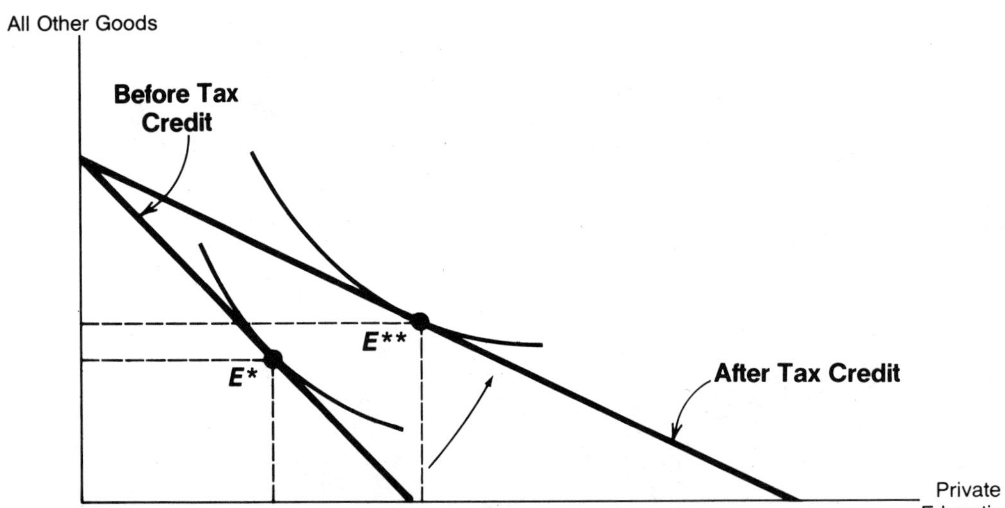

FIGURE 4.1

The preferences of a typical American family for education can be represented by an indifference map. Prior to passage of the tax credit bill, the equilibrium quantity demanded by a typicalAmerican family was located at the point of tangency (E^*) between an indifference curve and the family's budget constraint. The tax credit lowered the price of education relative to all other goods. This is represented by a rotation of the budget line. If education is a normal good, then the income effect reinforces the substitution effect and the quantity of education demanded rises from E^* to E^{**}. For a given amount of income, the family can afford to purchase more education, more of all other goods, or more of both.

(b) The income effect is depicted by a parallel shift of the family's budget line. The family jumps from one indifference curve to a higher indifference curve. The substitution effect is represented by a movement along an indifference curve in the direction of more education. In Figure 4.2, the income effect is the movement from point A to point B. The substitution effect is the movement from B to C.

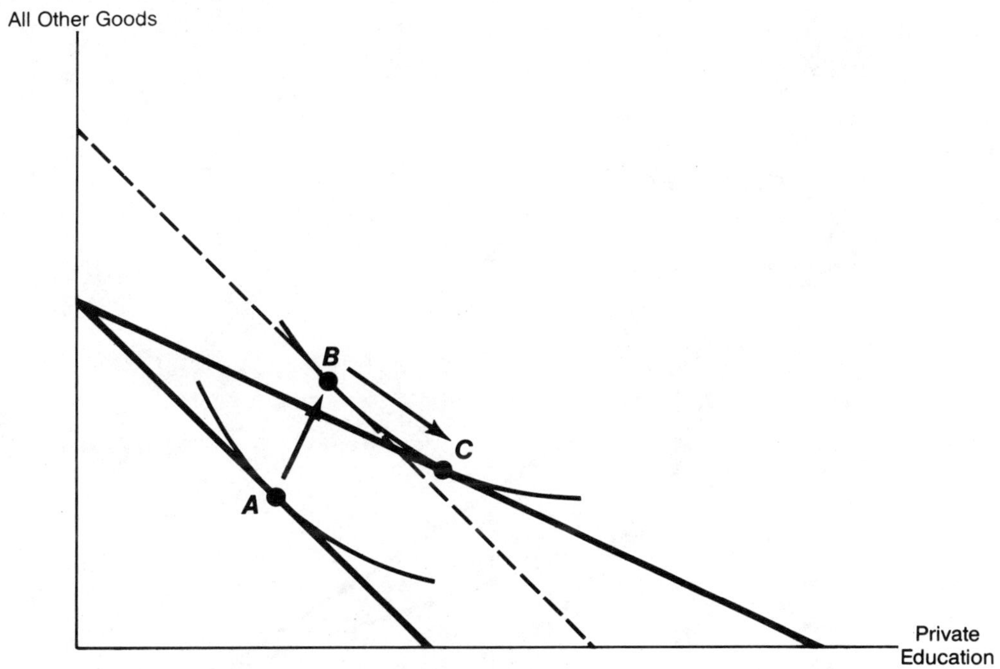

FIGURE 4.2

(c) Education is depicted as a normal good in Figures 4.1 and 4.2. The fall in the price of education results in an increase in the family's real purchasing power. This leads to an increase in the amount of education purchased. Further, the fall in the relative price of education causes the family to substitute more education in place of some of the other goods. The income effect reinforces the substitution effect. The total effect is therefore an increase in the quantity of education demanded.

2. (a) From 1965 through 1970, the average annual rate of inflation was 5%. But the price of gasoline charged at the pumps remained unchanged. The price of gasoline relative to all other

goods therefore fell.

(b) Suppose the relative price of all other goods was 100 in 1965. (Alternatively, the relative price of gasoline in 1965 was .01.) With a 5% annual rate of inflation, the relative price of all other goods was 105 in 1966, 110.3 in 1967, 115.8 in 1968, 121.6 in 1969, and 127.6 in 1970. The rise in the relative price of all other goods is represented by a rotation of the budget line. For any given amount of income, the consumer can buy the same amount of gasoline in 1970 that she could in 1965. But the amount of all other goods that she can afford to buy in 1970 is less than the amount in 1965. The equilibrium moves from E^* in 1965 to E^{**} in 1970 in Figure 4.3. The offer curve is the locus of equilibrium points.

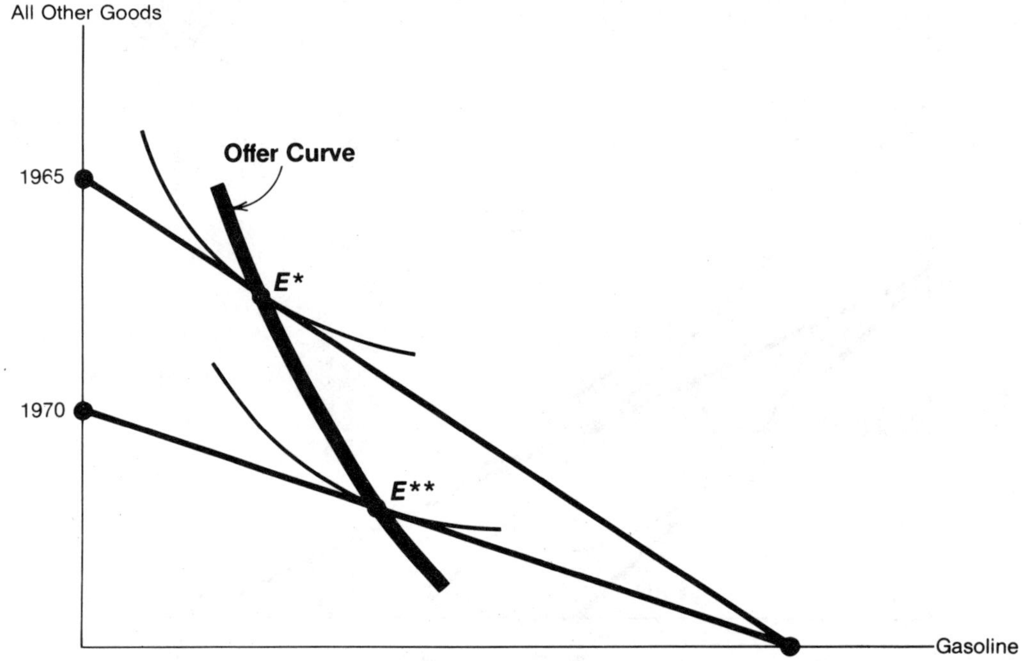

FIGURE 4.3

(c) The relative price of gasoline declined from 1965 to 1970. The quantity of gasoline demanded rose. This is depicted by the uncompensated demand curve in Figure 4.4. To construct the demand curve from the offer curve, read the quantity of gasoline demanded off the horizontal axis and plot this as a function of price. The uncompensated demand curve is not necessarily a straight line, even though the inflation rate was a constant 5%. The shape of the demand curve depends upon the shapes of the indifference curves.

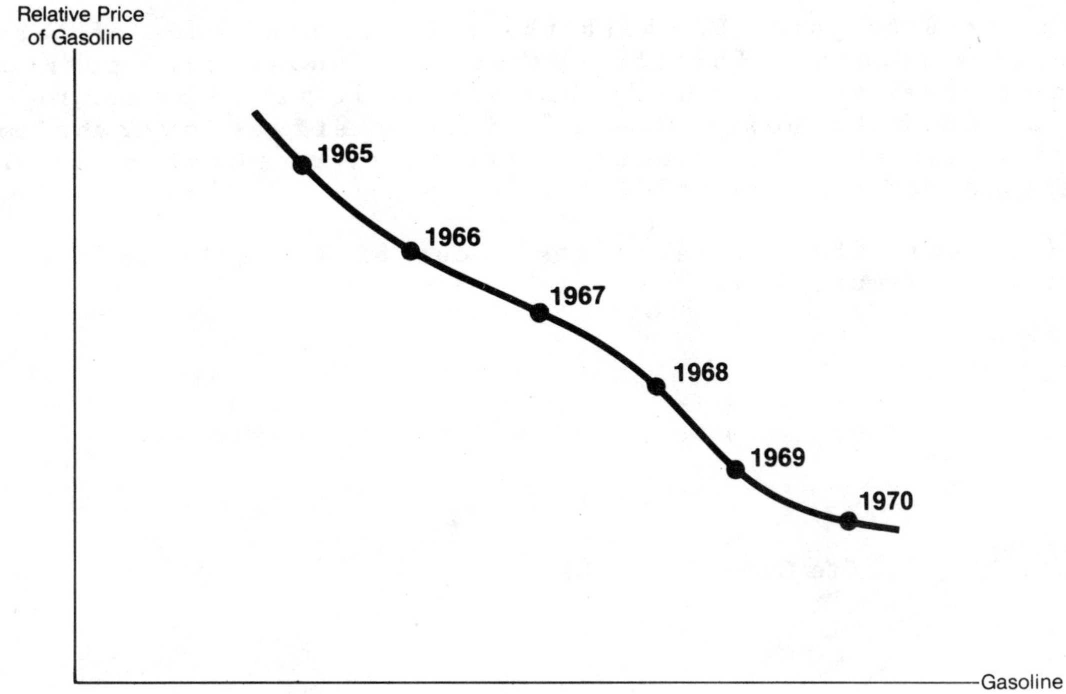

FIGURE 4.4

V. PROBLEM

(a) Figure 4.5 depicts the case of a Giffen good.

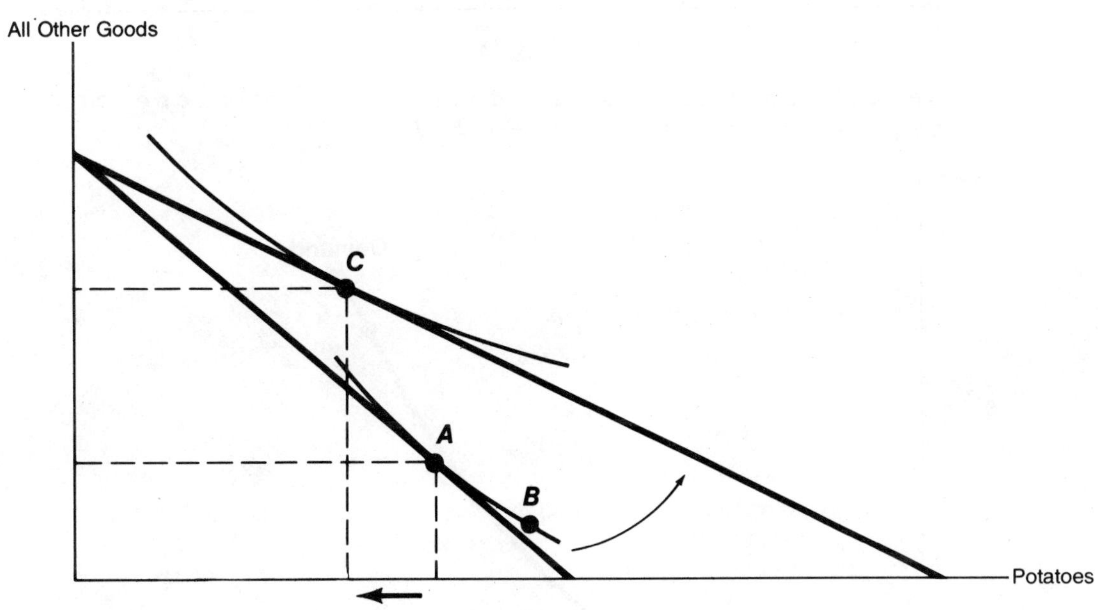

FIGURE 4.5

(b) In Figure 4.5, the substitution effect is the movement

from point A to point B. With the fall in the price of potatoes, there is a tendency for the consumer to substitute potatoes in place of other goods. The income effect is given by the movement from point B to point C. The income effect overwhelms the substitution effect, so that as the price of potatoes fell, the quantity demanded also fell.

(c) The offer curve is the locus of equilibrium points, as depicted in Figure 4.6.

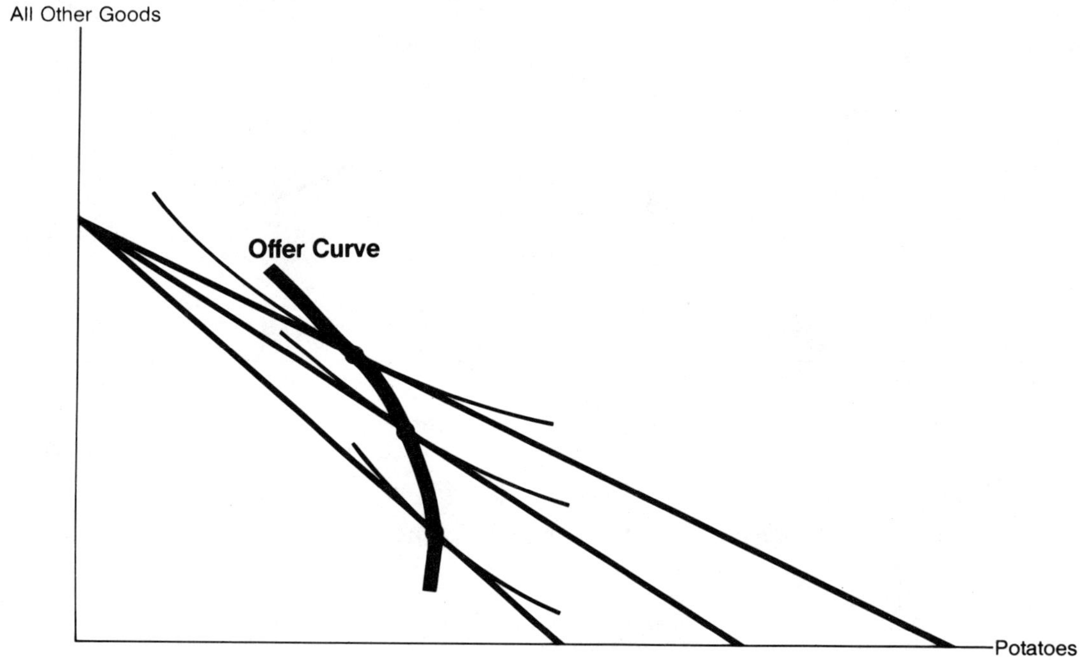

FIGURE 4.6

(d) The Giffen paradox leads to the perverse case of an upward sloping demand curve (Figure 4.7).

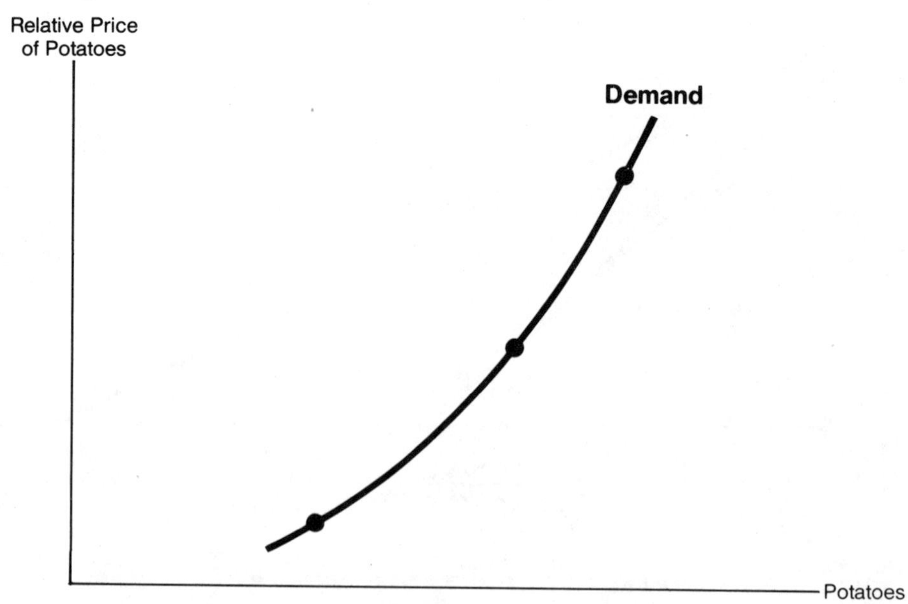

FIGURE 4.7

CHAPTER 5

III. MULTIPLE CHOICE

1 - a
2 - b
3 - d
4 - d
5 - a
6 - d
7 - c
8 - a
9 - c
10 - d

IV. EXERCISES

1. (a) Under the Reagan proposal, an efficient outcome will prevail. Recall that Adam Smith's theorem asserts that an efficient market equilibrium will prevail when exchange occurs in a free market of price takers. All mutually advantageous trades will be made. The problem is that efficiency is not equity. The market equilibrium depends on the initial distribution of income. The Reagan proposal -- which is the economist's proposal -- is to deal with the poverty problem directly and to alter the initial distribution of wealth. Once this is done, the market is permitted to achieve an efficient outcome without government interference. But this approach has its limitations. A principle objection is that the taxes that are required to redistribute income are themselves interferences in the market.

(b) The Marx approach emphasizes equity rather than efficiency. The advantage of this approach is that an equitable distribution of income will prevail in the economy. The problem with this proposal is that a socialistic structure is not led to an efficient outcome by an invisible hand in the same manner as a capitalistic structure. Extensive government intervention in the market is necessary and it is often difficult for the government to know precisely how to control the economy.

(c) Not necessarily. The Reagan approach attempts to alleviate the poverty problem directly. It then allows the market to achieve an efficient outcome with its additional benefits.

Under the Marx plan an equitable outcome might prevail, but it is not clear that the poverty problem will be alleviated. It is not certain that the equitable outcome will be one in which there is no poverty. The poverty problem is not directly dealt with. It is true that under a socialistic system the national income that exists is divided up equitably, but the size of national income might not be as large as possible. All of the benefits of an efficient outcome will not be reaped.

2. The U.S.-China trade negotiations are a good example of the benefits from trade. Trade is beneficial if one one party can be made better off without making the other party worse off. The fact that U.S.-China trade is expected to rise is an indication that both nations perceive the existence of possible exchanges that would be mutually beneficial. By trading with each other, the U.S. and China will move closer to an efficient outcome. They will move closer to a point on the contract curve (see Figure 5.1).

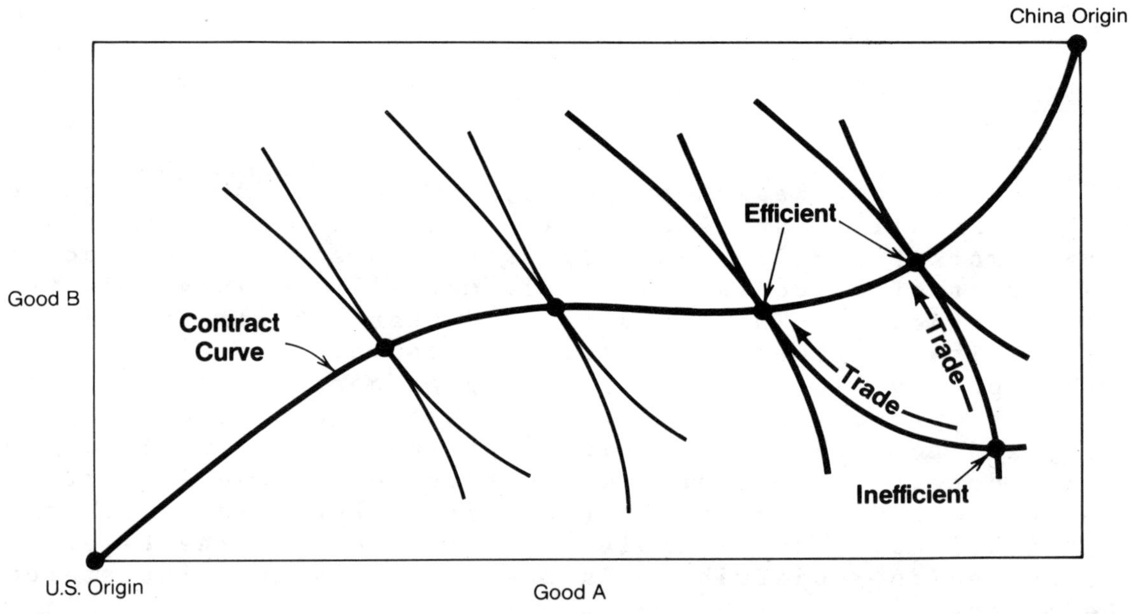

FIGURE 5.1

The U.S. hopes to improve global stability by improving trade relations with China. China hopes to modernize its economy and improve national security. Both nations recognize the benefits that they will gain from trade. A Pareto superior outcome can be achieved through trade. The final outcome will depend on the nations' initial endowments of wealth, resources, and technology, and on the bargaining abilities of both parties. In Figure 5.1, both point A and point B are possible efficient outcomes.

V. PROBLEM

The joint GM-Toyota venture is another example of the possible gains from trade. According to the data presented in the problem, both GM and Toyota are reporting record profits. But this does not mean that at least one of them cannot achieve better results without hurting the other. Consider Figure 5.2.

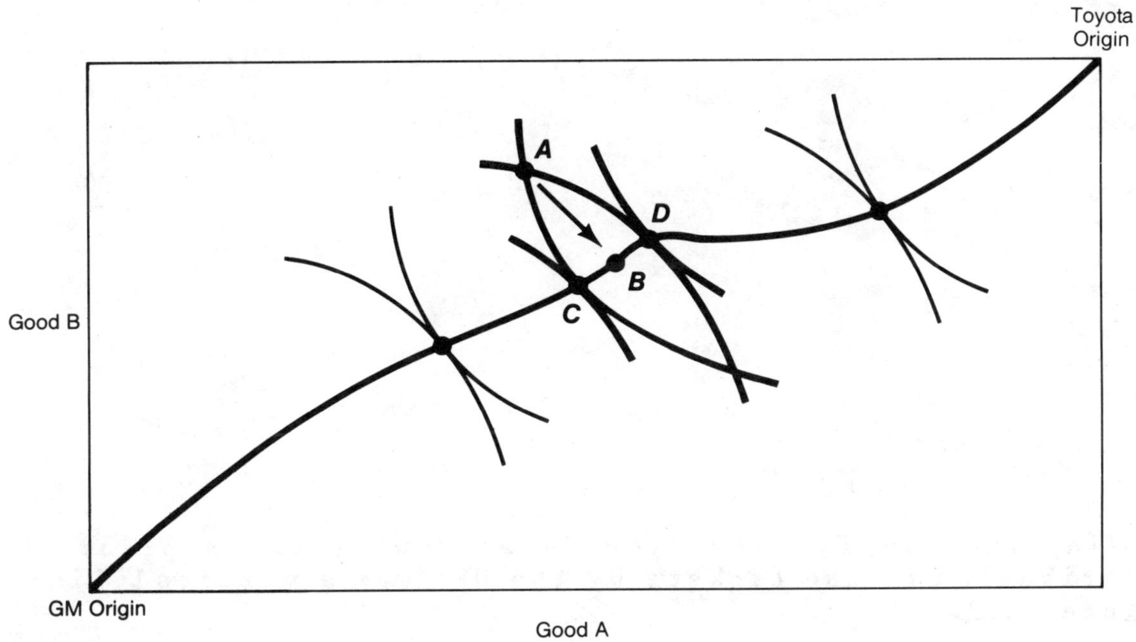

FIGURE 5.2

Suppose GM and Toyota were located at point A prior to their joint venture. At point A, both companies were competing and operating independently. Both were reporting record profits at point A. But the outcome is not efficient. Both firms can be made better off by moving to a point such as B. (Alternatively, a move to point C or point D would make one firm better off without making the other worse off.) The object of the joint venture is to try to achieve an efficient outcome like B. (Neglect for now the increase in monopolistic power that the firms gain by merging to gain a larger combined market share.) The way in which they plan to achieve this outcome is by jointly producing the Sprinter subcompact car. GM hopes to gain through trade Toyota's experience and expertise in small-car production. Toyota hopes to gain from the economies of scale GM enjoys in the U.S. market and from the circumvention of trade quotas. The joint venture is mutually beneficial.

CHAPTER 6

III. MULTIPLE CHOICE

1 - a
2 - c
3 - d
4 - d
5 - c
6 - a
7 - d
8 - d
9 - a
10 - d

IV. EXERCISES

1. (a) The supply curve for Super Bowl tickets prior to the distribution of the tickets by the NFL was a vertical line (see Figure 6.1).

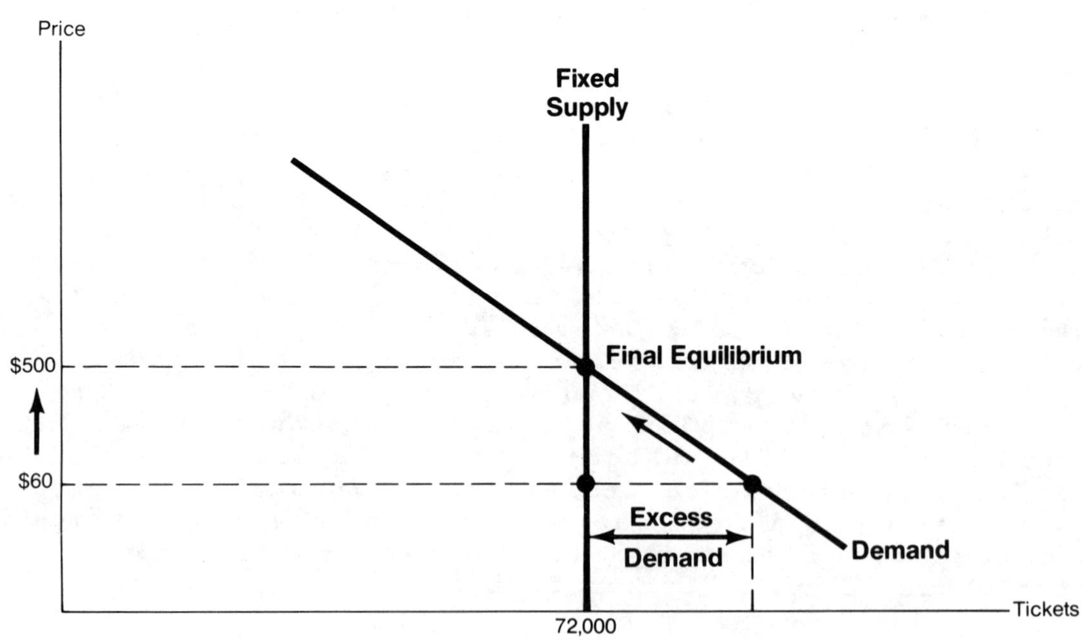

FIGURE 6.1

(b) The market demand curve is a downward sloping curve. The market demand curve intersects the market supply curve at some point above the $60 NFL price. The fact that people were able to resell their tickets at a price above the NFL price indicates that at the $60 price the quantity of tickets demanded exceeded the quantity supplied. A shortage of tickets existed at the $60 price. The market-clearing price was above the $60 NFL price.

(c) As tickets were resold, the market price for Super Bowl tickets began to rise. The final equilibrium was at the true market equilibrium price E^*. At this equilibrium price, quantity demanded was equal to quantity supplied.

(d) The people who received the tickets initially at the $60 NFL price benefitted. Dealers who were able to buy the tickets from the original ticket holders and then resell them at a higher price (at or below the equilibrium price) also benefitted. And the people who finally bought the tickets at the final equilibrium price of $500 also benefitted. The tickets finally ended up in the hands of those people who valued them the most. (The people who received the tickets at the initial $60 price but did not resell them also value the tickets highly because they decided to forego the opportunity of reselling the tickets at a higher price. There was an opportunity cost to holding the tickets rather than reselling them.)

(e) The reselling of tickets was not bad because it allowed the market to put the tickets into the hands of those people that valued them the most.

2. (a) The "gray market" exists because there is a shortage of silicon chips. The shortage exists because the producers of the chips are not able to keep up with the boom in demand for the chips. The price that these producers are charging is below the market-clearing price. This induces people to resell the chips that are either stolen or purchased legally at the market price.

(b) The existence of the gray market is not bad because it puts the chips in the hands of those people that value them the most. But the existence of <u>illicit</u> traffic in silicon chips is bad.

V. PROBLEM

(a) The law of demand says that the quantity of a good (such as energy) that is consumed, needed, required, or demanded depends on the price of the good. The law of demand says that the quantity of a good demanded is inversely related to its own price. The demand curve is a negatively sloped curve suggesting a whole series of alternative amounts that consumers "require" or "need," depending on the price.

(b) No. In a free market economy, quantity demanded always equals quantity supplied. The market always clears. The only exception is the case of perfectly inelastic supply and demand (see Figure 6.2).

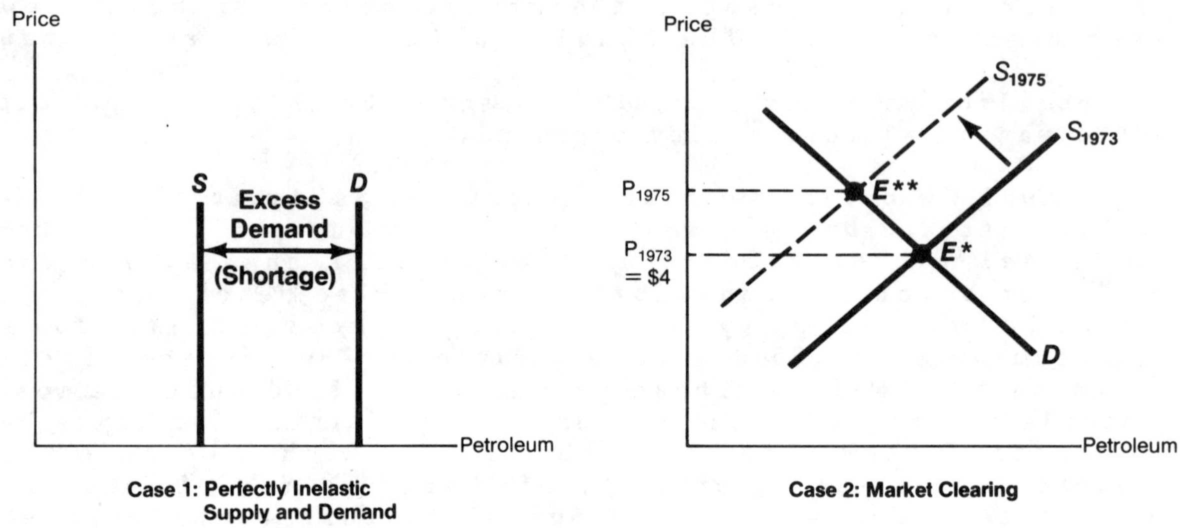

FIGURE 6.2

(c) Quantity supplied also depends on price. The supply curve is upward sloping, suggesting a whole series of alternative quantities of energy supplied, depending on price.

(d) The output restriction caused the market price for petroleum to rise from P_{1973} to P_{1975} (see Figure 6.2). Consumers' needs are still satisfied. The market always clears.

(e) If the government fixes the price of petroleum, consumers' needs will not be satisfied. A shortage will exist. The shortage will be equal to the difference between the quantity demanded at the 1973 price and the quantity demanded at the controlled price.

CHAPTER 7

III. MULTIPLE CHOICE

1 - b
2 - c
3 - b
4 - d
5 - a
6 - a
7 - c
8 - b
9 - d
10 - d

IV. EXERCISES

1. The total expenditures by purchasers (TE) are equal to the price of the commodity (P) times the quantity exchanged (Q). That is, TE=PQ. The law of demand asserts that there is an inverse relationship between price and quantity demanded. For example, when price rises, quantity demanded declines. But since price and quantity demanded move in opposite directions, the effect of the price increase on total expenditures is ambiguous. In order to determine the effect on total expenditures, one must know the degree to which price and quantity demanded change. This is exactly what the price elasticity of demand tells us.

Consider the case when demand is elastic and price falls by 5%. The law of demand says that the fall in price leads to an increase in quantity demanded. The price elasticity of demand indicates how much quantity demanded varies. Since demand is elastic (that is, demand is responsive to price changes), the percentage change in quantity demanded is greater than the 5% change in price. The rise in quantity demanded therefore outweighs the decline in price and total expenditures rise.

2. Since the price elasticity of demand is 0.5 which is less than 1.0, demand is inelastic. It is not very responsive to price changes. The law of demand says that the 5% rise in the price of apples will lead to a decline in the quantity demanded. Since demand is inelastic, the percentage decline in quantity demanded will be less than the 5% rise in price. The price increase outweighs the fall in quantity demanded. Total

expenditures therefore rise.

3. The negative income elasticity of demand indicates that to the people of Grand Fenwick, flour is an inferior good. As per capita income rises by 1%, the quantity of flour demanded falls. The share of flour in total expenditures declines.

4. The elasticity of demand is equal to the percentage change in quantity demanded divided by the percentage change in price. In an alternative form,

$$\text{price elasticity of demand} = (\Delta Q/\Delta P)(P/Q)$$

where the symbol Δ stands for "change in." (Note: When choosing which P and which Q to insert into the equation for the price elasticity, standard conventions say that the smaller of the two prices should be chosen and the smaller of the two quantities should be chosen.)

Between points A and B: The price elasticity of demand = (1/-1)(4/2.5) = -1.6. Since the negative sign is understood, drop it. The elasticity is therefore 1.6 and demand is elastic.

Between points B and E: The price elasticity of demand = (6.5/-3)(1/3.5) = -.62. The elasticity is .62 and demand is inelastic.

Between points A and D: The price elasticity of demand = (4.5/-3)(2/2.5) = -1.2. The elasticity of demand is 1.2 and demand is elastic.

V. PROBLEM

Physician Services

The total expenditures on any physician's services by the citizens of Sayreville are equal to the gross revenues received by that physician. Total expenditures are equal to the price of the doctor's services times the quantity of his services demanded. The law of demand says that the price of physician services is inversely related to the quantity demanded. But it does not indicate the degree of responsiveness of demand to price changes. The effect of price changes on total expenditures by consumers is therefore ambiguous. Whether Dr. Stanley's or Dr. Livingston's strategy is correct depends upon the price elasticity of demand for that physician's services.

Consider Dr. Stanley's strategy. He believes that higher fees will not result in lower gross revenues, even though quantity demanded will decline as his fees rise. This can only be true if the demand for his services is not very responsive to fee changes. Demand must be either inelastic or unitary elastic. If demand is inelastic, then fee increases will lead to higher revenues. If demand is unitary elastic, then revenues will not change as fees increase. But if demand is elastic, gross revenues will decline as fees increase.

Consider Dr. Livingston's strategy. He believes that he can charge lower fees because the quantity of his services demanded will rise. But the revenues he receives will rise only if the demand for his services is elastic. If demand is elastic, then quantity demanded will rise by a greater percentage than the fall in fees. Total expenditures will rise. But if demand is inelastic, gross revenues will decline as Dr. Livingston's fees decline. Unfortunately, Dr. Livingston's benevolence does not necessarily reward him with monetary gain.

CHAPTER 8

III. MULTIPLE CHOICE

1 - b
2 - c
3 - b
4 - a
5 - d
6 - b
7 - c
8 - b
9 - d
10 - c

IV. EXERCISES

1. A production function exhibits constant returns to scale if output changes by some constant t when all inputs are multiplied by t. If output changes by more than t, then the production function exhibits increasing returns to scale. If output changes by less than t, then the production function exhibits decreasing returns to scale.

Let t be a constant. In each production function, multiply each factor input by the constant t and then simplify the equation. Determine how much output changes when all factor inputs are multiplied by t.

(a) $25(tL) = t(25L) = tQ$. This production function exhibits constant returns to scale.

(b) $7(tK)(tL)(tM) = 7t^3(KLM) = 7t^3Q$. This production function exhibits increasing returns to scale. When all inputs are increased by t, output rises by more than t. (Similarly, when all inputs are decreased by t, output decreases by more than t.)

(c) $(tL)^2 = t^2L^2 = t^2Q$. This produciton function exhibits increasing returns to scale.

2. (a) Many of the fast-growing multinational companies from NICs came into being because these foreign firms developed comparative advantages in the production of certain products.

For example, the Caloi firm of Brazil discovered that it had special experience in the manufacturing of bicycles for small markets. It had learned efficient processes for running low-volume bicycle plants. It used this expertise to manufacture bicycles in Bolivia. Caloi also designed some of its own machinery to make small-scale manufacturing efficient.

The growth of these multinational firms from NICs does not imply that the traditional multinational firms are incapable of producing the same products. It simply indicates that the traditional multinationals can do other things better. The comparative advantage of the traditional firms is in the production of other types of output. The manufacturing skills of the new multinationals is usually most competitive in Third World countries that have small markets and low labor costs. In contrast, the traditional multinationals are better at producing output in larger markets in more developed countries.

(b) Existing American and Japanese firms have opportunity costs to production. These opportunity costs are equal to the output of other types of products foregone. The existing firms want to minimize their opportunity costs. It is therefore in the interests of these firms to operate jointly with the new multinationals if an efficient division of labor so dictates. If the existing firms recognize that the new multinationals have certain comparative advantages that are different from their own, then it is mutually beneficial for all of these firms to trade and operate jointly. For example, many of the new multinationals have been willing to share their special skills in exchange for skills in marketing and promotion.

V. PROBLEM

(a) The opportunity costs to society of committing $15 billion to the Synthetic Fuels Corporation is equal to the alternative goods and services foregone that could have been produced with the federal funds. When society commits taxpayer money to projects such as the Synthetic Fuels Corporation, it must make two fundamental decisions. First, it must decide whether the funding is being spent in such a way as to maximize social utility. Given the same level of expenditures, are there alternative projects that will yield a higher level of social utility? Second, once the fund have been committed to the project, are resources being used efficiently?

(b) With the establishment of the Synthetic Fuels Corporation, the Congress and President Carter made a decision that the project would ultimately yield the highest possible level of social utility. But the question still remained whether resources in society were being used efficiently.

The purpose of the project was to develop alternative forms of energy. The problem with this project was that many of the synthetic forms of energy were more costly than existing sources. Society would have to use more resources in the development of synthetic energy sources in order to obtain the same quantity of energy as from existing sources. Resources were being wasted. In terms of a production possibility curve, society was choosing to produce at a point inside its production possibility frontier. In efficiency terms, society was not doing as well as it possibly could.

The fact that private corporations were not willing to develop these alternative synthetic sources of energy without government assistance suggests that synthetic fuel development was not a profitable endeavor. Opportunity costs would not be minimized by producing synthetic fuels with existing resources. The formation of the Synthetic Fuels Corporation by the Congress and President Carter can only be rationalized if some other motivation or "externality" can be found. For example, one could argue for this project on the basis of "national security" considerations. President Carter may also have been concerned about the possibility of an oil embargo against the United States sometime in the future.

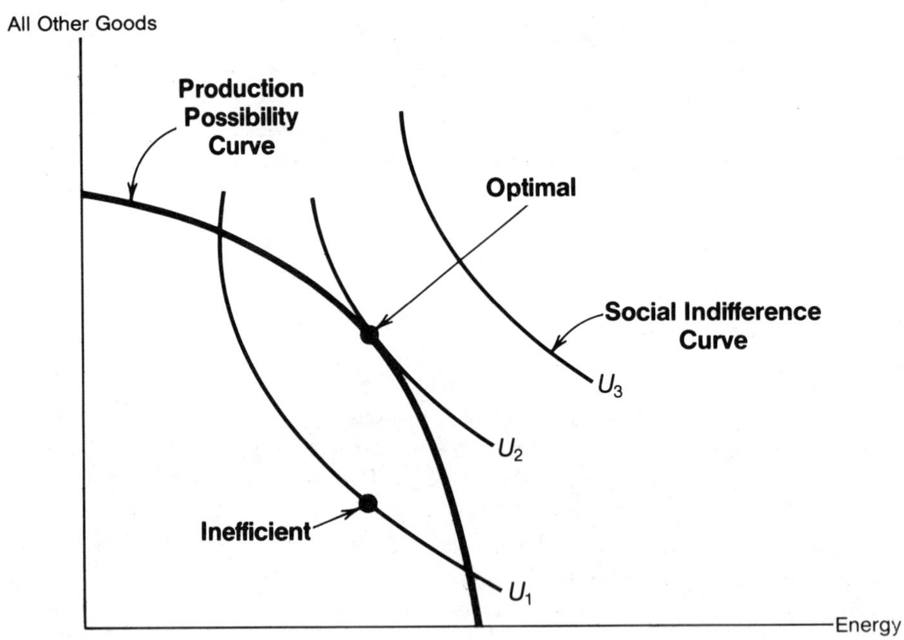

FIGURE 8.1

CHAPTER 9

III. MULTIPLE CHOICE

1 - b
2 - a
3 - a
4 - b
5 - b
6 - b
7 - d
8 - a
9 - d
10 - a

IV. EXERCISES

1. (a) State x and state y are both on the contract curve. They are both Pareto optimal points. At x and y, the marginal rates of substitution are the same for both people. Neither state is "better" than the other. States x and y are Pareto noncomparable to each other.

(b) States x and y are Pareto superior to state z. States x and y are on the contract curve. State z is off of the contract curve. States x and y are Pareto optimal points. State z is not a Pareto optimal point.

(c) Any state of the economy which results in an exchange at a Pareto optimal point is a candidate for a social optimum. States x and y are both Pareto optimal points and are therefore possible social optima.

(d) The Edgeworth box diagram indicates that state x results in utility level U_a'' for person 1 and U_b' for person 2. State y results in utility level U_a' for person 1 and U_b'' for person 2. Since both of these states of the economy are Pareto optimal points, they are both points on the utility possibility frontier. In contrast, state z leads to utility level U_a' for person 1 and U_b' for person 2. Since state z is not on the contract curve, it is inside the utility possibility frontier. These relationships are depicted in Figure 9.1 below.

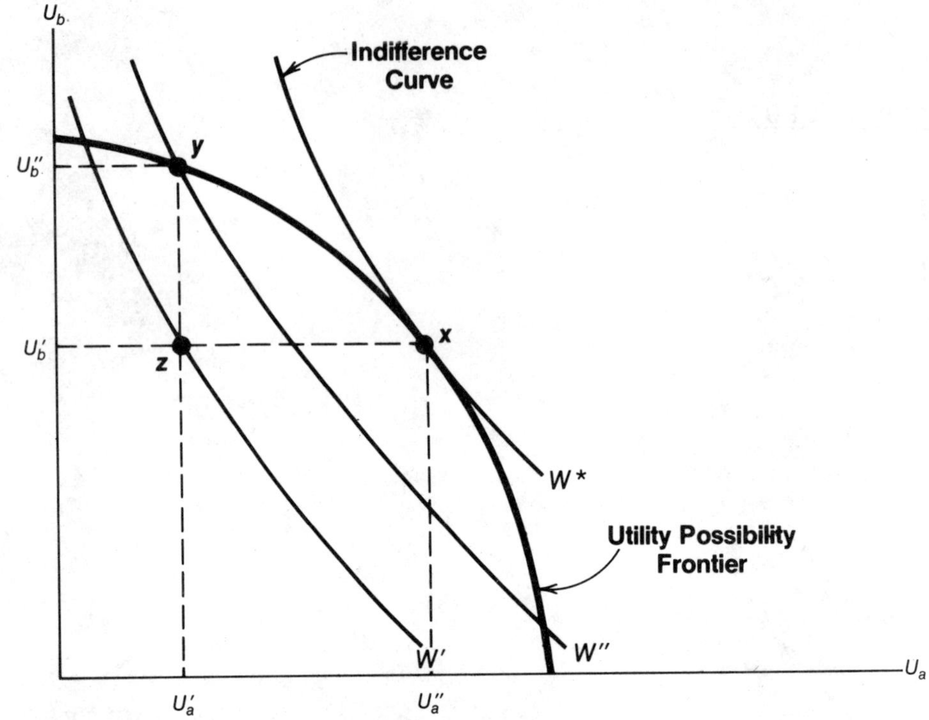

FIGURE 9.1

Figure 9.1 is drawn so that state x is the social optimum. States x and y are both Pareto optimal points and candidates for the social optimum. But the diagram is drawn so that the point of tangency between the utility possibility curve and the highest social indifference curve is at state x. State y is on a lower social indifference curve. State z is on the lowest indifference curve.

2. (a) The first social welfare function is the <u>classical utilitarian</u> social welfare function. Social utility is the sum of the individual utilities of the members of society. The second function is a <u>Rawlsian</u> social welfare function. Social welfare is determined by the utility of the worst-off member of society. Society is no better off than the poorest member of society.

(b) An indifference curve for the classical utilitarian social welfare function is a straight line with slope -1. An indifference curve for the Rawlsian social welfare function is L-shaped. This is depicted in Figure 9.2.

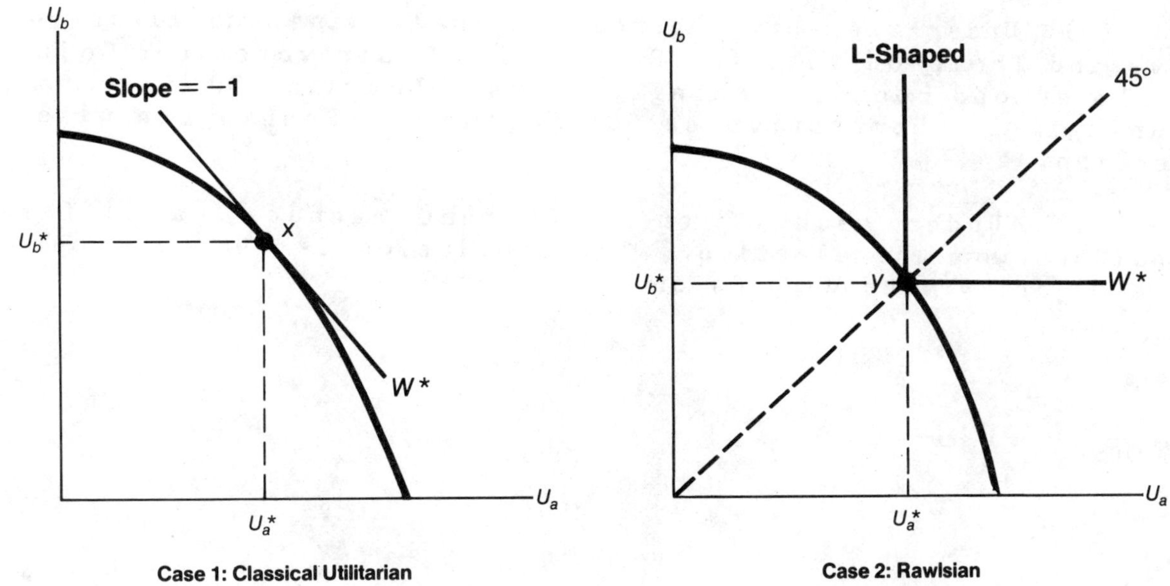

FIGURE 9.2

In the case of the classical utilitarian function, it is possible for the utility levels of the members of society to be quite unequal. An increase in the level of utility of either individual will raise the level of social utility. In the case of the Rawlsian function, social welfare cannot be increased by increases in either individual's utility beyond some minimum value. In Figure 9.2, social welfare will not be increased above W^* if only the utility of person 1 or the utility of person 2 is increased. In order to increase social welfare, the utility levels of both individuals must be raised.

V. PROBLEM

(a) In the first round of the election, Pennington beats Reginald. Levy and Blair both vote for Pennington. Thompson votes for Reginald. In the second round, Columbo beats Pennington. Levy votes for Pennington. Thompson and Blair vote for Columbo. Columbo wins the election.

(b) Under the new agenda, Columbo wins the first round. Levy votes for Pennington. Thompson and Blair vote for Columbo. In the second round, Reginald wins. Levy and Thompson vote for Reginald. Blair votes for Columbo. Reginald wins the election.

(c) Under the third agenda, Reginald wins the first round. Levy and Thompson vote for Reginald. Blair votes for Columbo. In the second round, Pennington wins. Levy and Blair vote for Pennington. Thompson votes for Reginald. Pennington wins the election.

(d) Under each of the different agendas, a different candidate won the election. The conclusion is that the outcome of a majority vote depends on the agenda.

CHAPTER 10

III. MULTIPLE CHOICE

1 - c
2 - a
3 - c
4 - b
5 - a
6 - c
7 - a
8 - c
9 - b
10 - d

IV. EXERCISES

1. (a) The quantity of gasoline demanded prior to the fall in price was q^0.

(b) The direct savings on the original quantity of gasoline demanded as a result of the fall in price is $(p^0-p^1)q^0$.

(c) q^1 is the quantity of gasoline demanded after the price decline. The extra consumption is the difference between the new quantity demanded and the old quantity demanded, q^1-q^0.

(d) Consumers are willing to pay the total area A for the extra consumption. The consumer is willing to pay $p(q^0)$ for the first small extra amount (Δq) of gasoline. She is willing to pay $p(q^0+ \Delta q)$ for the next Δq. She is willing to pay $p(q^0+ 2 \Delta q)$ for the next Δq, and so on. The consumer is willing to pay

$$\int_{q^1}^{q^0} p(q)\, dq$$

for the entire extra consumption. This is the value of the extra consumption. The net gain on this extra consumption is the difference between what the consumer is willing to pay and what the consumer must pay. The consumer must pay $p^1(q^1-q^0)$. The net gain is therefore

$$\int_{q^0}^{q^1} p(q)\, dq - p^1(q^1-q^0)$$

(e) Total consumers' surplus is the entire amount the consumer is willing to pay for the price movement from p^0 to p^1. This is equal to

$$\int_{p^1}^{p^0} q(p)\, dp.$$

2. (a) Let $e(p,u)$ be the expenditure function evaluated at prices p and constant utility level u. Let u_0 be Mary's original level of utility. She would have to be paid

$$e(p^1, u_0) - e(p^0, u_0)$$

to make her as happy as at the price p^0.

(b) Let u_1 be Mary's new level of utility. The amount of income that would have to be taken away from Mary to make her as well off as she would be at the price p^1 is

$$e(p^1, u_1) - e(p^0, u_1).$$

(c) The compensating variation is the maximum amount Mary would be willing to pay for the right to face the new price. Equivalent variation is the "bribe" that Mary would have to be paid to voluntarily accept the old price. The compensating variation and the equivalent variation are not equal.

V. PROBLEM

(a) The supply-demand diagram in Figure 10.1 shows the effects of rent controls on the Santa Monica rental housing market.

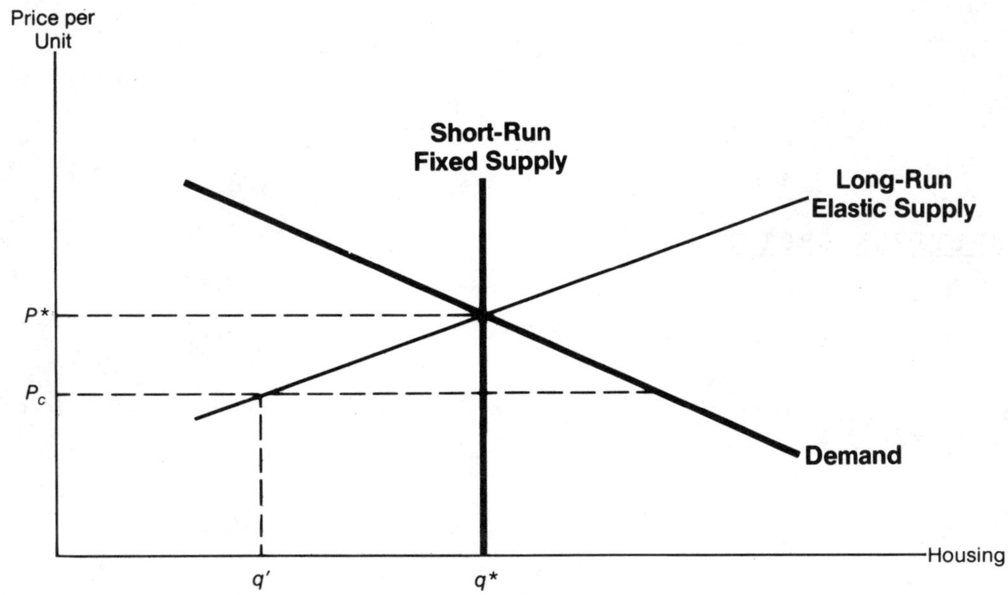

FIGURE 10.1

(b) At the controlled price p_c, quantity demanded exceeds short-run quantity supplied. The market-clearing price p^* is above the controlled price. This is what is meant by the "depressed value" of the property. The market is in disequilibrium. (Notice that the short-run supply of housing is perfectly inelastic. This is because houses cannot be quickly built or demolished. The long-run supply is more elastic. At the controlled price, landlords will continue to supply q^* in the short run. But in the long run, they will reduce the quantity supplied to q^1.)

(c) The landlord's opportunity costs are the returns from alternative investments foregone. In this case, the alternative investments include condominium apartments. By reducing the total revenue that a landlord can earn as rental income, rent controls reduce a landlord's ability to cover his costs. A landlord would want to demolish his building if he continues to lose money in the long run; that is, if total explicit costs plus opportunity costs exceed total revenues in the long run.

(d) The city is saying that the preservation of housing increases net social surplus. Landlords do not like rent controls because they incur a loss in producers' surplus. But the tenants get the gains from the rent controls. The tenants (at least in the short run) get the same amount of rental housing at a lower rental price. The city has decided that the increase in consumers' surplus exceeds the decrease in producers' surplus. Net social surplus has increased. (Unfortunately, this type of social choice often neglects the long-run implications for the total stock of housing.)

CHAPTER 11

III. MULTIPLE CHOICE

1 - c
2 - c
3 - b
4 - a
5 - b
6 - c
7 - d
8 - b
9 - d
10 - d

IV. EXERCISES

1. (a) Profits = Total Revenue - Total Cost.

(b) Profits are maximized at the point where the difference between total revenue and total cost is maximized. This corresponds to output level q_3 in the diagram. At this output level, the distance between the two curves is the greatest.

(c) At output levels q_1 and q_5, total cost exceeds total revenue. Profits are negative. The firm is losing money. At q_2 and q_4, profits are zero. Total revenue equals total cost. At q_3, profits are positive and maximized.

(d) At the point of maximum profits, the slope of the total revenue curve is equal to the slope of the total cost curve. The slope of the total revenue curve is marginal revenue. The slope of the total cost curve is marginal cost. Profits are maximized at the point where marginal revenue is equal to marginal cost.

Consider the slopes of the total revenue and total cost curves. To the left of the point of maximum profits, the slope of the total revenue curve is greater than the slope of the total cost curve. Marginal revenue is greater than marginal cost. If the firm increases output by one unit, the additional revenue it receives will be greater than the additional cost it incurs. The firm has an incentive to increase output. To the right of the point of maximum profits, the slope of the total cost curve is greater than the slope of the total revenue curve. Marginal cost is greater than marginal revenue. If the firm decreases output by one unit, the cost savings will be greater than the revenues foregone. The firm has an incentive to decrease output.

(e) Figure 11.1 below illustrates the point of profit maximization using the marginal revenue and marginal cost curves.

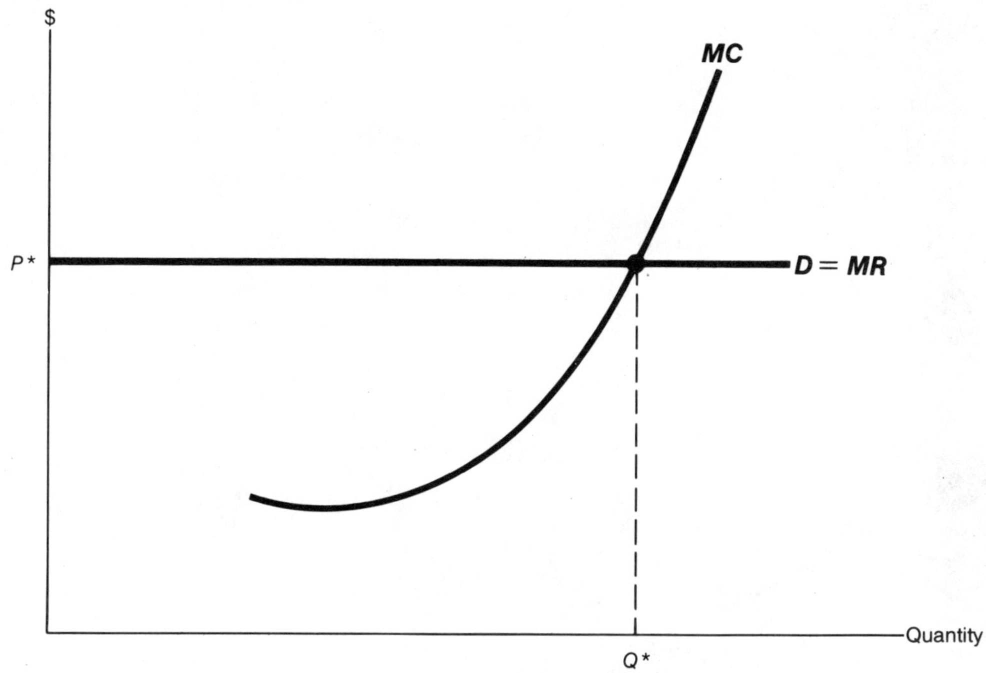

FIGURE 11.1

(f) To the left of the equilibrium point, marginal revenue is greater than marginal cost. Profits may be positive, but they are less than the maximum value they can become. If the firm continues to reduce output, profits will continue to shrink. The firm has an incentive to increase output.

(g) To the right of the equilibrium point, marginal cost is greater than marginal revenue. Profits may be positive, but they are less than the maximum value they can become. If the firm continues to increase output, profits will continue to shrink. The firm has an incentive to decrease output.

2. Total Costs = (Price of labor)(Labor)
 + (Price of plastic)(Plastic)
 + Fixed cost of capital

Substituting the given prices and fixed cost,

Total Costs = \$2L + \$1P + \$150

3. $TFC = 40$

$TVC = q^3 - 4q^2 + 20q$

$AVC = TVC/q = q^2 - 4q + 20$

$AFC = TFC/q = 40/q$

V. PROBLEM

(a) Consider Figure 11.2.

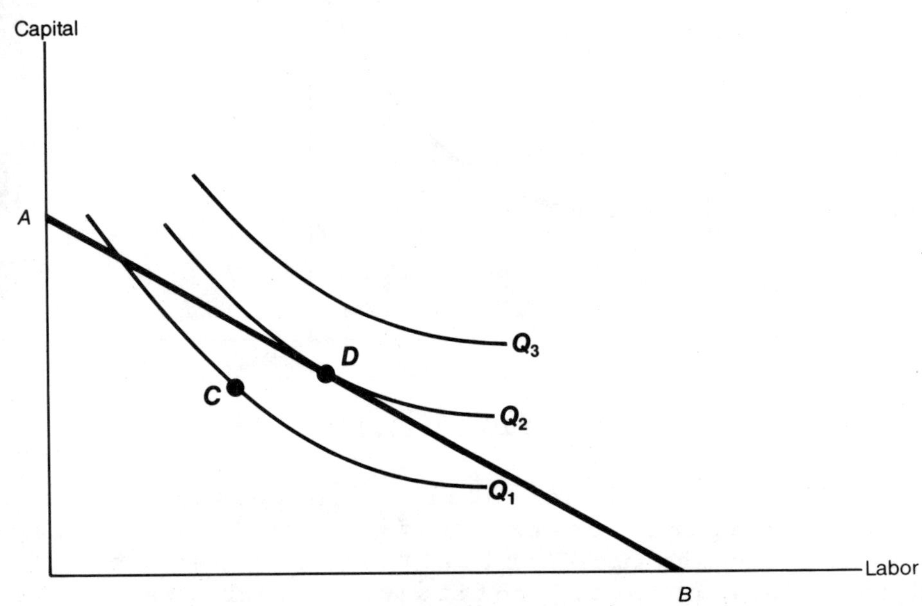

FIGURE 11.2

The firm's cost constraint is represented by the isocost curve AB. The level of output Q_3 is not attainable because the obtainable combinations of factor inputs are limited to those lying on, or beneath, AB. Interior points such as C are inefficient combinations of capital and labor because more output can be produced without exceeding the cost constraint. The optimal point of production is D, at which an isoquant is tangent to the isocost curve. The optimal level of output is Q_2. At D, the slope of the isocost curve is equal to the slope of the isoquant. This is the equilibrium condition.

(b) Consider Figure 11.3 .

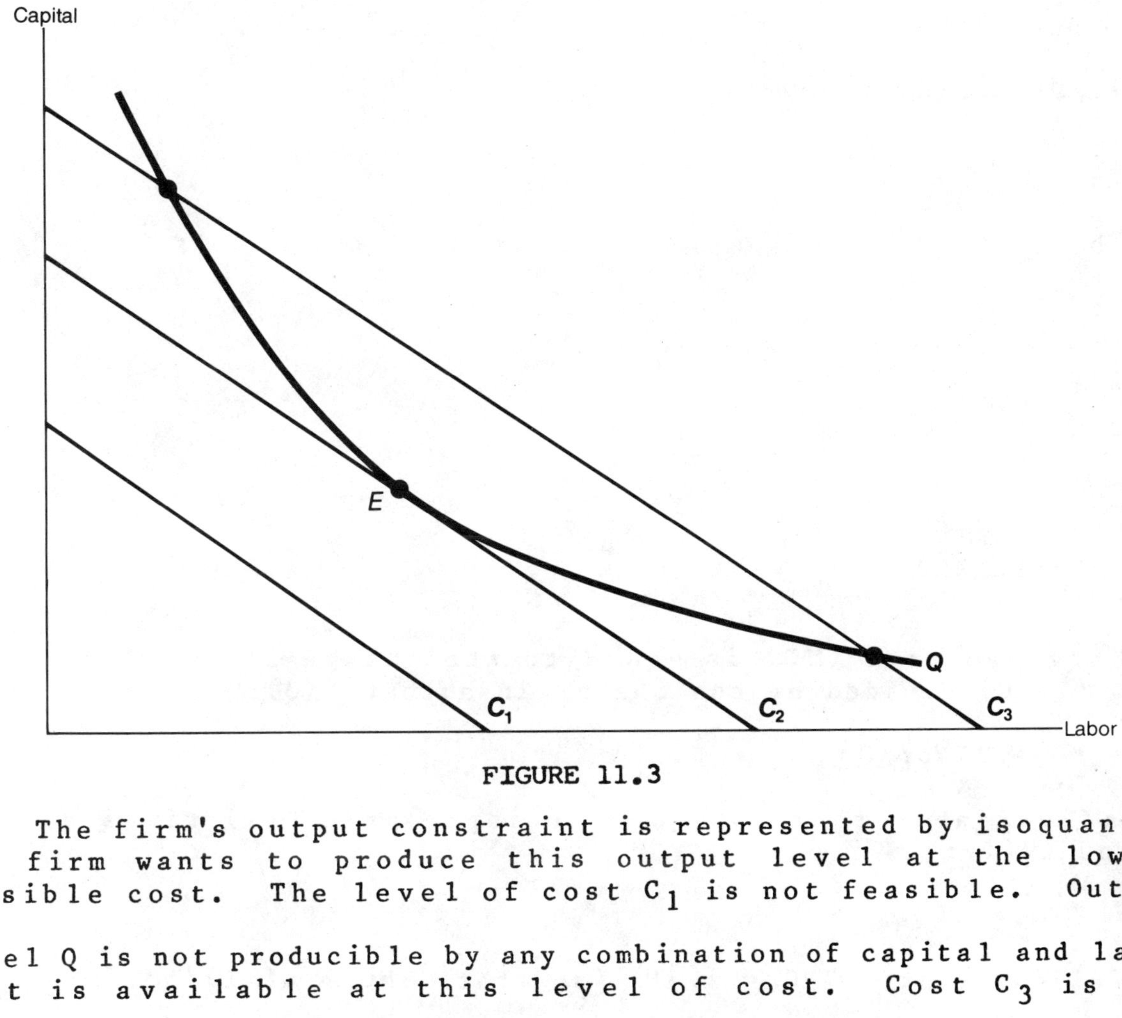

FIGURE 11.3

The firm's output constraint is represented by isoquant Q. The firm wants to produce this output level at the lowest possible cost. The level of cost C_1 is not feasible. Output level Q is not producible by any combination of capital and labor that is available at this level of cost. Cost C_3 is not efficient since output Q can be produced at a lower cost. The optimal point of production is at point E, where the given isoquant is tangent to an isocost curve. At the equilibrium point, the slope of the isoquant is equal to the slope of an isocost curve.

(c) The two equilibrium conditions are identical. In order to minimize cost subject to a given output constraint or maximize output subject to a given cost constraint, inputs should be employed at the point where the slope of an isoquant is equal to the slope of an isocost curve.

(d) Profits are maximized at both equilibrium points. The two equilibrium conditions are consistent with the condition that the firm produce where marginal revenue is equal to marginal cost.

CHAPTER 12

III. MULTIPLE CHOICE

1 - c
2 - b
3 - d
4 - b
5 - a
6 - c
7 - a
8 - d
9 - a
10 - b

IV. EXERCISES

1. Marginal cost (MC) is equal to the change in total variable cost (ΔTVC) divided by the change in output (ΔQ):

$$MC = \Delta TVC/\Delta Q$$

Total variable cost is equal to input price (w) times quantity of input (I):

$$TVC = wI$$

It follows that $\Delta TVC = w(\Delta I)$ so that $MC = w(\Delta I)/\Delta Q$.

Recall that marginal product (MP) is equal to the change in output divided by the change in input:

$$MP = \Delta Q/\Delta I$$

Hence $MC = w(1/MP)$.

Marginal cost and marginal product are inversely related. Marginal product normally rises, reaches a maximum, and declines. Marginal cost therefore declines, reaches a minimum, and then rises.

2. Total variable cost (TVC) is equal to the number of units of variable input (I) used times the unit price of the input (w):

$$TVC = wI$$

Average variable cost (AVC) is equal to total variable cost divided by output:

AVC = TVC/Q = wI/Q

Recall that average product (AP) is equal to total output divided by the number of units of variable input used:

AP = Q/I

Substituting:

AVC = w(1/AP)

Average variable cost and average product are inversely related. Average product rises, reaches a maximum, and then declines. Average variable cost falls, reaches a minimum, and then rises.

3. Bob Stone argued correctly. Fixed costs are not relevant to the decision of whether or not to shut the plant down. In either case, the firm still incurs the fixed costs. The relevant question is whether or not variable costs are covered. If the firm is able to at least cover its variable costs, then it will continue to produce, at least in the short run. By doing this it will be minimizing its losses and maximizing its profits (even though profits are negative). If the firm is not even able to cover its variable costs, then it will shut down. By shutting down it will be losing less money than if it produced any output at all. If the market price is below average variable cost, then the firm will lose even more money on every unit of output that it produces.

V. PROBLEM

(a) The average income level for the Stamford community in 1980 was $10,000. (Total income in the community was equal to $1,000,000.)

(b) Robert Shaun's marginal contribution was equal to his salary of $15,050. His marginal contribution was above the community average. Shaun's $15,050 salary raised the total income in the community to $1,015,050. The community now consisted of 101 citizens. Shaun's arrival therefore raised the average income level to ($1,015,050/101) = $10,050.

(c) Wilma Josephson's marginal contribution to the total income in Stamford in 1982 was $10,050. Since her marginal contribution was equal to the average at the time of her arrival, the average did not change from $10,050.

(d) Paul Blair's marginal contribution was $8,000. His marginal contribution was below the community average. This lowered the community average to $10,030.10.

(e) When marginal income is above average income, the additional (marginal) contribution pulls the average up so that the average will rise. When marginal income is equal to average income, the average will not change. When marginal income is below average income, the additional contribution pulls the average down so that the average must fall.

CHAPTER 13

III. MULTIPLE CHOICE

1 - c
2 - c
3 - c
4 - d
5 - b
6 - c
7 - a
8 - c
9 - d
10 - b

IV. EXERCISES

1. (a) Brett's decision to stay in business after six months was correct. He is unable in the short run to cover his average fixed costs of production. But these costs will be incurred whether or not he stays in business. The decision to stay in business depends on whether or not average variable costs are covered. If marginal revenue is below average variable costs, then the firm loses money on every unit of output sold. Brett is able to cover his average variable costs. Brett therefore made the correct decision to stay in business.

(b) Brett's rationale for staying in business after one year was not correct. If marginal revenue is below average total costs in the long run, then the firm is losing money by being in business. It is earning negative profits. The correct decision is to shut down the firm. Brett's decision to increase the volume of his sales will result in larger and larger losses as output increases. Every time he sells another tire he will lose more money.

2. A competitive firm maximizes its profits by producing the level of output at which marginal revenue is equal to marginal cost. If the Getcha Paper Supply Company produces an amount of output that exceeds this profit-maximizing level Q^*, then it will be producing at a point where marginal cost exceeds marginal revenue (see Figure 13.1). Production of the extra amount of output will reduce total profits because the additional cost of

producing every unit of output above Q^* will exceed the additional revenue received.

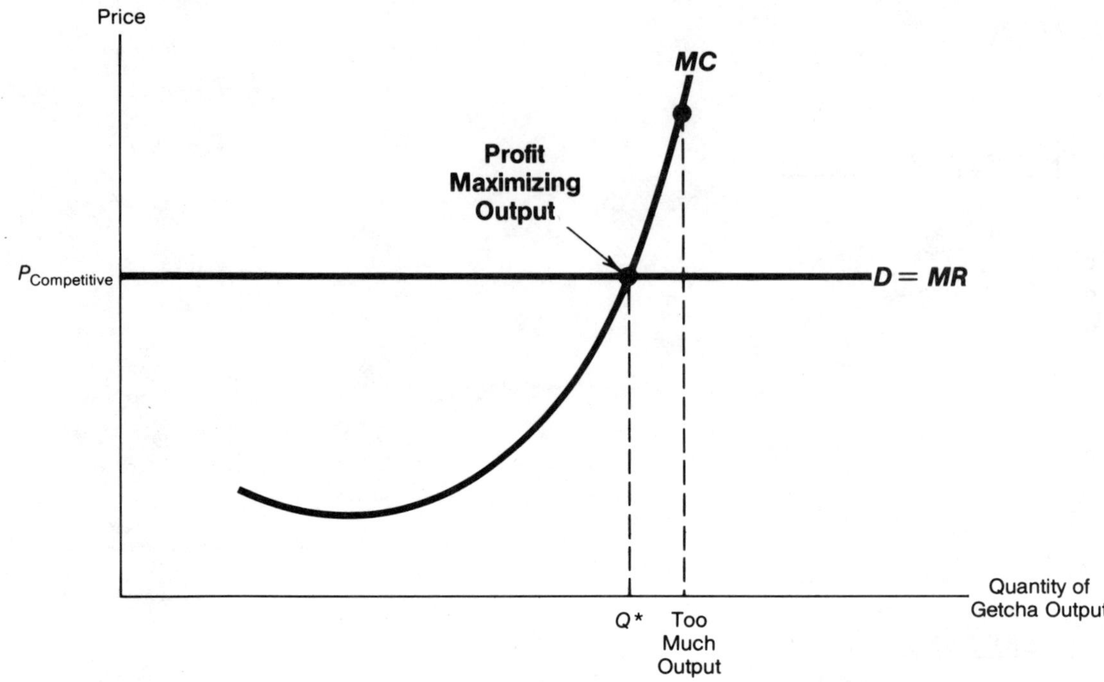

FIGURE 13.1

3. Market supply is equal to the sum of the supply curves of the individual firms in the industry. If Tastem Foods leaves the hamburger market that is on George Street, total industry supply will be reduced. The market supply curve will shift to the left (see Figure 13.2). The market must clear. The new equilibrium will result in a higher market price for hamburgers. At this new equilibrium price, fewer hamburgers will be bought and sold. The remaining firms in the industry will continue to maximize profits by producing where marginal cost is equal to market price. Since the market price is higher, each of the remaining hamburger joints on George Street will produce, cook and sell more hamburgers (see Figure 13.3).

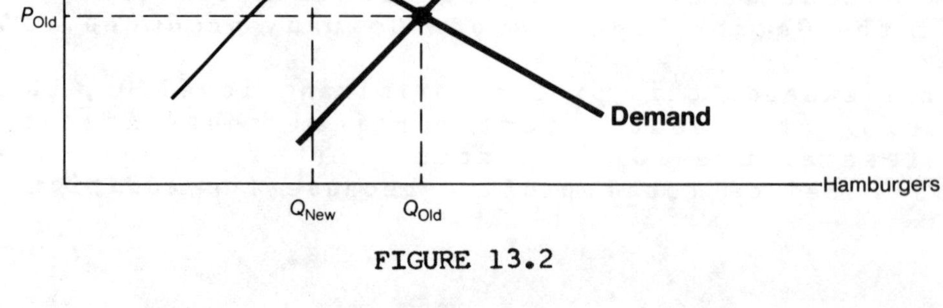

FIGURE 13.2

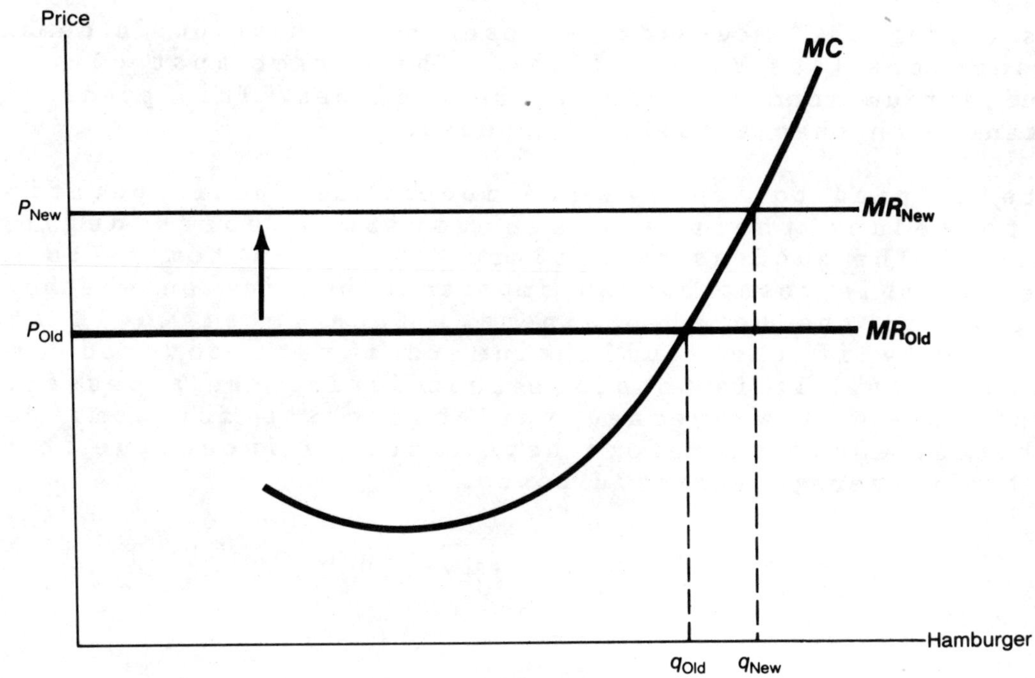

FIGURE 13.3

V. PROBLEM

(a)

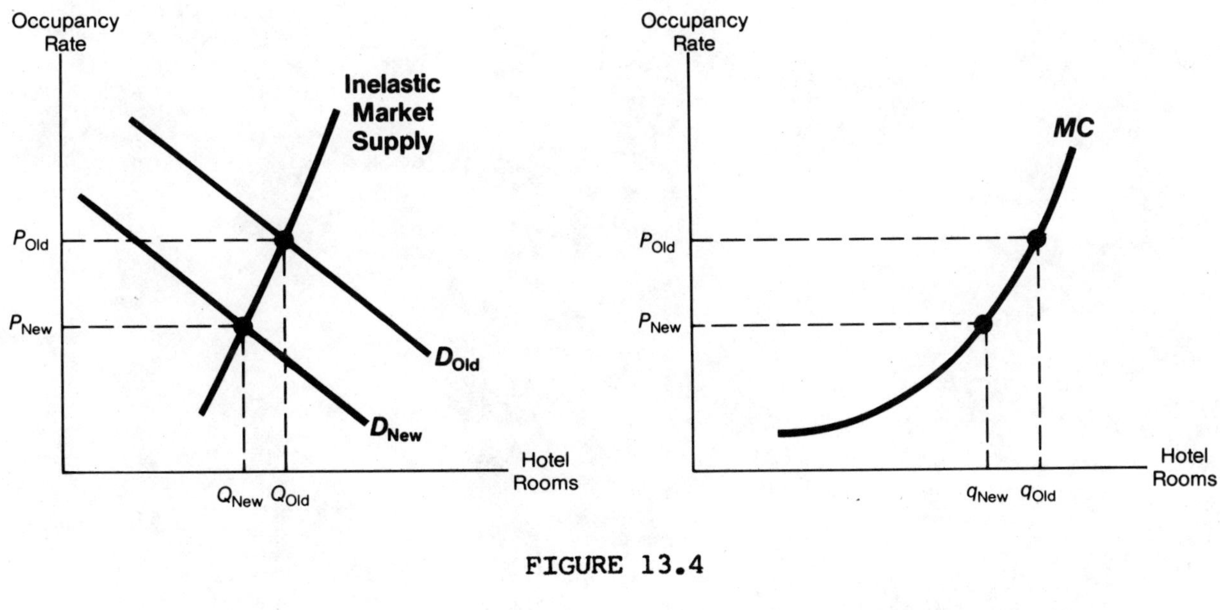

FIGURE 13.4

(b) The decline in the number of visitors to the city of New

Orleans during the recession represents a reduction in demand for hotel services (see Figure 13.4). The market must clear. The new equilibrium room rate therefore declines. This prediction is consistent with what actually happened.

(c) Hotels tried to improve and modernize their operations in order to reduce their average variable costs during the recession. The success or failure of their attempts to reduce average variable costs had an important bearing on whether they would stay in the hotel business. Each hotel would stay in business only if the equilibrium room rate covered average variable costs. It is possible that during the recession, the room rate was below average variable costs for some hotels. These hotels would therefore have a strong incentive to try to reduce their average variable costs.

CHAPTER 14

MULTIPLE CHOICE

1 - d
2 - b
3 - c
4 - a
5 - d
6 - c
7 - c
8 - b
9 - b
10 - b

IV. EXERCISES

1. The gasoline stations on the northbound side of the Garden State Parkway are in a different industry than the stations on the southbound side. The concrete divider in the middle of the highway separates the two sides of the highway. Automobiles cannot cross the highway to purchase gasoline from stations on the other side. The northbound stations serve a different group of customers than the southbound stations. The northbound market is different than the southbound market. Both are competitive, but the market-clearing prices are different.

2. WARNING: If the writer of the article is so smart why isn't he rich? There is free entry into the Japanese stock market. The principle of entry and exit should make the reader skeptical of the existence of any unexploited profit opportunities in the Japanese stock market. USA Today is also a nationwide newspaper which thousands of people read. Every reader is a potential entrant into the market and has an opportunity to exploit any supernormal profits.

3. Barry Whitman's proper response should be: "If I were that smart I would be rich." Economists are no different than any other potential entrants into the stock market, including the thousands of readers of the national business magazine. There is no reason to believe that economists have any greater ability than say, business executives, to see unexploited opportunities for profit. Further, by the time John Thompson asked Barry for his opinion, any profit opportunities that might have existed

would have already been exploited and eliminated.

V. PROBLEM

(a) Prior to the introduction of minilabs, the photo processing industry was at a long-run equilibrium (see Figure 14.1). The prevailing market price was P^* and the equilibrium quantity transacted was Q^*.

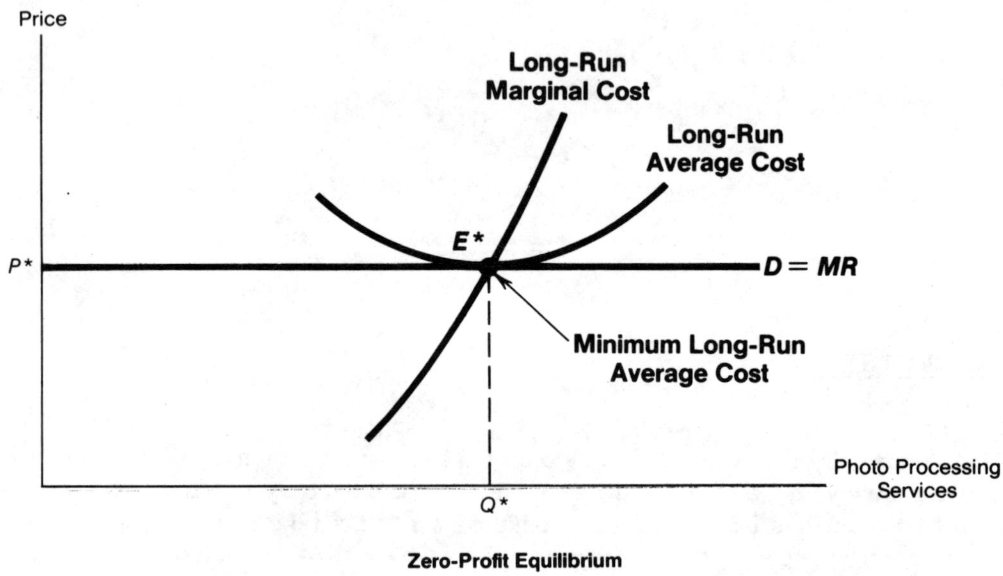

FIGURE 14.1

(b) The introduction of Kis minilabs which sold for one-third the cost of existing equipment, had the effect of lowering the minimum point on the long-run average cost curve (see Figure 14.2)

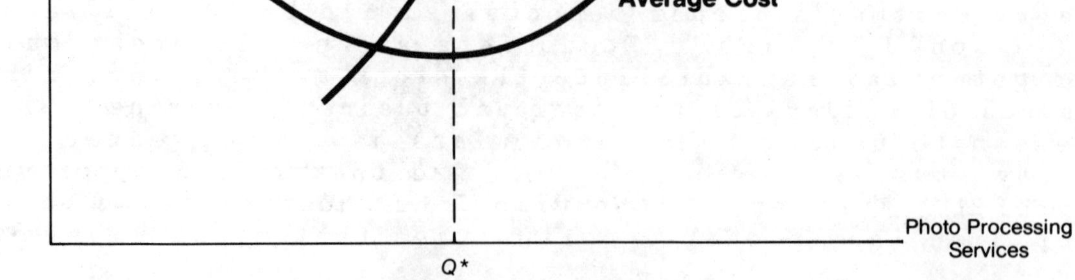

FIGURE 14.2

At the prevailing price P^*, new firms that enter the industry with the new Kis technology make positive short-run profits (see Figure 14.3).

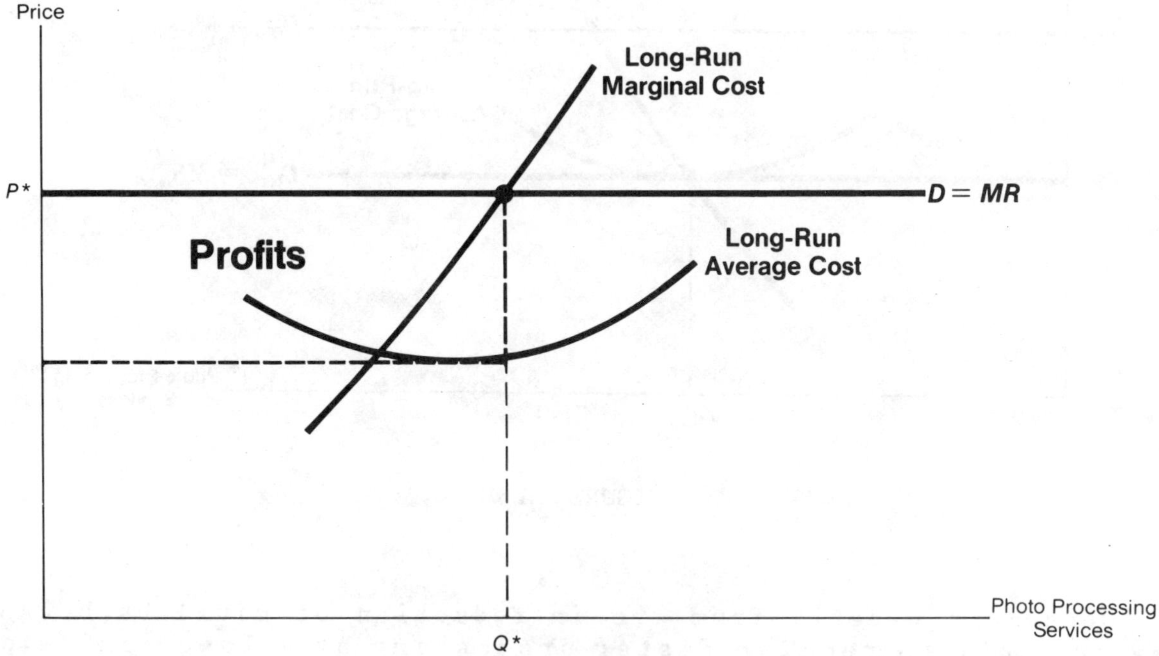

FIGURE 14.3

(c) The appearance of this <u>pure economic profit</u> in the industry (that is, a return in excess of that obtainable elsewhere), attracts entry into the industry. This entry expands industry supply and reduces the prevailing market-clearing price. This process will continue until all economic profits have been eliminated (see Figure 14.4). Some firms that were unable to reduce their average costs through the introduction of new capital will exit from the industry.

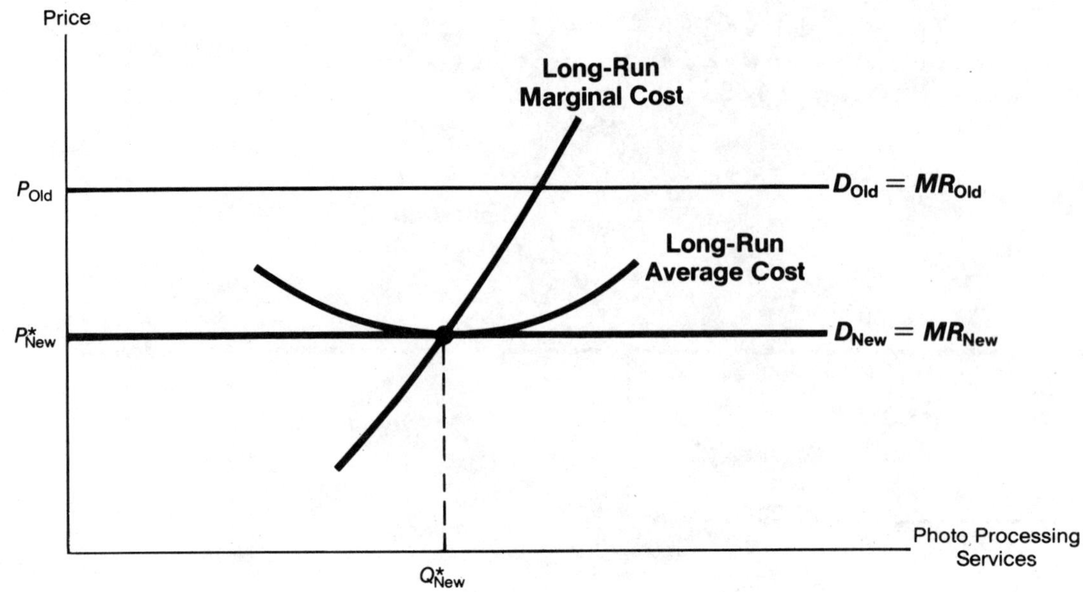

FIGURE 14.4

(d) Consumers benefit from the introduction of minilabs because they are able to receive faster processing at a lower price per roll of film. The new entrants into the industry also benefit because they gain a share of the total photofinishing market and are able to earn normal profits.

CHAPTER 15

III. MULTIPLE CHOICE

1 - c
2 - d
3 - d
4 - d
5 - a
6 - d
7 - d
8 - a
9 - a
10 - d

IV. EXERCISES

1. (a) Private corporations are not entities that are distinct from middle class America. Corporations are people. Recall that the "firm" lies between the individual consumer and the economy. The people within a firm are agents of other people who own, work for, sell to, and buy from it.

(b) The reduction in corporate taxes does not stay entirely where they are initially put. The taxes fall where they fall. The burden of the tax is eventually also borne by people outside of the corporate sector. The degree to which the burden is shifted depends on the price elasticities of supply and demand.

(c) The analysis of a corporate tax is not complete until the incentives to enter or exit the industry are considered. A reduction in corporate taxes will create short-run profits above normal. The tax reduction increases the normal return to corporate ownership. This causes entry into the corporate sector. The relative prices of goods produced in the corporate sector declines and raises wages and the employment of resources. Entry will continue until all profits are normal.

(d) The debate is meaningless. The burden of a tax falls where it falls, not where politicians or lawyers puts it.

2. The tax increase will have the greatest effect on goods with a high price elasticity of demand. The demand for cigarettes and

gasoline tends to be inelastic (at least in the short run). A tax increase on these goods will have little effect on the quantities that people will purchase. But the demand for chocolate bars is elastic. A tax imposed on chocolate bars will have a larger effect on the quantity of chocolate bars bought and sold.

3. (a) The tax credit lowers the price of parochial and private school education. This will increase the quantity demanded. Further, more families will want to substitute private education in place of public school education (causing an upward shift in the demand curve for private education). But the supply of classroom space in parochial and private schools is fixed in the short run. The short-run supply curve is almost perfectly inelastic. More children are willing to attend private school than there are spaces for. The number of children attending private schools will not change much in the short run.

(b) The price of private school education must rise in order to restore equilibrium to the market. Many of the funds from the tax credit are passed on to the private and parochial schools. This is another example of a tax falling where it falls, not where policy makers put it.

V. PROBLEM

(a) There is a deadweight loss to society resulting from the tax. The tax money that consumers pay is revenue gained by the government. But the tax revenue does not completely offset any losses to society. National income still falls because the tax puts a wedge between the marginal cost of electricity and its marginal valuation.

(b) The tax on electricity raises the unit price of electricity. Quantity demanded will fall. At the higher price, excess supply exists. The quantity of electricity sold and the price must fall to remove the excess supply. At the new equilibrium, consumers pay more per unit of electricity and electric utilities receive less than before the tax.

(c) If the tax creates profits below normal, then exit from the electric utility industry will occur (neglecting the effects of regulation). Exit will continue until all profits are normal.

(d) Social welfare declines. The fall in national income is an indication (though imperfect) that social welfare is reduced. The fact that policy makers want to spread the tax out nationally is unimportant to society as a whole. Some local regions might benefit at the expense of others. Society as a whole is worse off. But the tax is justifiable. Pollution is an externality. Society as a whole may decide that the elimination of the acid rain problem is worth the costs in inefficiencies that it will incur due to the tax.

CHAPTER 16

III. MULTIPLE CHOICE

1 - a
2 - d
3 - b
4 - d
5 - c
6 - a
7 - c
8 - a
9 - b
10 - a

IV. EXERCISES

1. Coase's Theorem warns us that the "cause" of the sewage is not always the best place to put the liability. The sewage originates at the Littletown Electric Company. Notice however, that the location of the homes close to the Electric Company is as much a "cause" of the problem as is the Electric Company.

The best place to put the liability for the sewage depends upon the costs of transacting deals. If the costs of making deals is low, then the party that can most cheaply avoid the hurt from the sewage can be induced to do so. In this case, it does not matter for efficiency where the liability is placed. Adam Smith's generalization guarantees that the liability will find its way to the correct party. But if the costs of making deals are high, then it does matter where the liability is placed.

If the costs of making deals between the Littletown Electric Company and the homeowners on Gates Road are low, then the Electric Company faced with a $500,000 bill for pollution abatement equipment will be able to bribe the homeowners to pay for the installation of new pipes from the Water Company to their homes. The Electric Company might, for example, pay the homeowners $250,000 to install the water pipes plus a $100 bribe. The sewage will no longer be a problem and the Electric Company will not have to pay for the installation of the pollution abatement equipment. If transaction costs are low, the exchange of rights will lead to the social optimum. If the costs of making deals are high, then the Electric Company will not be able to bribe the homeowners and will be forced to install the pollution abatement equipment at a social cost of $500,000.

Placing the liability for the pollution on the Electric Company does not achieve the social optimum when the costs of making deals are high.

2. (a) The ration coupon system would be effective in eliminating the long lines at the gasoline stations. Only those individuals who held coupons would be allowed to purchase gasoline at the stations.

(b) A rationing system that prohibits the resale of coupons would result in a social loss due to the allocation of any gasoline to the wrong individuals. An alternative system that would permit the resale of coupons would be more efficient. If the coupons are exchangeable, then they will end up in the hands of those individuals that value them the most. All individuals will end up having the same marginal rates of substitution for all pairs of goods in the economy.

3. It is not at all surprising that cases of bribery occur. When consumers are prevented from freely purchasing commodities that they desire, wasteful nonmarket competition will occur. It is often the case that unlicensed and nonunion workers are willing to do plumbing and electric wiring for builders of homes. But the law prevents the builders from purchasing these services even if they so desire. To circumvent the market, bribery often occurs.

V. PROBLEM

(a) Consider Figure 16.1. If the current controlled price of natural gas is below the equilibrium price, then the actual quantity transacted will be less than the equilibrium quantity. Recall that when the market price is not equal to the equilibrium price, quantity exchanged is equal to the lesser of quantity supplied and quantity demanded.

(b) Consumers who are able to purchase the natural gas at the regulated price gain from the price controls. But shortages exist because quantity demanded exceeds quantity supplied at the controlled price. People who would be willing to purchase the natural gas at the regulated price but are unable to do so, incur a loss from the controls. There are foresaken opportunities for exchange. The loss from price controls on natural gas is equal to the value of the foregone opportunities for exchange.

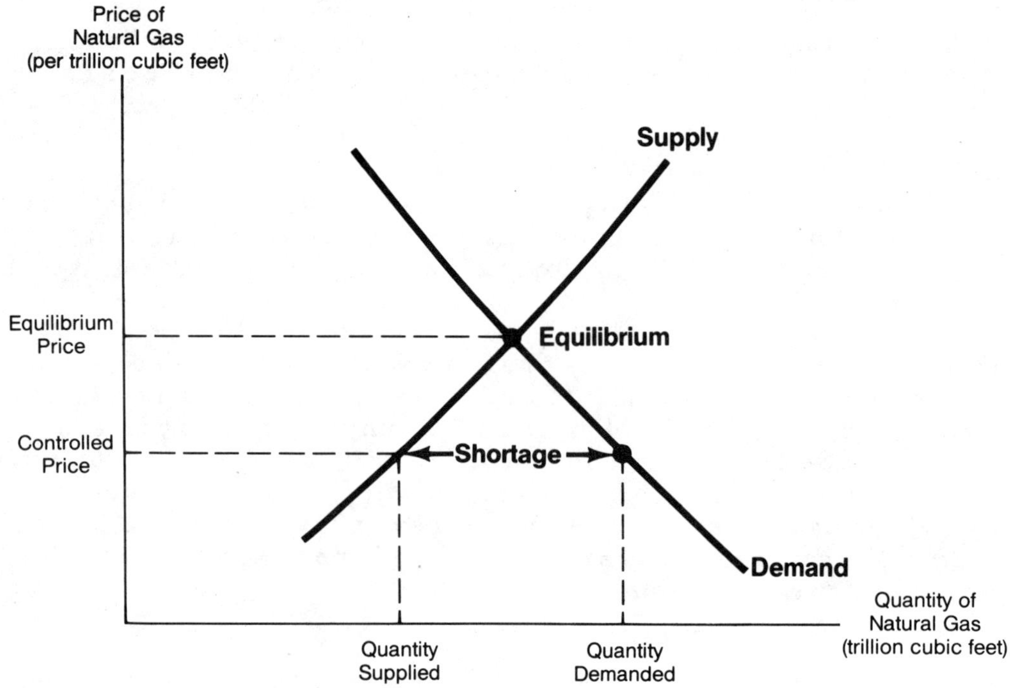

FIGURE 16.1

(c) Consider Figure 16.2.

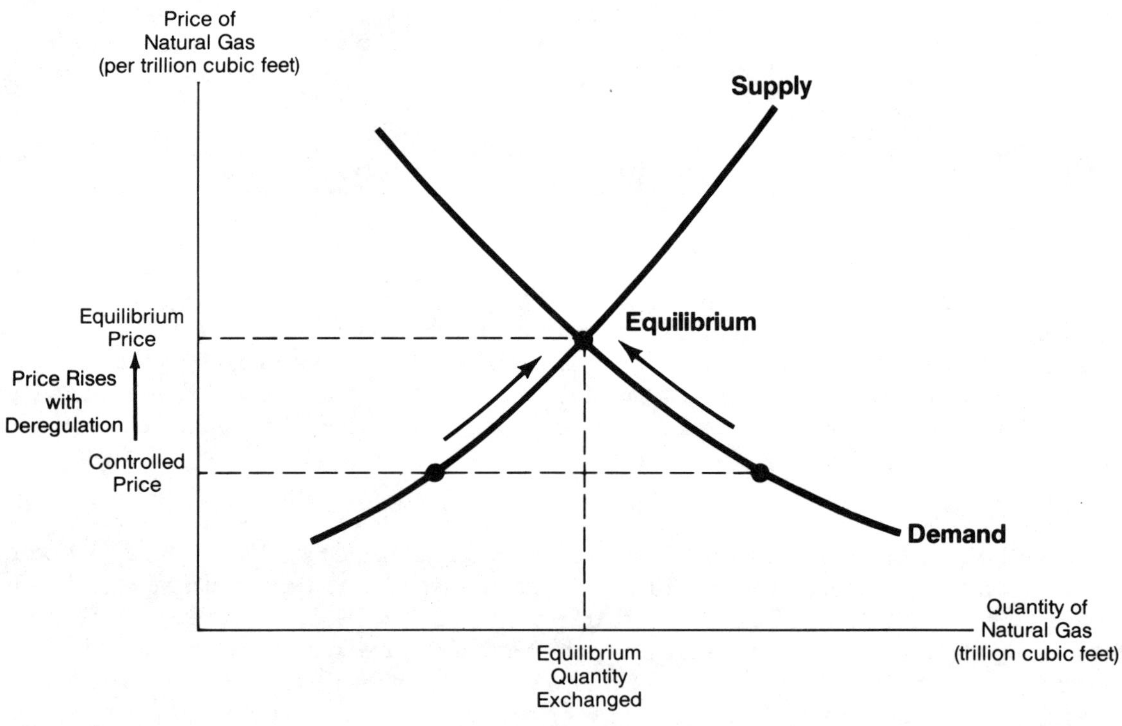

FIGURE 16.2

Passage of the Reagan administration bill would have allowed the market for natural gas to finally clear. The market price would have risen to the equilibrium price and the quantity exchanged would have risen to the equilibrium quantity. Consumers who are willing to pay the equilibrium price for natural gas, who previously were unable to get the gas because of the shortages, would have gained. Consumers who previously were able to obtain the natural gas at the regulated price would have lost.

(d) If the alternative bill had been passed, the shortages of natural gas would have worsened. Although some lucky consumers would have been helped, people as a whole would have been hurt.

(e) If there are no restrictions on the resale of natural gas, then one would expect a secondary market for natural gas to develop. Prior to any reselling of the natural gas, a gap exists between what some people are willing to pay for it and what it actually costs at the controlled price. The gap is supernormal profits to whoever can claim it. People are rent seekers. The lucky individuals who were able to buy the gas at the controlled price have an incentive to resell it at a higher uncontrolled price. Rents are transferred from the original producers of the natural gas to the people who are able to resell the gas.

CHAPTER 17

III. MULTIPLE CHOICE

1 - a
2 - b
3 - d
4 - a
5 - d
6 - d
7 - d
8 - d
9 - a
10 - d

IV. EXERCISES

1. (a) The monopolist will produce at the point where MR=MC. This is point B in the diagram. The demand curve indicates the price that consumers are willing to pay for any level of output. From point B, move vertically up to the demand curve (point A) and then read off of the vertical axis the monopoly price. Price P is the monopoly price.

(b) Output Q is the monopoly output. The demand curve indicates that at monopoly price P, consumers are willing to purchase output Q.

(c) The cost per unit, or average cost, is represented by the distance OC. Total costs are equal to the area of rectangle OCBQ. The area of this rectangle is equal to the average total cost ($OC) times the monopoly output Q.

(d) Total revenue is equal to the area of rectangle OPAQ. Short-run monopoly profits are equal to total revenue minus total cost. Total profits are equal to the area of rectangle CPAB. The area of rectangle CPAB depends crucially on the elasticity of the demand curve. The more elastic is market demand, the smaller will be monopoly profits.

(e)

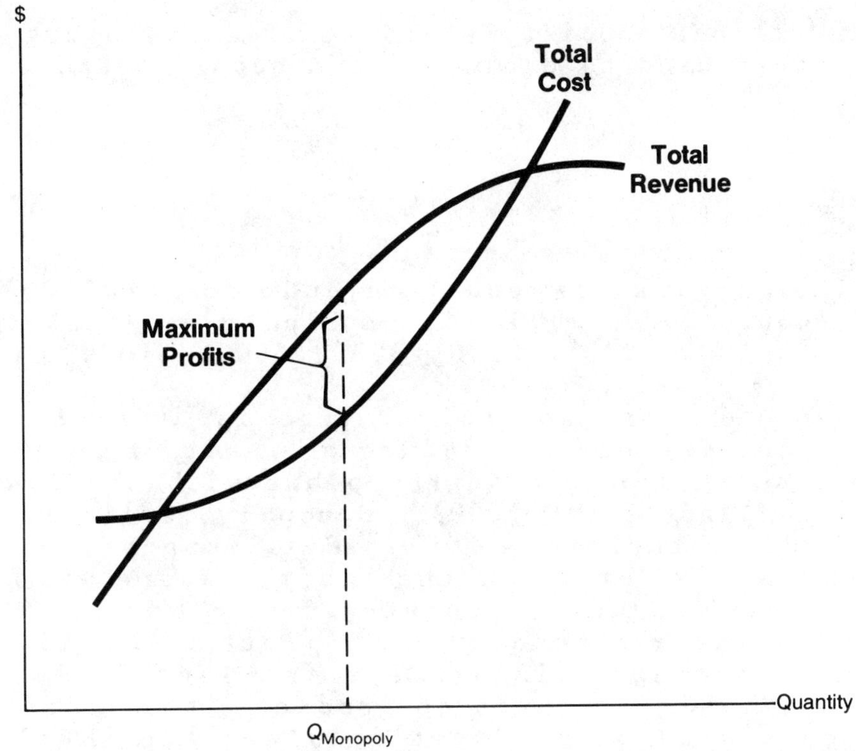

FIGURE 17.1

2. (a) The monopolist will produce at the point where marginal revenue is equal to long-run marginal cost. In the diagram, monopoly output is Q and the monopoly price is P.

(b) Per unit costs are $OH. Total costs are given by the area of the rectangle OHGQ.

(c) The maximum long-run monopoly profits are equal to the area of rectangle HPFG.

(d) The optimal size plant is given by short-run average cost curve SAC. The optimal plant is the one whose short-run average cost curve is tangent to the long-run average cost curve at the point corresponding to long-run monopoly output. At this point, short-run marginal cost is equal to marginal revenue.

(e) Under perfect competition, production occurs at minimum long-run average cost and minimum short-run average cost. The monopolist chooses his output and then utilizes the plant capable of producing this long-run output at the least unit cost. But this plant is not associated with absolute minimum cost. Society's resources are used more efficiently in perfectly competitive markets.

The perfect competitor produces where price is equal to marginal cost. The monopolist produces at a point where price is greater than marginal cost. Under monopoly, the marginal social valuation of monopoly output is greater than the marginal social cost of production. Society would benefit by having more of its scarce resources used to produce the monopoly output.

V. PROBLEM

(a) The marginal revenue schedule is $10000, 7000, 7000, 6000, 5000, 4000, 3000, 2000. The monopoly marginal cost schedule is 1000, 1500, 1900, 2001, 2100, 3000, 3000, 3100.

(b) Suppose total monopoly output is initially zero. The monopolist then decides to produce one unit of output. It will produce this unit of output in the plant with the lower marginal cost. This is plant 1 (MC=1000). Monopoly marginal cost for one unit of output is therefore 1000. Next suppose the monopolist wants to expand output by another unit. Where will it produce this second unit? It will produce it in plant 1. The marginal cost of producing a second unit in plant 1 (MC=1500) is still lower than producing a single unit in plant 2 (MC=1900). Now suppose the monopolist wants to produce a third unit of output. The third unit will be produced in plant two (MC=1900) rather than plant one (MC=2001). And so on.

(c) Profits will be maximized at the point where monopoly marginal revenue is equal to monopoly marginal cost, which in turn is equal to the marginal costs in both plants. In this example, the monopolist will produce seven units of output. At seven units, monopoly marginal cost equals $3000. Marginal revenue also equals $3000.

(d) Marginal cost in plant 1 is equal to $3000 at an output level of five units. Marginal cost in plant 2 is equal to $3000 at an output level of two units. Monopoly output will be allocated so that plant 1 produces five units of output and plant 2 produces two units of output.

CHAPTER 18

III. MULTIPLE CHOICE

1 - c
2 - a
3 - b
4 - d
5 - b

IV. EXERCISES

1. (a) These price elasticities are consistent with the observed behavior. The price elasticity of demand for a book club member is higher than for a retail buyer. One would expect that the retail buyer, who is willing to pay the higher retail price despite the existence of book clubs, would be less responsive to price changes.

(b) It is possible to determine how much more a retail buyer would be willing to pay by using the Fundamental Equation of Discriminatory Monopoly. Substituting the given values for the price elasticities of demand:

$$(\text{book club price})(1-1/2) = (\text{retail price})(1-1/1.5)$$

$$(\text{retail price})/(\text{book club price}) = .5/.33 = 1.52 \ .$$

The buyer of books at retail is willing to pay 1.5 times as much for the same book.

2. Yes, the licensing agreement is rational. Trancomp Computer Corporation is price discriminating. It recognizes that different groups of computer owners have different price elasticities of demand for the Trancomp program. It is not legal for them to charge different groups of consumers a different price for the same program. It circumvents this legal obstacle by signing the licensing agreement.

3. (a) Perfect competition does not imply zero profits. It implies zero supernormal profits. The observed $25,000 annual profits might be a normal return for an aspirin manufacturer.

This might be the amount necessary to cover the firm's opportunity costs of being in the industry.

(b) A large number of firms does not always prove that a market is perfectly competitive. But in the case of the generic aspirin market, the firms are all producing a homogeneous product. None of the products is differentiated from any other product. None of the firms is gaining monopolistic power by differentiating its product. There are no apparent barriers to entry in this market. One would expect the four-firm and eight-firm concentration ratios to be very small for this market.

V. PROBLEM

(a) The Solar Beater Food Company is a monopoly. A monopoly is said to exist if there is only one seller in a well-defined market. In this case, the market is that for solar-powered blenders. A monopoly exists because Solar Beater received a patent for its product. This patent represents a barrier to entry of potential competitors.

(b) A market concentration ratio would be a good measure of Solar Beater's market power. It would indicate that the entire market belonged to Solar Beater. The market concentration ratio measure usually fails to consider the existence of potential entrants. But in this market, entry is barred completely by the existence of a patent.

(c) It is not true that there are absolutely no constraints on Solar Beater's behavior. The actions of any monopolist might be constrained by (1) the indirect competition of reasonably adequate substitute goods, (2) the indirect competition of all goods for the consumer's dollar, and (3) the threat of potential competition if market entry is possible. In this particular case, there is no immediate threat of entry because of the patent. But Solar Beater must still be conscious of the existence of substitute products, such as ordinary blenders, and other products competing for the consumer's limited money.

(d) The company's managers will try to maximize the firm's profits. This is done by following the Rule of Rational Life. They will choose to produce the level of output at which marginal revenue is equal to marginal cost (see Figure 18.1).

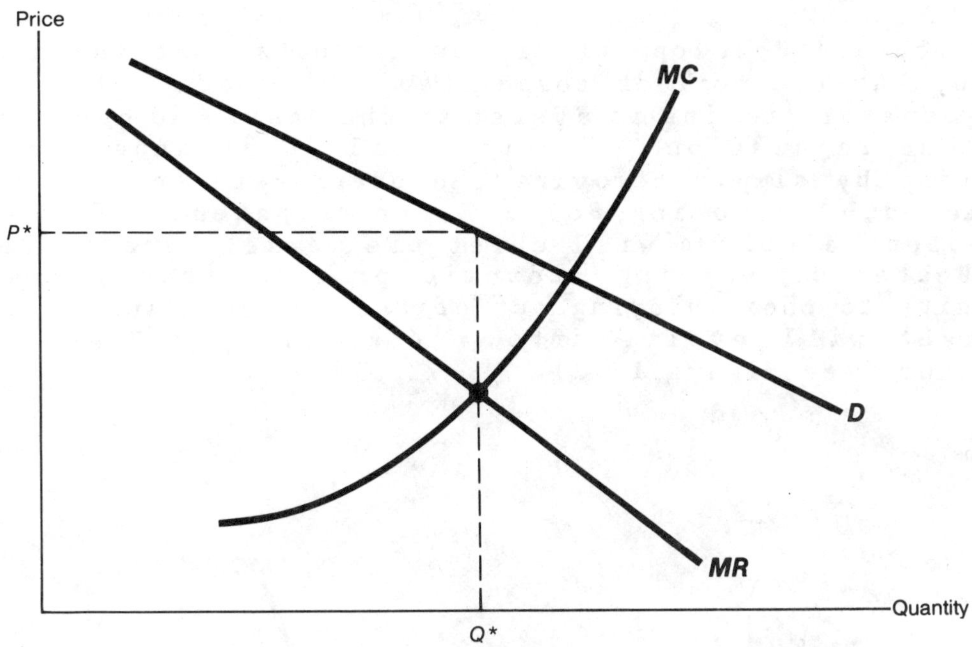

FIGURE 18.1

(e) It is meaningless to speak of a unique supply curve for a monopolist. Monopoly supply does not have a precise meaning like competitive supply. The quantity supplied by a monopolist depends on the shape and location of the demand curve. Different demand curves have different marginal revenue curves, which lead to different quantities supplied at any given price.

(f) There are apparently regional differences in demand for solar-powered blenders. The price elasticities of demand for Solar Beater's product differ between regions. The regional differences in prices reflects price discriminatory behavior by Solar Beater. This type of behavior is perfectly rational for a profit-maximizing firm.

(g) From society's point of view, the type of regulation proposed by Senator Helpman might be desirable. Under perfect competition, production occurs at the output level corresponding to minimum long-run average cost. Under monopoly, the firm chooses its profit-maximizing output and then utilizes the plant size capable of producing it at the least unit cost. But this plant is not necessarily associated with absolute minimum unit cost. In a sense, society's scarce resources are used more efficiently in perfectly competitive markets. Society as a whole would benefit by having more of its scarce resources used in producing the commodity.

(h) Senator Ralph Pickins is apparently in agreement with Senator Helpman that social welfare tends to be promoted through a more competitive market organization. (Senator Pickins has decided not to consider certain other factors such as the amount of research and development of new products that the monopolist might do, but the perfect competitor might not.) The difference is that Senator Pickins is averse to the costs and bureaucracy of government regulation. His proposal is intended to promote competition by simply removing the barrier to entry. Entry can be promoted by revoking Solar Beater's patent. Once this is done, potential firms will enter the market because they know Solar Beater is earning economic profits that represent an opportunity to their staying out of the market. In the long-run, the market will evolve into a competitive ("zero profit") equilibrium (see Figure 18.2).

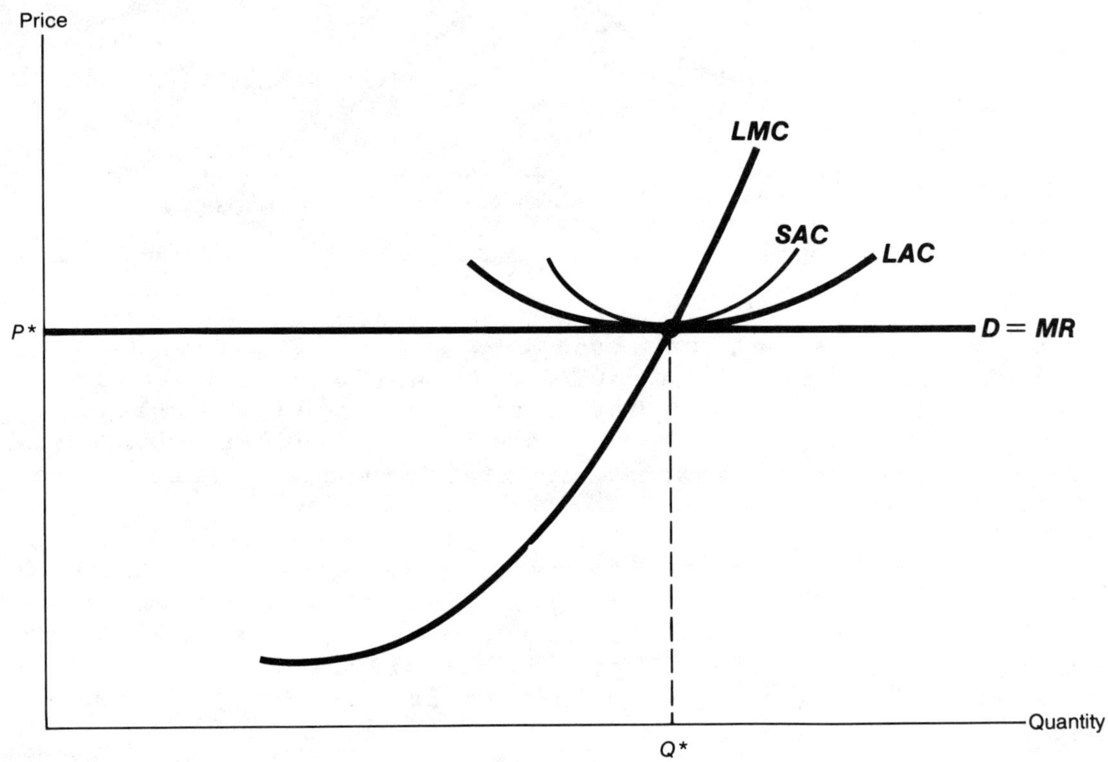

FIGURE 18.2

CHAPTER 19

III. MULTIPLE CHOICE

1 - a
2 - d
3 - a
4 - a
5 - c
6 - d
7 - b
8 - a
9 - b
10 - a

IV. EXERCISES

1. No. The perceived "minor league" status of many college football teams is not a compelling argument for subsidization. In general, if the owners of a major league sports team do not pay for the training of players in the minor leagues, the players will pay for it themselves. This is the case with college football teams. It is tempting to argue that the monopoly profits that many professional football teams make could be justified by such a subsidization program. But subsidization is irrelevant to deciding about the justification of monopoly profits.

2. If demand for such an automobile really existed and it could be profitably produced, it would be produced. The manufacturer would sell it at the value of the infinite series of ordinary automobiles that it would replace. It is probable however, that such an automobile would be so expensive that nobody would buy it.

V. PROBLEM

(a) Static economic theory cannot conclusively say whether a competitive environment or a monopoly is more innovative.

(b) Local phone service will no longer be subsidized by

long-distance service. Proponents of the breakup have argued however, that the higher costs for local service will be offset by new efficiencies in other communications services. Static economic theory cannot resolve this question. Many defenders of monopoly argue that large monopolies can benefit from increasing returns to scale. To the degree that this is true about AT&T, the breakup is bad. The old AT&T had an impressive organization with inherent efficiencies, such as the ability to invest in areas that needed it the most. Further, the old AT&T supported Bell Laboratories, which was an important haven for basic research. All of these benefits that existed under the old AT&T might be lost under the new system.

(c) Subsidization of local service may be desirable. This is a decision that must be made by society. Many proponents of monopoly argue that it permits the subsidization of unprofitable customers. This was the case with the old AT&T. But if subsidization is determined to be desirable, one must question the rationale for breaking up AT&T. The old AT&T was a <u>regulated</u> monopoly that subsidized local service, possessed expertise in management, and supported important basic and applied research efforts.

CHAPTER 20

III. MULTIPLE CHOICE

1 - d
2 - c
3 - c
4 - a
5 - a
6 - a
7 - a
8 - d
9 - a
10 - a
11 - b
12 - c
13 - c
14 - a
15 - d

IV. EXERCISES

1. (a) Monopolistic competition best describes industries in which many heterogeneous products exist.

(b) Sternovsky is correct. Productive efficiency is not achieved under monopolistic competition. Firms do not produce at their lowest attainable cost. Monopolistic competitors face downward-sloping demand curves. They can earn monopoly profits in the short run. Freedom of entry and exit forces profits to zero in the long run. The absence of long-run profits requires that each firm's demand curve be nowhere above its long-run average cost curve. The absence of losses in the long run also requires demand to be equal to average cost at some level of output. These two requirements together imply that in a long-run equilibrium, monopolistic competitors will produce where their demand curves are tangent to their average total cost curves. At the tangency, both curves are downward sloping. Each firm is producing <u>less</u> output than the one for which long-run average cost reaches its minimum point.

(c) Product diversification exists in the United States because people have different tastes. Some people prefer one differentiated product to another. Product differentiation is not necessarily bad. There is a tradeoff between producing more products to satisfy diverse tastes and producing any given set of products at the lowest possible cost.

(d) A stable equilibrium exists for markets like this. The equilibrium is at the point where the marginal gain from adding one more differentiated product is equal to the marginal loss from having to produce each existing product at a higher cost.

2. (a) Productive efficiency is not achieved under monopolistic competition. As explained in (1b) above, each monopolistic competitor produces less output than the one for which long-run average total cost is at its minimum.

(b) Consider Figure 20.1.

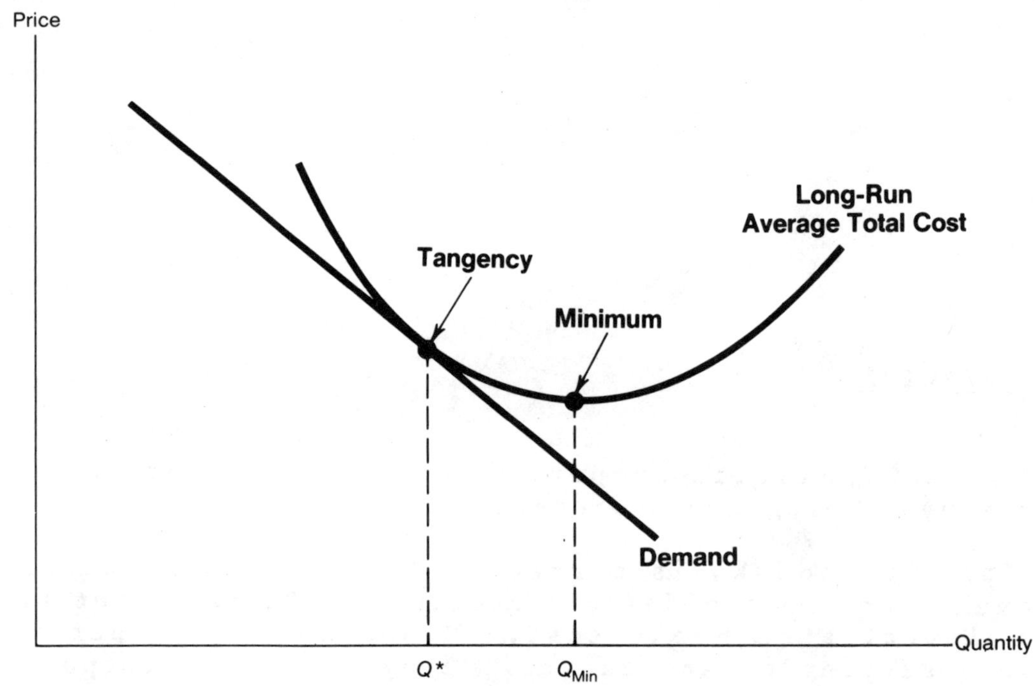

FIGURE 20.1

In a long-run equilibrium, monopolistic competitors produce where their demand curves are tangent to their average total cost curves. At the tangency, both curves are downward sloping.

(c) Productive efficiency is not necessarily desirable because people have diverse tastes. Differentiated products exist to satisfy those diverse tastes. Consumers' satisfactions are not maximized by increasing production of each product until it is produced at its least-cost point. A tradeoff exists between producing more differentiated products and producing any given set of products at the lowest possible cost. The more there are of differentiated products, the further to the left of the least-cost output the production of each product will be.

But at the same time, more diverse tastes will be satisfied.

(d) The conclusion is that monopolistic competition does not necessarily waste society's resources.

V. PROBLEM

(a) Consumers have different tastes for automobiles. Some people prefer one differentiated automobile to another. Alfred Sloan's objective was to satisfy these diverse tastes. This approach went to such extremes in 1984 that Chevrolet's Citation was available in 32,000 versions (each with a different combination of engine, transmission and optional accessories), and the Ford Motor Company's Thunderbird came in over 69,000 versions.

(b) Lloyd Reuss' comment also recognizes the fact that people have diverse tastes. His argument is that in order to survive in the American automobile market, a firm must differentiate its product from all other cars. Many consumers do not simply want a black sedan. Any of the automobile companies can sell a consumer a black sedan. But to survive in this market, Reuss claims, an automobile manufacturer must convince the consumer through advertising that its product is different and better than competitors' products. It must differentiate its product.

(c) Overhead is a fixed cost. It does not vary with the quantity of cars produced. Recall that total cost consists of variable cost and fixed cost. The addition of $1,000 to overhead cost raises fixed costs and total costs. Average total cost is total cost spread across (or divided by) total output. The rise in total cost also raises the average total cost of production.

(d) Recall that one of the objections to the model of monopolistic competition is that pointless differentiation of products through advertising is supported at the customer's expense. The purchaser of an American automobile bears some of the cost of product differentiation. This product differentiation is not necessarily bad though, if it is satisfying heterogeneous consumer tastes for automobiles. (The very fact that many different models of cars have been sold during the past twenty years attests to this benefit.) But as we will see below, if too much advertising and product differentiation is done, the automobile manufacturer also bears some of the burden in the form of lost sales.

(e) If the recent study is correct, it would suggest that GM's optimal point of production is closer to minimum average total cost than it thinks. The model of monopolistic competition concludes that the level of output that maximizes social welfare is to the left of minimum long-run average total cost. The optimal number of differentiated cars is at the point where the marginal gain from adding one more differentiated car is equal to the marginal loss of having to produce each car at a higher cost. If the study is correct, then GM has moved too far to the left of minimum long-run average total cost.

(f) The Japanese experience also suggests that the American companies have moved too far to the left of minimum average total cost; that is, they are producing too many differentiated automobiles.

(g) The Japanese strategy of conducting market surveys of consumer preferences is a very good one. A major uncertainty in any market is the size and distribution of consumer tastes. The American manufacturers' strategy appears to be based on the belief that consumer tastes for automobiles are very broad and diverse. It further seems to indicate a belief that the distribution of consumers across the spectrum of tastes is fairly even. The Japanese approach of conducting market studies is intended to verify or refute these beliefs. Their experience so far suggests that consumer tastes may be distributed more densely at particular points on the spectrum of tastes.

(h) The smaller variety of Japanese cars gives the Japanese companies greater economies of scale in production. They can realize greater economies of scale in engineering, manufacturing, and distribution systems.

(i) The lower prices for comparable Japanese cars are not surprising given the greater economies of scale that the Japanese companies have realized. In addition to being able to price their cars lower than their American competition, the Japanese have also been able to use some of the savings from the economies of scale to improve the quality of their automobiles.

CHAPTER 21

III. MULTIPLE CHOICE

1 - c
2 - b
3 - c
4 - d
5 - d

IV. EXERCISES

1. (a) Aggregate supply to the market = X+Y.

(b) Firm 1's total revenue (TR) function is $TR=p(X+Y^*)X$, where p(·) is the price function and Y^* is the level of output for firm 2 that firm 1 takes as fixed. Its profit function is

$PROFIT = p(X+Y^*)X - C(X)$.

(c) Firm 2's total revenue function is $TR=p(X^*+Y)Y$. Its profit function is $PROFIT = p(X^*+Y)Y - C(Y)$.

(d) The actions of the two firms will be consistent when their choices are compatible with each other's expectations.

(e)

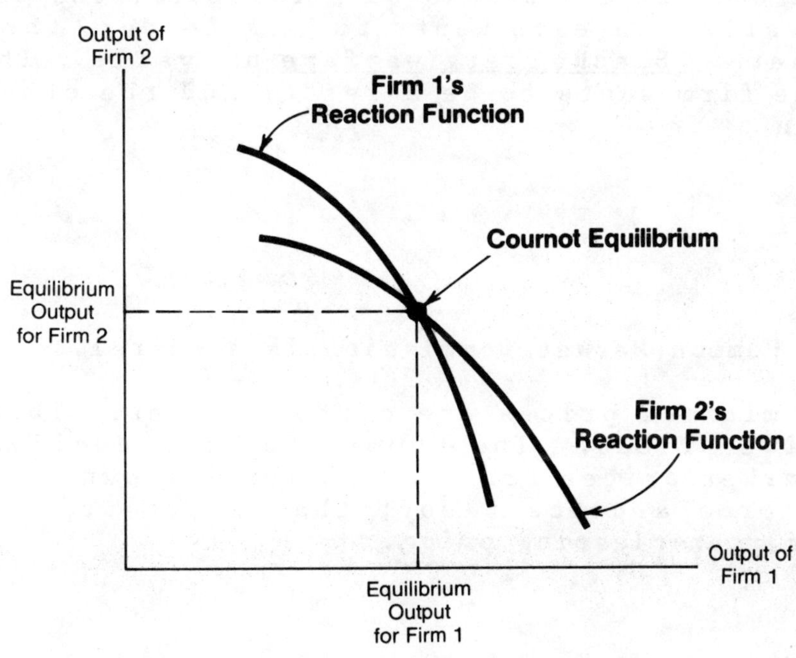

FIGURE 21.1

2. An equilibrium for the duopoly is an output pair (X,Y), such that the two reaction functions are simultaneously satisfied. Substituting for Y in firm 1's reaction function:

$$X = a + b - X \qquad \text{or} \qquad X = (a+b)/2 \quad .$$

Substituting this expression for X back into firm 2's reaction function:

$$Y = (b-a)/2 \quad .$$

These two expressions for X and Y in terms of a and b represent the Cournot equilibrium.

3. (a) Firm 1's profit function is:

$$\text{PROFIT} = p(X+Y^*)X - C_1(X) \quad ,$$

where $p(\cdot)$ is the price function and Y^* is the level of output for firm 2 that firm 1 takes as fixed.

(b) Firm 2's profit function is:

$$\text{PROFIT} = p[X(Y) + Y]Y - C_2(Y) \quad .$$

(c) Firm 2 "leads the way" by setting its level of output. Firm 1 "follows" by then choosing its profit-maximizing level of output. This type of behavior is known as <u>Stackelberg behavior</u>.

(d) Whether a firm should be a follower or a leader depends on the relationship between the two cost functions. Each firm must compare its own profits under the different possible scenarios. If each firm wants to be a follower, the Cournot-Nash solution prevails. If each wants to be a leader, the situation is indeterminate. <u>Stackelberg warfare</u> prevails. There is nor problem if one firm wants to be a leader and the other wants to be a follower.

V. <u>PROBLEM</u>

(a) The Common Market Commission is a cartel.

(b) The minimum prices are cartel prices. These are not the competitive prices. The Commission has decided that the prevailing market prices are too low for its own tastes. It is trying to enforce a price floor; that is, a price above the competitive, market-clearing price.

(c) It became neccesary to set new prices because the competitive equilibrium price fell. Demand for steel products fell, leading to the fall in the equilibrium price levels. The leftward shift in the demand schedule also led to a price war among makers of steel in the European Community. This price war was not surprising. Recall that in a contracting industry, firms have excess capacity and want to compete for the existing market demand.

(d) One would not expect the agreement to survive, given the existing market conditions. As long as the price floor is above the equilibrium price, excess supply of steel will exist. Steel producers will have an incentive to cheat on the cartel agreement in order to sell their excess supply and increase their market share. The firms in each nation are faced with a tradeoff. They have an incentive to charge the cartel price in order to maximize joint profits. But they also have a conflicting incentive to cheat on the agreement, cut their own prices below the cartel price, and increase their market share.

(e) The financial sanctions are a form of punishment intended to bring about cooperation. The Community recognizes that each member nation is faced with a prisoner's dilemma. The financial sanctions are intended to solve the prisoner's dilemma by imposing punishment on cheaters and defectors from the agreement. By imposing sanctions, the matrix of payoffs that each nation faces changes. If detection of cheating is possible and the sanctions are enforceable, this change might make it worth the nation's while to cooperate rather than to cheat.

CHAPTER 22

III. MULTIPLE CHOICE

1 - a
2 - b
3 - c
4 - d
5 - a

IV. EXERCISES

1. The economic value to the airline of Ryan's service as a pilot is not determined by total product, or the product taken away if the pilots' services are taken away. In a competitive marketplace, the value of a pilot's services is determined by the marginal product of one extra pilot.

2. (a) No, the Braves are not irrational. Ted Turner and the Braves' management have offered these players such lucrative contracts because they believe that the players will earn the club an amount equal to, or greater than, their salaries. When a baseball player signs a lucrative contract with a team, the deal is mutually beneficial.

(b) The actions of other teams does not justify the Braves' strategy. Behind the willingness of the Braves to offer lucrative contracts is the willingness of the Atlanta fans to pay Ted Turner to see the players play baseball. Other baseball teams are willing to offer lucrative contracts because their own fans are willing to pay them to see the players play. Atlanta's willingness to pay is a derived demand. The Braves demand the services of players in order to satisfy the demands of its fans for a better and more exciting baseball team. (Ted Turner is also trying to satisfy the demands of subscribers to his cable television network for more exciting baseball games.)

IV. PROBLEM

Consider stage 1. Average product is increasing over this range of output. The wage rate is constant. The rising average product implies that the cost per unit of output decreases as more output is produced. The firm would never want to remain at any point in stage 1 because it can always increase output and reduce unit costs. By expanding output, the competitive firm can increase its total profits. Consider stage 3. The firm never produces in stage 3 because marginal product is negative. More output can be produced by employing less labor.

The conclusion is that efficient production for a competitive firm occurs somewhere in stage 2.

CHAPTER 23

III. MULTIPLE CHOICE

1 - a
2 - d
3 - b
4 - d
5 - c
6 - b
7 - d
8 - c
9 - c
10 - a

IV. EXERCISES

1. Average product is equal to total output divided by the quantity of the factor input employed. Consider the average product of labor, Q/L. For the linear homogeneous Cobb-Douglas production function:

$$Q/L = AK^{a}L^{-a}$$

$$= A(K/L)^{a}$$

$$= \text{average product of labor}$$

$$= f(\text{factor input ratio}) \quad .$$

A similar exercise reveals that $Q/K=A(L/K)^{1-a}$.

2. Consider the Cobb-Douglas production function $Q=AK^{a}L^{b}$. Increase capital and labor by the same proportion t:

$$f(tK,tL) = A(tK)^{a}(tL)^{a}$$

$$= t^{a}(AK^{a}L^{a})$$

$$= t^{a}f(K,L)$$

$$= t^a Q \quad .$$

When capital and labor are increased by the same proportion t, output rises by more than t.

V. PROBLEM

(a) $Q = f[A(t)K,\ A(t)L]$

$$= A(t)f(K,L) \quad .$$

(b) Let Q^* be the time derivative of Q, K^* be the time derivative of K, L^* be the time derivative of L, and A^* be the time derivative of A. Then

$$Q^*/Q = (A^*/A) + A(\partial f/\partial K)(K^*/Q)$$
$$+ A(\partial f/\partial L)(L^*/Q)$$

(c) $Q^*/Q = (A^*/A) + w_k(K^*/K)$

$$+ w_1(L^*/L)$$

(d) If all factors are classified as either K or L, then the factor shares should always add up to one.

(e) If one assumes that factors are paid their marginal products, then the production function is homogeneous of degree one.

(f) Note that $q^*/q = (Q^*/Q) - (L^*/L)$, and so on, where the * superscript signifies time derivatives.

$$q^*/q = (A^*/A) + w_k(k^*/k) \quad .$$

(g) The conclusion is that to obtain A(t), one needs time series data for output per man hour, capital per man hour, and the share of capital.

CHAPTER 24

III. MULTIPLE CHOICE

1 - b
2 - a
3 - d
4 - c
5 - d
6 - b
7 - a
8 - c
9 - b
10 - c

IV. EXERCISES

1. Consider the case of a monopolist in a product market who employs one variable factor called labor, and one fixed factor called capital. A monopolist hires factors of production at the point where the marginal revenue product is equal to the marginal cost of the factor. The marginal revenue product is lower than the value of marginal product. The quantity of the factor input employed is less than under perfect competition. It is less than desirable in view of the value of the marginal good produced and the value of the last unit of input used to produce it.

2. (a) If there is a positively sloped supply curve for a factor input, then input price is a function of input demanded.

(b) The input price is equal to the marginal expense of the input.

(c) The marginal expense of input schedule is 10, 23, 32, 40, 48, 56, 64.

(d) Columns 1 and 2 represent the labor supply schedule to the monopolist.

(e) Column 3 is the additional expense of increasing the factor input by one unit.

PROBLEM

(a) Prior to the entry of the Postal Service, one would expect a perfectly competitive market to have existed for multiple-unit mail boxes.

(b) The post office became a monopsonist. It quickly became the only buyer of cluster mail boxes.

(c) The entry of the post office drove down prices. The Postal Service encouraged suppliers to undercut each other.

(d) With the fall in prices, profits fell in the industry. Manufacturers of cluster mail boxes recognized that there was an opportunity cost to staying in the industry. They realized that they were not covering their total costs, including opportunity costs, and exited from the industry.

CHAPTER 25

III. MULTIPLE CHOICE

1 - d
2 - b
3 - a
4 - d
5 - c
6 - b
7 - a
8 - a
9 - b
10 - c

IV. EXERCISES

1. (a) The segment of the labor supply curve that is relevant to this question is backward-bending. As the wage rate falls, the quantity of labor supplied rises. This seeming contradiction with standard supply-demand analysis arises because the income effect due to a wage change dominates the substitution effect. Assume labor is a normal good. If the substitution effect dominates, then a fall in the wage rate will cause the quantity of labor supplied to fall. But if the income effect dominates, then the quantity of labor supplied will rise. (Recall that the substitution effect is due to the change in the relative price of leisure to all other goods. The income effect is due to the change in the worker's real income.)

(b) With the fall in the wage rate, it is likely that workers will exit from the market. These workers recognize that there is an opportunity cost to staying in the market.

(c) It is likely that the exit of workers from the market will offset the desire of the other workers to increase the number of hours worked. The conclusion is that although the backward-bending labor supply curve is theoretically possible, it is not likely to be observed in markets with no barriers to entry or exit.

2. (a) Franco Harris was worth $600,000 per year to the Steelers. This offer was not "exorbitant." Had the deal been made between Harris and the Steelers, it would have been a

mutually benecial agreement. The Steelers are willing to pay him $600,000 because they think this is the minimum amount of money that he will earn for the club. Their demand for Harris' services is a derived demand. Their willingness to pay him $600,000 reflects the willingness of Steeler fans to pay the team to watch him play.

(b) The Steeler's decision to cut him from the team was not inconsistent with their earlier valuation of his worth. The Steeler's time is money. There was an opportunity cost to the time they waited for him to sign a contract with the team. The cost eventually became too high and they decided not to wait any longer.

(c) The $600,000 offer from the Steelers reflected Harris' worth specifically to the Steelers. Harris' worth to other football teams can be determined by observing the offers made to him when he became a free agent. If the demand from fans to see him play was the same throughout the country, one would expect to observe a single wage offered to him by the clubs.

V. PROBLEM

Consider Figure 25.1 below.

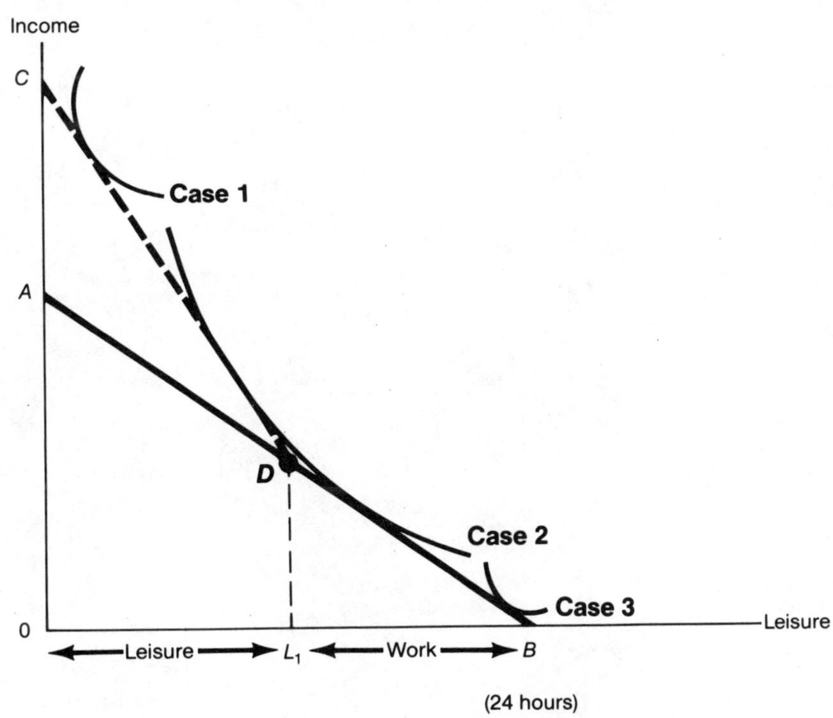

FIGURE 25.1

Assume that the overtime wage is higher than the regular wage rate. The price of leisure to the worker rises. The original budget (of time) constraint for the worker is AB. Suppose that in the absence of overtime pay, the worker chooses to work L_1B hours per day. OL_1 ($=24-L_1B$) is the number of leisure hours.

The rise in the price of labor due to the overtime wage rate is represented by the new budget line CD. Three possible outcomes may prevail. If the worker's indifference curve looks like case 1, then she will choose to work overtime. If her indifference curve looks like case 3, then she chooses leisure over overtime. If her indifference curve is case 2, then the worker is indifferent between leisure and labor.

The conclusion to be drawn is that if a worker is free to choose the number of overtime hours she wishes to work, an overtime wage rate above the regular wage rate will have uncertain effects on the quantity of overtime labor she will supply.

CHAPTER 26

III. MULTIPLE CHOICE

1 - d
2 - a
3 - b
4 - c
5 - b
6 - a
7 - d
8 - a
9 - b
10 - a

IV. EXERCISES

1. (a) Tommy Ryan's opportunity cost is equal to the $50,000 annual salary he has decided to forego.

(b) Ryan is a capitalist. He is augmenting the capitalized value of his labor by investing in more education. He is borrowing on the promise that his skills will be improved.

2. Roberta is smart. She realizes that there is a trade-off between the benefit of obtaining a discount ticket and the cost of foregoing interest on her money. If Roberta were to invest her money in a bank account for four months instead of buying a discount ticket, she would earn 3% of her $218 or $6.54. If on the other hand, she buys the discount ticket by September 1, she will benefit by saving $280-$218=$62. Her savings today far exceed the interest she would earn on her money tomorrow. Roberta should buy the discount ticket.

V. PROBLEM

Solar Ray's advertisement is enticing. It superficially appears that if a family invests $250 it will save $300. But the $300 savings is spread over three years. The savings are not immediately forthcoming. The problem with this is that a dollar tomorrow is worth less than a dollar today. The $300 savings must be discounted to reflect the price that a family should be willing to pay for the future savings. This can be done using the general discounting formula. For a 10% rate of interest, the formula is:

$$P = 100/(1+.1) + 100/(1+.1)^2 + 100/(1+.1)^3$$

$$= 90.91 + 82.64 + 75.13$$

$$= 248.68 \quad .$$

The discounted value of the future savings is $248.68. This is less than the $250 price for the solar panel. The family therefore should not invest in a solar panel.